8/01

DATE DUE
Fecha Para Retornar

THE LIBRARY STORE #47-0100

THE
TALKING CURE

THE
TALKING CURE

A MEMOIR OF
LIFE ON AIR

MIKE FEDER

SEVEN STORIES PRESS
New York | London | Toronto | Sydney

A Seven Stories Press First Edition

Excerpts from *New York Son: Stories by Mike Feder.* Copyright © 1988 by Mike Feder. Reprinted by permission of Crown Publishers, a division of Random House, Inc.

Seven Stories Press
140 Watts Street
New York, NY 10013
http://www.sevenstories.com

In Canada: Hushion House, 36 Northline Road, Toronto, Ontario M4B 3E2

In the U.K.: Turnaround Publisher Services Ltd., Unit 3, Olympia Trading Estate, Coburg Road, Wood Green, London N22 6TZ

In Australia: Tower Books, 9/19 Rodborough Road, Frenchs Forest NSW 2086

Library of Congress Cataloging-in-Publication Data
Feder, Mike.
    The talking cure / Mike Feder.
       p. cm.
    ISBN 1-58322-041-0
    1. Feder, Mike. 2. Authors, American—20th century—Biography. 3. Radio broadcasters—United States—Biography. 4. Storytellers—United States—Biography. 5. Parents—Death—Psychological aspects. 6. Queens (New York, N.Y.)—Biography. 7. Storytelling. I. Title.

PS3556.E235 Z474 2001
813'.54—dc21
[B]
                                                                00-050953
9 8 7 6 5 4 3 2 1

College professors may order examination copies of Seven Stories Press titles for a free six-month trial period. To order, visit www.sevenstories.com/textbook, or fax on school letterhead to (212) 226-1411.

Book design by Cindy LaBreacht

Printed in the U.S.A.

To J and B,
who are always with me

To Ralph,
who never stops trying

and

To my wife,
once, now, always

CONTENTS

"It's a strange and beautiful world."
—Jim Jarmusch, *Down by Law*

PART ONE
LAURELTON

CHAPTER ONE

When my sister was born, I was exiled to an upstairs bedroom and spent the next seventeen years of my life, till the day I moved out of my mother's house, looking out at Mount Sinai, the largest Jewish cemetery in Queens. I watched it for hours, day and night. I watched it in the slow, sad afternoons when my sick, crazy mother was holed up in her room, and I watched it in the dead middle of the night when the moon was full and I couldn't sleep.

It could be grim—to say the least, especially the funerals, shrieks, wails, moans—the terrible music of the grieving and bereaved. I must have seen hundreds of people lowered into the earth.

But, after all, *they* were dead and we were living; and life, even in such a strange, sad family as mine, had to go on.

On Sundays during the summer, we often had barbecues in my backyard. Some of my aunt's friends came by; there was me, my sister, maybe one or two of her little pals, and my mother, wearing dark sunglasses, set up in an aluminum lawn chair with a cool glass of lemonade, quiet for a while.

We put up a badminton net and listened to the radio or the hi-fi through the open window of my mother's bedroom: Frank Sinatra, Sammy Davis, the make-believe ballroom—big bands and crooners from the forties and fifties.

My uncle Myron (who lived next door with my aunt Erma) stood over a round black barbecue grill, wearing a big white apron decorated with colorful pictures of a dog on a bun, a bottle of ketchup, a steaming burger, and the helpful words "What's Yours?!" printed on it. Myron turned the dogs and patted the burgers with a spatula. He had grown up in rural West Virginia and had spent most of World War II on a destroyer escort as a cook, so he was pretty handy at the grill. My aunt, wearing her new red bathing suit with big yellow daisies on it, came out of her kitchen door carrying a big tray of mustard, ketchup, various other condiments, buns, potato chips.

Ten yards away, hidden by the vines growing on the fence, there was a funeral beginning. Car wheels crunched...car doors opened and closed.

"So, Erma—you heard?" asked my aunt's best friend, Dora. "Marilyn's girl, the little one, Roberta, is taking dancing lessons: I don't know who she thinks she is with her fancy *lessons*."

Subdued crying from behind the fence.

The badminton birdie sailed back and forth over the net.

"You're not playing for real," my sister whined. "Play for real!" I put down my racket and sloshed some lemonade.

A rending sob burst into the backyard; my mother, already strung as tight as a badminton racket herself, clutched her drink in her shaking hand.

"Michael," said my aunt, "don't gulp your lemonade!"

"Yeah, OK."

From the fence the rabbi spoke, *Those of you who were privileged to know Seymour Greenbaum...*

"Myron, is my hot dog ready?"

"Just a minute, Erma...."

Seymour was more than a successful furrier, he was also a kind father, a loving husband.... More crying, more sobbing.

"Michael," said my uncle, "how do you want your burger?"

Oh God, Why did he have to die?!!

"Well-done, please."

Take me too, God!!

Grab her, Sol, she's jumping into the grave!! Piercing shrieks, gasps, shouting.

Spilling her lemonade, my mother sat straight up, her sunglasses falling sideways over her nose. She's had enough: "Erma, goddamnit, those people are driving me crazy!"

"Ruthie," shushed my aunt, "just calm down. We're having a nice barbecue...."

A moan like a wounded animal started low, then soared into the sky. *Seymour, come back! Don't leave me!!*

"So," asked my aunt cheerfully, "who's having seconds?"

I guess, in the modern world, in our bright shiny American world, you could live most of your life without thinking about death, much less having to see or hear anything about it—except of course for whatever pops up on television or in the movies. But for better and for worse, death, dying, fear, and suffering—in fact, extremities of most every sort—have surrounded me since childhood.

I was four years old when my sister was born.

My mother had disappeared, it seemed like weeks before, and then suddenly reappeared, coming in the front door, moaning, crying, shaking. She was supported on one side by my father and on the other by my grandmother.

Immediately behind my mother was a large, sour-faced nurse in a white uniform and hat, holding a white bundle with a screaming red face. I know it was red-faced because the nurse lowered the package to my midget level for me to see—"Look, it's your new baby sister. Her name is Sandy." I took a quick look and was repelled, disgusted, and deafened by the screaming. It sounded like this creature was being stuck with a butcher knife.

My grandmother and my father guided my mother into her bedroom and shut the door. The nurse and my aunt Erma took the creature into *my* bedroom—adjacent to my parents' room—and shut the door.

From inside my mother's room, mostly muted words. I also heard crying, yelling, groans, sobs...the sounds that were to be my mother's music for the rest of her life. Once in a while I heard my grandmother's sharp irritable voice, "Ruthie, just be quiet." And from my room, the horrible wailing and screaming continued.

In the living room my uncle and my grandfather fidgeted and said nothing—their usual MO—while I stood outside the two closed doors, alone in the dark hallway.

My mother never recovered from her postpartum depression, and from that point on she was crazy on and off for the rest of her life: in and out of mental hospitals, on massive doses of pills. Despite brief periods of calm, she was never much more than an outpatient.

In the first couple of weeks she didn't leave her bed except to wander briefly through the house, mumbling, crying, her fists clenched and tears pouring down her cheeks. My grandmother or my aunt and uncle from next door had to get her and put her back in her room. Sometimes doctors came and gave her injections. The rabbi came and sat with her for hours. Sometimes, when she was calm for a while, and under guard as always, she would see the baby.

I slept, though from then on I never really slept well, in my old room—but now I shared it with my screaming sister in her crib, and whatever grown female was there to try, hopelessly, to comfort her.

About two months later, my mother was sufficiently regulated or drugged to try to resume the position of wife and mother, but my aunt and grandmother were always around, cooking, helping with the baby, talking to my mother in her room.

My father, always given to fits of violent temper alternating with long, grim silences, suddenly got very busy. He was an engineer with a degree from City College, and sometimes he traveled for his work. Now he came and went more often and was sometimes gone for a week or two at a time. When I think about it now, I realize he probably volunteered for every out-of-the-city job he could get, just to get a break from the madhouse.

When he was home, my father had very little to say to me. He had never been an extensive talker, but before my sister arrived, he was sometimes enthusiastic and would tell me all manner of things about the world—pointing out constellations in the night sky, veins in the leaves of trees, different kinds of dirt and minerals in the backyard: *that red color in the dirt is iron, that's mica, this is granite.* He was like a natural-history encyclopedia. Though honestly, even before the devil-sibling arrived, my father wasn't all that thrilled by my existence. There had definitely been times when my very presence seemed to drive him into a rage. I remember jumping into bed one morning between him and my mother (I was probably about two). Suddenly he rolled out of bed, his face turned red, and he was yelling while my mother held on to me. Other times he was just silent and brooded in the living room for hours. Now, with *two* little kids *and* an insane wife, he did no more talking than was absolutely necessary.

I got the feeling that he blamed me for what happened—that somehow my mother and I were in league with each other and had done these terrible things to him. Soon after my sister arrived, he was always up in our attic—bringing up lumber and tiles, tearing things apart, drilling, hammering, sawing. I had no idea what was going on up there: it was off-limits, and my father declined to comment.

Then, in the fall, about five months after my sister was born, my father took me upstairs to show me what he had been doing in the attic. He had finished half of it and made it into a bedroom. My bedroom. Downstairs, where I had slept for the past four years, fifteen feet from my parents' bed, was now my sister's room. I was banished to the tower like a cursed prince in a fairy tale.

A few weeks later, my father left and never returned. My mother relapsed. She wandered the house in her nightgown, her hair all wild, screaming, scratching her hands bloody, yelling incomprehensible words, cursing—in language that usually made her blush when she heard it from other people.

The doctors came more often, and the rabbi was there, it seemed, every day.

My grandmother, who until then had always been amused and entertained by my nonstop banter, now told me I had to be quiet as much as possible because my mother was so upset. She slept—alternating with my aunt—in the room with my mother, watching her, bringing her chicken soup and pills. My sister cried or let out full, blood curdling screams.

At four, I blamed my sister for everything. She was the poisoned apple, the snake in the garden, the all-consuming curse that had suddenly descended on my perfect family and destroyed it forever. Of course, now that I've been married and have my own kids, I can understand what went on with me and my sister. When my son was born, my daughter was jealous and angry and often mean to him—something that continued for years. Using myself as an example to try to get her to give her brother a break, I told her about the way I had treated my sister, "I was awful to her and, after all this time, she still feels bad about it, and *I* still feel bad about it."

When I was a child, though, everything was very clear to me: I had a wonderful life, then my sister was born. And what made all this infinitely worse for my sister was that my mother felt the same way.

My mother blamed this new baby for the loss of her husband and her nervous breakdown. It was obvious she wished my sister had never been born. If we were sitting at the kitchen table and Sandy asked my mother for a glass of water, my mother would just as likely bring it to me as her. My mother talked to me as if Sandy weren't even at the table. When Sandy threw her inevitable fits over this unfair treatment, she was told to shut up or go to her room. She spent most of her childhood making scenes, yelling, and crying. The more she yelled and cried, the more nasty my mother and I were. It was a conspiracy of petty torture. There were times when even I realized how gratuitous and brutal my mother was to my sister, and I stuck up for her. But those times were few and far between.

I lived in that house as if my sister didn't exist. I read books, watched TV by myself, and ate by myself whenever I could. In the house were my mother and me and this *stranger*—a loud, irritating intruder. Once, when I was fifteen, I came home from school and found the front door locked. I rang the bell, and my sister opened the door. I didn't recognize her. I stared at her for a couple of seconds, thinking I must have gone to the wrong house.

One time I blasted a dollhouse of hers completely to smithereens with my BB gun. Mom and dad, sisters and brothers viciously gunned down, furniture, teacups, little doll clothes smashed to pieces. When I got done shooting, the dollhouse looked like it had gone through the Battle of the Bulge. When my sister discovered the massacre, she burst into tears and complained to my mother. My mother laughed and told me I should apologize. I never did, and my mother couldn't have cared less.

Just a few years ago, my sister told me that my mother had actually attacked her a few times when I was out at school, and that she had to be pulled off her by my grandmother and my uncle.

THE TALKING CURE / 19

Sandy has always been a painful part of my life story. Now, decades later, I finally talk to her. We speak on the phone (she lives in California), and sometimes we trade e-mails. She just recently sent me a box full of old letters and family pictures covering thirty years of family history.

In my haunted house in Laurelton, Queens (I was five), up in my attic room, very late one night, I was awakened by something that sounded worse than the usual demented chaos downstairs. I heard thumps, cries, threats, people on the telephone. My uncle rushed in from next door. All the lights were on. I went to the doorway of my room and looked down. My mother was running around half-naked in the hallway downstairs, trying to claw her way past my grandmother, my aunt, and my uncle to run outside. She was cursing at them. My grandmother was yelling, "Ruthie, the children!" They didn't see me up there looking down at them.

A few minutes later, there was a loud knocking at the door and two men in white jackets, white pants, and white shoes came in and grabbed my mother, twisting, clawing, and screaming. They picked her straight up off the floor and took her out.

My grandmother was crying, something which I had never seen her do before. She looked up and saw me there at the top of the stairs. She came up, took me by the hand, and put me back in bed. When I was tucked in, she told me that my mother was very upset and had to go away for a rest and that she, my grandmother, would be staying over for a while.

Fifty years later, I close my eyes and see that scene again. I don't even have to close my eyes. It's not just seeing it as if it were a photo in an album. I hear it, smell it, feel my heart pounding.

A few weeks passed.

Things remain unexplained to me. My mother is someplace, I have no idea where, could be the moon. She's "resting." The question in my mind is: why would, how could my mother, who is virtually everything to me—especially since my father has gone off—leave me, too? Did I do something wrong? Maybe she was forced to go—after all, I saw big men come and take her. Maybe some witch or monster had her. I didn't bother my grandmother about it because she seemed too upset and she had already made it clear that my questions would get no answers.

One Saturday afternoon, my grandfather said we were going for a ride to visit my mother. I was happy to hear it but scared, too. My grandfather was nervous, his hands gripped the wheel of the car. He was mute. He didn't say where she was. He never did say much, but now not so much as a word as we drove and drove. All this silence and secrecy was difficult for me to bear. When I was two and three, I was a nonstop talker and asked an endless stream of questions like most little kids do. If the adults were slow with answers, I might handle that end of the conversation too.

My aunt Clarice, my mother's oldest sister, told me decades later that I had a very peculiar habit: when she put me to bed, I'd talk about something—an idea or a story I'd made up. I'd fall asleep in the middle of a thought or a word, wake up the next morning, and begin exactly where I had left off the night before.

My grandfather drove on what seemed like an endless trip into the countryside. As always, he had on shined shoes, a pressed suit, snappy tie, sharp hat. He was a salesman for a cotton and lace clothing company. He was (as the great old joke goes) "in ladies underwear."

Eventually, we stopped outside a huge wrought-iron-fenced estate; long, wide, trimmed green lawns and several large brick and wood buildings were visible behind hedges and trees. He parked the car outside the entrance, got out, and pressed a buzzer at the gate. A man in a uniform came out of a little guardhouse and the gate was opened. We drove through and up to one of the buildings. It was quiet and pretty there; a couple of people sat in some chairs in the sun. My mother could rest pretty well, I thought, in one of those chairs.

My grandfather got out again, told me to wait in the car, went into a building, and came out a few minutes later to get me. He was more nervous than before, sort of pushing me through the door and up some steps to the second floor. We knocked on a door; a nurse opened it and asked us to come in. I walked in—no mother in sight. My grandfather was fidgeting, the nurse was smiling hard at me. We all stood there waiting.

Then I heard the familiar sound of my mother talking. Maybe I heard a little crying. "Here's mom," says the nurse, and into the room comes my mother. But *that* wasn't my mother—it was an old woman with lines all over her face and gray hair. She smiled at me, a twisted, scared, awful smile, and held out her arms. "Michael, sweetheart, come to Mommy." Oh, no. No way on this earth. This was not my mother—this was a witch, an impersonator, a woman with an ugly mask on. *My* mother was young with long black hair and beautiful green eyes.

I hid behind my grandfather and grabbed onto his pants. He tried to pull me around in front of him. My mother kept telling me to come to her; the nurse reached out for me, "Go kiss your mommy." I stayed right where I was, hiding, looking around my grandfather's leg and staring at this crazy strange old lady. She started to cry, to become, as they say on psychiatric wards, "agitated." She was scratching one hand violently with the other, her smile turned to a grimace, then she laughed and burst into tears. The nurse took her arm and moved her out the door. As my mother was almost out, she twisted around, looked at me, and said, "Michael, Michael, look what they've done to me! Michael…"

After a minute or two, my grandfather took me downstairs and put me in the car. He went back inside and returned a minute later. In his clear blue eyes were tears.

He got behind the wheel and we drove out of the compound and back to the city, again wordless. I was looking out the car window at the world passing by. It looked different in a way: the buildings, the trees, even the air and the sunlight seemed to be shimmering and unreal.

I found out later, when I was teenager, that they had given her massive shock treatments in the hospital. It turned her hair gray overnight and etched deep creases in her skin. She was twenty-eight years old.

A few weeks later my mother returned from the hospital and went, as usual, straight to her room, accompanied by an attendant. A few minutes passed and then they sent for me to come into her room. She lay on her bed, not so scary-looking now, obviously calmer; her hair was combed and her face didn't look so ravaged. I let her hold me and cry, but I really didn't want to touch her. I felt as if I had two mothers now, one the strange old woman lying on the bed, and the other up on the wall in a college graduation photo in a cap and gown, young, pretty, with long wavy black hair—the one who had been my mother only a few weeks before.

This was a time when silence again became an absolute requirement of my daily life, important and fearsome like one of the ten commandments. I was cautioned every few hours to keep my voice down, not to yell or create even the slightest disturbance. Usually it was my grandmother who told me this, but finally every grown-up who walked in the house said the same thing: my mother's friends, visiting relatives, not to mention the rabbi and the doctor. They told me that if I made a lot of noise or disturbed her, she would get "sick" again.

Being told *shut your mouth—keep it to yourself* was agony to me. All my soaring thoughts—all my words—now had nowhere to go and could only bounce around in my head. It started to get very crowded up there, like there was a nest of bees inside trying to get out. I began to develop all sorts of physical symptoms, random, unexplainable fevers, rashes. I had trouble breathing and was seized with mysterious aches and pains.

CHAPTER TWO

At eight, I was a very skinny kid who talked in jags (when someone would listen) or was silent for hours on end. I spent a lot of time playing alone in my room or in the dirt in my backyard. My mother did what she could to keep sane, but it was obvious that she was always living right on the border of some nameless disaster. She stayed in her room most of the time, and when she came out I had to be wary and watch for the signs; if I said the wrong thing she'd snap like a vicious dog. A loud laugh, a wrong word, or sometimes no word at all—the sound of sneakers running up the front stoop, or the screen door being pushed open—could send her into a shaking rage.

She would loom up over me and my sister, her eyes blazing, her body shaking, point her bony white finger at me, and say: *"You are driving me crazy!! Do you understand me, Michael?! Crazy!! You better shut up or I'm going to kill myself!!"*

I'm not sure I really understood what she meant, but I knew one thing. Killed meant dead—just like the people in the big cemetery right behind my house—and if she were dead, she'd be gone. She wouldn't be walking around my house anymore scaring me, threatening me, casting a giant black shadow over everything.

There were moments that I wanted to get rid of her myself—just shoot her or stab her and throw her over the fence into the cemetery.

My mother had one more out-and-out breakdown, when I was nine. It may have been because she had received final divorce papers from my father. Once, around that time, I was snooping in her closet when she wasn't around and found them.

In all the years my father had been gone my mother believed that he was going to come back; maybe that was why she tried as hard as she did to be sane. When the court papers arrived, the truth became official: he was never coming back.

She started getting worse by the week. She was seeing a psychiatrist in Forest Hills, a fancy part of Queens. He gave her more and more drugs at higher and higher doses: the top of the dressing table in her bedroom looked like a pharmacy. I don't know how she could tell one pill from another.

Half the time she was a zombie, her eyes dull and her speech slurred. When she was finally persuaded by her regular doctor to cut down on the drugs, the screaming and cursing started again. She walked around downstairs half-dressed, hair uncombed, bumping into the walls, calling my name as if she or I or both of us were lost in some dark forest with the night closing in fast.

I'm nine and hiding behind the door to my room but holding it open a little to see what's going on down there. Just like the last time, the whole family is trying to grab hold of my mother, who is screaming and cursing. Emergency calls are made, the doctor comes, but the situation is beyond him, and once again an ambulance comes to take her away.

I awoke very early the next morning and went downstairs. Everybody else was still asleep. There were dried bloodstains—long dark red smears —covering the walls of the hallway. My mother had tried to kill herself by cutting her wrists with a kitchen knife.

This time she stayed in the mental hospital for three months. It seemed like years—I forgot what her face looked like. When she finally came home, she was remote and drugged like the first time, but after a few weeks some kind of regular family life resumed. By now I was permanently wary of her. I lived in my own private world and whoever this woman was or might want to be, I kept her on the outside. I particularly avoided physical contact. Her touch was repellent to me—she seemed like a demon or a vampire—her hands like claws.

In the beginning, I told her to leave me alone, then I pushed her away, even tried to hit her if she came near me. From then on, I never let her kiss me or hug me.

Through the magic of psychiatry and psychopharmacology, and whatever willpower was available to her, my mother came to approximately resemble the other fifties mothers in my neighborhood out there on the edge of Queens. She did a little cooking, a little cleaning; once in a while, when she was feeling brave, she walked the three blocks to Merrick Boulevard to do her own shopping.

As before, though, she spent most of her waking hours in her bedroom, lying on her single bed in the corner, reading novels or history books, watching television, or simply chain-smoking and staring out her bedroom window into our backyard.

Sometimes, I came home from school to signs of normalcy. The vacuum cleaner was propped up in the hallway, and my mother was sitting, like any good suburban mom, on the couch in the living room, watching soap operas on television.

I often sat and watched with her.

These were precious moments, states of grace, both of us suspended in unreal TV time. Me in the big stuffed chair that used to be my father's, my mother on the couch, watching intently to see if Mandy could convince Tom to stop drinking or whether Bob would be able to save little Timmy, who had fallen down the well.

It was the great secret of soap operas—concentrating on *other* people's problems got you a temporary break from the everyday darkness of your own life.

These brief respites aside, my mother was perpetually nervous, or "high-strung," a phrase from those days that I have always loved—it calls to mind a violin tuned too high and tight. My mother was high-strung all right. She always had a lit cigarette in her mouth, Camels or Pall Malls, vacuuming great gasps of smoke into her lungs. Her fingertips were stained yellow, her lips were always flecked with bits of brown tobacco and white specks from all the tranquilizers she took. She bit her lips, twisted her hair obsessively in her fingers, picked at her fingertips with her nails until they bled. Her teeth were also yellow from nicotine, coffee, and forgetting to brush. Her hair was a sick-looking shade of yellowish-gray.

She wore old, creased house dresses and once in a while—sad recollection of her girlish beauty—she put on some bright-red lipstick, more smeared than applied.

When she could manage it—and I believe she tried as hard as she could—she came out of her room to cook supper that always ended up burned or otherwise ruined. She stood at the stove and shouted: "I hate cooking!" while my sister and I sat at the table in gloomy silence. More than once she put water on to boil and forgot about it, burning the pot so that for days the kitchen stank.

We ate cold hard baked potatoes and tasteless Green Giant vegetables out of cans. Even TV dinners arrived on the table half-cooked.

Once in a while my mother would be overcome with remorse and something like shame for how she was acting. Then we might have lamb chops, or real homemade mashed potatoes. "Don't run off to watch TV until you finish all your food," she'd tell us, proud of herself. And we were proud of her, too. We were always willing to forgive and forget so long as once in a while she tried to do the right thing.

So, on the good nights, my sister and I went along—we washed our hands, grumbling like real children, and we ate all our vegetables (or at least pretended to: do all kids think they invented the ruse of hiding lima beans under mashed potatoes?).

These moments of normalcy never lasted very long. In a little while, after a few minutes, or maybe as long as an hour or two, something, we never knew what, would turn her strange or sad or angry again, and we were right back to zero—feeling like simple-minded suckers.

My mother had been a little genius when she was growing up in the twenties and thirties in Brooklyn. She skipped three grades and entered Hunter College (in those days, before open admissions, you had to be a top student to get in) when she was fifteen years old. She graduated at nineteen, and by then she was already nervous, spoiled, and far too sensitive.

Years later, after my mother died, I went out to Long Island to visit my aunt Frances, my father's sister. She told me she had been against my father (her younger brother) marrying my mother. "Should I tell you a story, Michael?" said Frances, a little warily, not wanting to speak ill of the dead.

"Look," I said, "don't worry about it—who's gonna care now?"

"All right, Michael," said Frances, holding up her forefinger, giving me to understand it was my own fault for asking.

"One night your father comes home from a dance and says, 'I met the girl of my dreams.' So, being the oldest, I was sent to Brooklyn to see this 'wonderful' girl. I get to the house in East New York, the lights are on all over the block, but your mother's house is dark. I knock—no answer. I knock again and still nobody comes to the door. I called earlier and made an appointment, mind you, so I don't know what's what here.

"I knock one last time and finally somebody comes to the door—it's your grandmother. I introduce myself and your grandmother says, in a whisper, 'Come in, but be very quiet.' I come into the foyer and I see people running up and down the stairs, whispering to each other, carrying bottles of medicine and hot water bottles and I don't know what else. Your grandmother goes upstairs, and after a long time she comes down again. I ask her, 'What's wrong?' and she says, 'Shhh—Ruthie's having her period.'"

I went to the local public school, PS 132, about six blocks from home. Despite everything, my mother woke herself each school day morning, crawled out of bed, and called upstairs to wake me. "Miiichael!!!" I can still hear the sound of her voice. Its effect on me was chilling. I knew she was down there in her bathrobe, at the bottom of the steps leading up to my room, her hair all over the place, shaking, disoriented. The first thing I would see was her pale, sick face. And worse, I knew—though she never said the words—that she really didn't want me to leave the house. I knew that simply by going to school I was abandoning her, leaving her to her demons.

If I was lucky she would be back in her room with the door closed by the time I got to the bottom of the stairs. If I wanted anything to eat, I got it myself. I usually slurped milk straight out of the bottle and ran out the door with my books. Anything to get out of that house. When I hit the street I felt like I had been let out of prison. A wave of relief and pure happiness surged through me. Sky, sun, air, birds chirping, kids walking to school. Out into the great life-stream—yes, Lord!

When I first read Kipling's *Kim*, at fifteen, I loved naturally all the adventure, the spying, the battles, the magic, the colorful characters. But what I liked the best were the scenes on the road: the Grand Trunk Road, wide and warm and dusty, on which "all India" traveled. Rich and poor, saints and villains in great caravans or all alone, on horse, or on foot. All journeying in both directions, to shrines three hundred miles away or just to visit a relative in the next village. At night they camped at the side of the road, cooking, singing songs, telling stories, and then up with sun and on the road again. A whole country, ceaselessly moving: the road itself was home.

I liked being out of my house, but at school I writhed in my seat, got kinks in my arms and legs, pains in my backside. I was a small kid, smaller than even the girls in my class—a midget—and all the teachers knew I came from the only divorced-parent household in the neighborhood: they knew my mother. In fact, the principal of my elementary school, Mrs. Flinker, had been a classmate of my grandmother's at Hunter College, class of 1911. With my known familial handicaps, my runt stature, and my undisputed need to talk (and, probably, my *in* with the principal), the teachers called on me all the time. I didn't mind at all. It was my chance to unleash all the words that got stopped up at home.

Now, I wasn't a fool. I knew I risked getting the dread reputation of teacher's pet, but I *needed* that attention. The teachers, all women, doted on me, and of course, there was no danger that by talking too much I could drive my second-grade teacher crazy or make her commit suicide.

Whatever my ambivalence, I was as glad as the rest of the inmates when school let out. Three o'clock meant springing out the door with hundreds of other kids and hitting the streets: basketball, punchball, handball, marbles, flipping baseball cards, hanging out at the candy store, or almost killing yourself swinging from an old tire on a rope in the vacant lot. Play till you drop—what else was the world for?

Eventually, though, you had to go home: it was the law. Milk and cookies, homework, a bath. A lot of kids dawdled, of course, especially the boys, but I was one kid who *really* didn't want to go home. I was the last one to leave the playground, taking one more shot at the basket or stuffing one more Tootsie Roll in my mouth, doodling along the sidewalk at a snail's pace, occasionally dropping down to the ground to examine an anthill or a strange plant; I was in no hurry to get anywhere near my house.

As often as not, when I finally did walk through the front door, my mother would be waiting for me in the living room—lying on the couch, the TV off, the room dark.

As soon as I appeared, she fixed me with her strange, shiny eyes, her sick, scared smile, and said: "How is everything outside today, darling?" And well she might ask. The blinds were always drawn, the windows closed. If it was bright May or June outside, *she* wouldn't know it. It was as if she had launched me earlier that morning into space, an intelligence probe from the mother ship looking for signs of life in the darkness of the universe. I hated these moments. Her staring eyes, her raw, overwhelming *need*. I felt helpless, trapped, unable to pull away.

One bright, beautiful spring day, I came into the house feeling pretty good. I had just raced Stuie Kornreich home from school and beat him by at least half a block: he was hopelessly slow. Not only that, but I got a ninety-five on a story I wrote about dinosaurs for Mrs. Elliot, my second-grade teacher. I had completely forgotten about my lurking mother. I banged open the screen door, headed for the steps leading up to my room, and there she was in the dark living room. "Hello, darling, how is everything outside today?"

I wanted to leap to the steps and run upstairs to my room, but I turned and, holding my books, looked into her anxious, crazy face. She stared at me for a long time, and I began to talk: "Well, you know the crocuses are up, and…and it's very sunny out and windy. I saw Stuie Kornreich and

Eric and Stanley and we all walked to school together, and Eric punched Stuie in the arm and called him a dork and I raced Stuie after school and beat him, and there was a giant moving van up near Two Hundred and Twenty-second Street—I don't know whose house it was. And—you know that really big maple tree in the Collins's yard? There was a red bird in it, maybe it was, um, a cardinal, or a finch—is that right? Can finches be red? Anyway, then, at school, we did astronomy, you know, distances from us to the moon and the sun. And—I found out the sun is only a *small* star! Isn't that incredible?"

My mother would go from a prone position to sitting upright, stop picking at her fingers, and the lines in her face would soften. I kept talking.

"So then we, at lunch, we played basketball and some kid, Anthony, said nobody could jump from this low roof in the schoolyard—and, he's so stupid, I told him anybody could—that I knew three kids who did it already and then he climbed up and jumped off! He twisted his ankle and had to go to the nurse. What a dope."

My mother seemed to grow calmer, her fidgety hands were still, her nervous smile more genuine. Dropping my books on the floor so I could use my hands for description, I went on.

"And me and Butch saw *two* new Buicks! A black one and a green one. I like that green color, you know, they were really shiny—really new— with whitewalls...and Mrs. Wagner was watering her lawn and I said hello and she said hello—and they are painting their house—bright white in the front and blue, like a robin's egg, near the windows...."

I talked and talked and talked, and when I ran out of things that I had actually seen and heard, I made things up. "Also, Ma, I saw, right down the block, a chain of ants on the sidewalk, walking, what do you call it, single file, a giant chain of ants, No! It's true! They were holding onto each other like elephants do in the circus, you know, with their trunks and tails—and the ant chain stretched for three houses!"

I talked almost without taking a breath, throwing my arms around, pointing, making the noises *whooooshhhh, brrrppp!*, my hands grabbing the back of the next ant in the chain to show how they did it.

And often, when I was done, my mother laughed—a real laugh. She got up off the couch, went into the kitchen, poured me a glass of milk, and gave me some cookies on a plate. She raised the blinds in the kitchen and we sat at the table with the afternoon sun pouring through the window.

CHAPTER THREE

No matter how earnest and dramatic they were, my passionate monologues and my fairy tales failed as often as they succeeded. My mother sank back into the living-room shadows, worried, completely self-absorbed even as I stood there, ten feet away, ready for another round of lifesaving entertainment.

What to do then? Nothing. I'd walk up the stairs to my attic bedroom, drop my books on the floor, stand at the window, and stare out at the afternoon sun and shadows—the backyard, the flowers, aluminum lawn chairs, the clothes line…and beyond that, just past the chain-link fence, the cemetery. Rows and rows of tombstones, old and new graves, low bushes, grass half-burned from lack of watering, and, about thirty yards away in the center of my view, a large dark tree, which never could seem to grow leaves. On the tree, always, were two or three motionless crows.

It struck me that life and death could be only a matter of distance, and not much distance at that. Only twenty minutes ago, a hundred feet from where I was standing, I was on the street saying good-bye to my friends, laughing because one of them had made a stupid joke about a teacher at school, and then, right outside my bedroom window—a hundred feet in the opposite direction—were graves, tombstones, dead grass, dead trees, dead people, silence.

The cemetery was ringed with small two-story houses almost exactly like ours. They'd been cheaper to buy than other new houses in the neighborhood—for obvious reasons. I suppose some parents didn't want their kids growing up right next to an active burial ground. Who knew why my parents chose it?

I used to stand at the window, looking at the lights in back of the houses on the other side of the cemetery. Since the layout was the same as my house, I knew they probably had finished attics that were bedrooms like mine. And I knew that, probably, other kids lived in them. I watched these lights every night of my life. In my loneliness, they became magic places where happy families lived. They were like beacons on a happy shore, and I was watching them from out in the dark sea, adrift, as if prevented by a dark spell, a curse, from reaching the safety of those lights.

When I was fifteen my aunt got me a telescope and I used it to study the cemetery.

I discovered where all the rabbit holes were. There were lots of rabbits in the cemetery, fast, small, gray or brown rabbits. I tracked the various kinds of birds, watched their nests; saw all the takeoffs and landings, worms or insects in their beaks. Loud, harsh bluejays, pretty cardinals, big nasty crows, starlings, thrushes, sparrows, and robins. I carefully observed the occasional green or black snake shimmering through the grass and even saw a few tortoises. On summer nights you could see bats flicking through the air. The place was teeming with wildlife and a hundred different plant types, weeds, creepers, wildflowers, bushes, and trees.

On weekday afternoons, when I arrived home from school, and, of course, almost all day Sunday, there were funerals. Our house was next to a newer part of the cemetery, fresh ground for new graves.

Sunday, about eleven in the morning, I'd look out my open window, and in the distance I'd see a chain of cars slowly approaching: black limousines, then normal-sized cars of different colors winding their way toward me. I'd get my telescope.

The cars stop and everybody gets out. The casket is taken from the back of the hearse and placed on low wooden blocks near the open grave, which is surrounded by black velvet ropes attached to polished brass stands. The mourners line up, ladies in black, some with scarves or veils covering their heads, white handkerchiefs held in gloved hands or pressed to faces. I focus the scope and see the faces more clearly, some red and distorted with tears, some completely frozen and sad, others just quiet, and still others bored or irritated. Occasionally there is a dressed-up little boy or girl, confused, looking like a big doll, holding a grown-up's hand. I bet myself who would be the first to leave. *Yup—the guy with the red vest and yellow tie looking at his watch, puffing up his cheeks and rolling his eyes as the rabbi talks; absolutely, he'll be first off the mark.*

The gravediggers stood in the back, at a discreet distance, their shovel blades resting on the ground. Once everyone was gathered around the grave, the coffin was lowered slowly down. That's when I'd begin to see the breakdowns, hear the sobbing, the shrieks.

"Oh, God, No! No!" "Please don't—oh, please!"

A woman would sink and have to be held up. A man would press one hand to his face and reach blindly with the other one for something or someone. Sometimes, someone seemed to slip or attempted to jump into the grave. Usually it was a woman.

When the rabbi would finish speaking, there'd be a suspended moment, the pinpoint turn when it was clear, finally, that the dead person wasn't coming back, that this was not a nightmare, not a cruel joke. Life with the person lying in that coffin—down in that deep hole—was over forever.

People start to leave, from the fringes first, then slowly from the center. The last ones are helped back into the cars and limousines. The doors shut, the cars drive slowly over the dirt path, the hearse is the last one in the parade. I hear the wheels crunching on the rocks and pebbles, kicking up a little dust if it hasn't rained for a while.

The last car disappears behind a distant group of trees. More silence. The grave diggers advance to the pile of fresh dirt next to the grave. The first clumps of dirt hit the coffin—*parrump, palumpp*—then it gets quieter as dirt hits dirt. The grave diggers are professional shovelers and in no hurry. Sometimes they make jokes. One of the diggers pauses between shovelfuls and flicks his half-smoked cigar into the grave, then finishes up, pats down the fresh earth. They carry the ropes and stands over to the pickup truck parked near the bushes, load them in, toss shovels in after them, and drive off. The breeze lightly ruffles the bushes. The birds call— a sweet chirping conversation. Far away I hear the engine whine of an airplane.

There were times I'd find myself having a hard time breathing when I watched the coffin disappear into the earth and the dirt pile up on it.

Whatever the cemetery represented, it was peaceful, and given the special circumstances of my house—the knife-sharp tension, screaming fits, and arguments—I would escape into the backyard, crawl past the bushes, and wriggle through a hole in the chain-link fence. I'd walk a few yards in, sit on the uncut grass, pull up a long piece, carefully remove the hard yellow outer part, and suck on the sweet green stalk inside. My back rested against the warm granite of a headstone—BELOVED UNCLE, AUNT, FATHER, MOTHER, part of a happy, peaceful family.

I was always respectful—remembering to say hello and ask permission (which they never refused) to sit there among them. Sometimes I dozed off.

Twenty-five years later, when my wife was five months pregnant with our first child, I scouted out a newer, bigger apartment for us. With the low vacancy rate in Manhattan, I felt pretty lucky to find, in just a few days, a big, clean apartment in a good building. I checked the closets, looked at the walls to see if there were any water leaks, turned the valves on the radiators, checked the doors—whatever you do to make sure you aren't being totally hornswoggled by the real estate agent.

I liked the place, mostly because of the copious sun pouring in. I assured the agent that I'd be taking it and signed some note of intent.

The next day I bring my wife to look at the place. She goes to the kitchen window and calls me over. I stand next to her and look out. Directly across the street stands The Westside Memorial Chapel, and at that very moment mourners are getting out of their cars to attend a funeral service. "Nice place," says the wife. "Should be interesting for our child."

I hadn't even noticed it the day before. So, I got to watch another couple of hundred Jews receive their last rites. More veils, black cars, and tears.

CHAPTER FOUR

Despite all my tales of nightmare and depression, my life was not one relentless melodrama. I went to school, I had clean socks and T-shirts, I mowed the lawn in the summer and shoveled snow in the winter, saved my nickels, dimes, and quarters, and bought a bike. I had adventures like any normal kid. My friends and I flipped baseball cards, rode our bikes all over the neighborhood, lay in the grass looking up at the sky, and speculated on the nature of all things.

Almost every morning before school, my best friend, Butch Bayliss, and I played ping-pong in his basement, and in the afternoons we'd sit in his kitchen while his mother made us iced tea and fed us home-baked cookies. I often wished I didn't have to go home—that Butch's mother or somebody would just phone up my house one day and say that I was going to move in with them.

One school day afternoon, I walked into the house and there she was, in the dark living room, looking at me. "How is everything outside today, darling?"

I looked at her and something elemental twitched inside me. I thought: *No. That's it. I'm not doing this anymore.* "I don't know," I said.

"What?" She moved closer, hovering like a bad dream. "What did you say, Michael?!"

I stood there, refusing to speak.

She stared at me. "Michael, I'm asking you."

I stared back at her, blurted out, "I'm not telling!!" and ran upstairs to my room.

Bedlam reigned. I was upstairs, quivering with fear and sheer amazement at my rebellion. My mother punched the table downstairs, upsetting a lamp, and ran, crying, into her room. She dialed up her mother, my grandmother, and was yelling on the phone. "He's going to kill me…oh, God, I wish I'd never had children!!"

Resigned and yet strangely elated, I walked over to the window and contemplated the cemetery, tombstone shadows, crows circling. My mother was downstairs crying brokenheartedly in her room. Her door was open so I got the full effect. My aunt arrived with hot compresses, tourniquettes morphine…my grandmother was on her way.

To my great surprise, no one came up to my room to yell at me. They left me alone. I almost felt lonely, as if the absence of punishment for what I had done was a punishment in itself. Nothing would be the same again. I would never stand in that hallway again, never be forced to tell her my stories. I was happy with my new freedom but sad to have no one to talk to about it.

I entered the unfinished part of the attic, where a few old cardboard boxes of my father's were stacked. And, as I had done many times before, I crouched down and reverently removed objects from the boxes, examining them carefully.

I was fascinated by a slide rule that my father had gotten as a present when he graduated from City College in 1944. It was made of ivory and came in its own red velvet pouch. By the time I was ten years old, it had acquired a very slight creamy tinge. On the surface of the slide rule there was a small, delicate square of crystal, a magnifying glass with a thin red line etched down the middle—which slid smoothly across the length of the ruler, enlarging a small universe of brightly colored numbers and symbols. Beyond one to twelve inches, the stuff on the slide rule made practically no sense to me, but that didn't stop me from playing with it for long stretches. I measured, I computed, I made up my own values and distances, slid the crystal across, poised it over a green symbol that looked Greek. Maybe I imagined that if I found the right magical combination of numbers, my father would materialize right there in the attic.

Certainly the best things in these boxes, better even than the slide rule, were my father's books. Not the college texts; they were boring. No, the real stuff was a set of Mars books by Edgar Rice Burroughs. Everyone knows Edgar Rice Burroughs for Tarzan, but the Mars books are far better, more imaginative. The hero is a guy named John Carter and the first book in the series is *The Warlord of Mars*.

John Carter was a former captain in the Confederate Army, a "dashing, noble Virginian" who embodied the finest of manly virtues. Captain Carter, like so many other fighting men throughout history, grew bored with peace and decided to seek his fortune as a gold prospector in the Wild West. Out west he is pursued by "bloodthirsty" Indians, but just before his capture and certain death he is magically transported to the planet Mars.

Once on the Red Planet, it takes him only a few weeks to master the difference in gravity, the languages, and even the use of the Martian weaponry. Less than four months after his arrival he has overcome the greatest villains and married the most beautiful princess on the planet. He has become the warlord of Mars!! There were several books in this series—nonstop adventures in which John Carter encountered astounding beasts, underwent unbelievable trials and tribulations, saw things no man had ever seen before. Naturally, because of his innate nobility and fighting prowess he emerged victorious.

I read these books in wide-eyed wonder. My father had bought and read them when he was a kid—I could see his name scrawled in some of them. My wandering father who by the time I was nine had taken a series of engineering and construction jobs all over the world, built dams in Alaska, bridges in India, and oil refineries in Ceylon.

The times he did come back to see me, home for a couple of days from his world adventures, he brought me exotic presents. One Sunday afternoon, his usual visiting time, he pulled up in his big green Packard convertible and honked the horn for me to come out. I got in the car and he burned a little rubber pulling away from the curb. It was already late October, getting cold, but my father had the top down.

There he was, bigger than life, fuming cigar stuck in his face, hands on the white plastic steering wheel. "Where do you want to go, kid? How 'bout we take a ride on Southern State?" He cruised the car through my quiet neighborhood. The men were out on their lawns raking leaves. Their eyes shifted over to us. My father's huge two-tone convertible was definitely not the Laurelton style.

We pulled onto the highway at forty miles an hour and were soon doing seventy in the left-hand lane, the cold air whipping me in the face, freezing my right arm where it leaned on the door. We drove like that for about twenty minutes, then he pulled off the exit to Hempstead Lake State Park.

We rolled to a stop near the lake. Nobody around. The wind pretty brisk and most of the leaves off the trees. He turned toward me on the seat and pulled an object out of his jacket pocket. It was a long thin box with foreign writing on it. "That's Hindi, an Indian language," my father said. "I brought this back from India." I removed the top of the box and saw something wrapped in pink tissue paper. I ripped away the paper. It was a curved dagger in a scabbard!

I held it in my hand for a moment, hypnotized—it was like something out of *The Arabian Nights*. The handle and the scabbard were made of wood, painted in a multicolored pattern, lacquer-brilliant greens and golds, and with jet-black lines snaking through the other colors. I tried to pull the knife out of the scabbard, but it wouldn't move. "Here, let me show you how to do it," said my father, taking it out of my hand. I leaned closer to him and watched him. "See," he said, "there's a lock on it, you just have to push this part down with your thumb as you pull it." And out it came, curved, polished, gleaming steel. I took it from his hand. "Watch yourself now," he said, "it's not a toy." I gripped it in my hand and held it up, twisting it back and forth so that the sun glinted off the blade. God, it was beautiful!

I practiced putting the blade back in the scabbard, taking it out, putting it back in. It was perfect. A seed for a million daydreams. I looked up at my father. Ah, how I loved him at that moment. "Do you like it?" he asked. I nodded. We sat there for a while, looking at it on the lake. Then he turned the key in the ignition and we drove back out onto the highway.

We rode for another half hour or so, found a Carvel stand, and got ourselves some double-chocolate cones.

An hour or so later, after another wind-whipping ride on the highway, we pulled back up in front of my house. The sun was going down and it had gotten colder. I sat in the front seat of his car, pulling the dagger out of the scabbard and clicking it back in again. "Well," he said, after a couple of minutes. "Guess I got to be going." I sat there with the knife in my hand, looking up at him. It didn't feel to me that we had spent more than a minute together. And now he was going. "Here," he said, "take the box for the dagger." He handed it to me. My fingers brushed his.

I sat there for another second, then I opened the door and got out, standing on the grass near the curb. He leaned over and pulled the door shut. "OK," he said. "I'll call you. If I have to go out of town, I'll let you know, and I'll write you letters from wherever I am." He started the car and pulled out, made a U-turn, then drove away. I stood there looking at the car as it disappeared down the street. I had no way of knowing if I would see him the next weekend or months later. In a couple of days, he might be twelve thousand miles away.

I walked back into my dark house, clutching the dagger in my hand.

True to his word, my father sent me letters, and when he was too busy to write, he sent postcards.

I remember one from Burma. A photograph of my father on the front of the card, dressed in complete white-hunter getup: khaki hunter's shirt, long khaki shorts, kneesocks, high boots, steel watch on his arm, and a white pith helmet. Standing next to him was a little half-naked brown man and behind them, the jungle. Through the vines and leaves I could just make out the shape of a ruined temple. On the back of the postcard it said, "Dear Mike, The jungles of Burma are very hot this time of year. How is everything in Laurelton? Love, Dad."

CHAPTER FIVE

The last thing my father bought for me before he left our house for good was a small Zenith table radio. Over the years it became my permanent lifeline. This radio, a small, dark-brown plastic box, sat on a night table right next to my bed, no more than a foot from my right ear. It was there when I was four and it was virtually the only thing I took with me when I moved out of the house. It was a radio with tubes that took a few seconds to warm up before the sound came on.

In the center of the band the Zenith people (no doubt knowing how much it would mean to me) had painted a fire, friendly and warm like a campfire, that lit up red-orange when the tiny bulb behind it started to glow. Up in my room, with madness downstairs and death out the back window, I huddled over that little radio fire, like a caveman on a vast dark plain.

And what did I listen to? Men's voices, of course. Anything: weather, news, comedy, baseball broadcasts of course, and *The Lone Ranger* and *Amos and Andy*.

The Lone Ranger was a little like John Carter of Mars—a real stand-up guy. I didn't care for Tonto's tone, though; I believe that sometimes he was actually making fun of the Lone Ranger—who could tell what those grunts meant? I mean, after all, you couldn't see the man's face.

Just around dawn there were hog and cattle price reports from some far-away place. Why anyone thought people in New York City wanted to know what pigs and cows were selling for was a mystery to me—but I listened anyway.

In those days, there weren't that many women on the radio, just ladies like *Miss* Arlene Francis and *Miss* Pegeen Fitzgerald. They interviewed novelists and told other ladies when there were sales on at Bonwit's and Lord & Taylor.

I loved my little radio, because in the daily reality of my life I existed in a world of women: my mother, my sister, my aunts, and my grand-mother. True, I had an uncle next door and my grandfather lived two blocks away. They both went to work, brought home the money, ran errands for the women, and spoke only when spoken to. But it was on the radio that I found a daily dose of what I was missing.

On Sundays, after two or three hours of "Yes, Jesus!" and "Bless us, Lord!" programs, I listened to foreign-language broadcasts, usually Spanish and Greek. I understood a couple of words of Spanish (because I watched *Zorro* and *The Cisco Kid* on television) but Greek, well, it was Greek to me.

Aside from the fact that they were men talking, maybe I thought these foreign voices brought me closer to my father. I even listened to the Yankees games in Spanish sometimes. It sounded like this to me: "Mantle elcapeto-decaballo-deplato...yobingotopo...ehhhhh-tchk!! (that was the bat hitting the ball). Biquita! Biquita! Scatolpo!! Bambadebandomente! Gobotoledo-decompresiento!! [cheers]."

I remember one Sunday morning, my grandfather came into the house and stood at the bottom of the stairs, listening to me listen to the radio. It was a Greek station.... "Efkerstopho Kalata...Kosmoplako—Helas Kostas...Kroastotahpose—Dramatikos...Astoria, Quins." I heard my grandfather say to my mother: "Ruthie, mark my words, that boy has a facility for languages!"

My two favorite radio personalities, when I was thirteen or so, were Long-John Nebel and Jean Shepherd, both on WOR. Later on in his career Nebel moved to NBC and had a syndicated show, but that wasn't the real deal. His earlier and by far his greatest programs were on WOR in New York. The show started at midnight and ran till five A.M., every weekday night. It began with an eerie musical theme that instantly let you know that the day was over and you were entering…*The Night.*

Long-John always had his regular bunch of pals, a gang of old-time cigar-chomping, whiskey-guzzling men. I don't remember all of them. One was Will Ousler, a well-known radio writer, and then there was Keigh Deigh, a character actor in the movies. There were a couple of chefs from famous midtown restaurants, and reporters just having wrapped up their stories for the early editions. Jackie Gleason, the television star, would show up now and then.

And what did they talk about for five hours every night, five days a week? …Anything they felt like. The news, who was going to win the pennant, UFOs, the best bars and grills in New York; one night they traded stories about the best shoeshines they ever had—for five hours! And it was terrific. These men were part of a now vanished type—raconteurs, bullshit artists, cigar-store philosophers. They had all traveled and worked all manner of jobs in their lives, high and low, and they could tell long stories about any damn thing and make it sound fascinating.

You could hear the glasses clinking and the smoke blowing from their mouths. "Light that for you, John?" (sound of a cigarette lighter clicking). "Thanks, Will" (puff puff). "You're a gentleman and a scholar…ah, that's a smoke.…"

And it was an even better smoke if the brand was one of the sponsors.

Long-John, in his early years, had been a carnival barker and a traveling salesman. He could sell anything. I remember once he did a commercial for dog food, I think it was Alpo.…

"Now, ladies and gentlemen, let me take just a moment of your time to tell you about a fine, fine product. This product, Alpo dog food, is top-quality goods. I'm holding a can of this fine product in my hand at this very moment. Made from the finest ingredients, the choicest chunks of beef, the finest spices, and succulent gravies. Yes, ladies and gentlemen, this is, beyond dispute, the very best dog food on the market today. Get some tomorrow for your dog—I guarantee you he will love it." Forget the dog—*I* wanted a can of that succulent product for myself, right then and there. Long-John took time out for a station ID, and the show continued where it left off.

"You know, boys," says John, clearly on the cusp of a story, "this fine cigar reminds me of a time I was in the Porter House in Chicago. You know it?"

"Know it well, John, know it well. Finest steaks this side of the Mississippi."

"True, very true...well, there was a man walked in and sat down next to me at the bar...he was about fifty or so, looked like he had seen better days, but still, you could tell by the cut of his cloth, a real gent in his time...." And, off he'd go with a long, rambling story, like Damon Runyon.

Right before Long-John was Jean Shepherd. Shepherd was a Midwesterner who every night, five nights a week, came on by himself and just talked. I don't know how he kept it up. The show was on for years, from maybe the late fifties to the mid-seventies. Later on, when radio got more homogenized and robotic, he did some television specials and wrote a couple of successful screenplays. He also wrote for *Playboy* and had a couple of books published, but radio was his true metier. Shepherd was an artist of talk—a born storyteller. He spoke right up against the microphone, in a hushed, intimate voice tinged with dry humor and charged with appropriate melodrama when called for. He told of his youth, growing up in a lower-middle-class suburb of Chicago, right near the steel mills; of his sad mother and his pompous old man; of his friends and their days on the streets. Life in the mills, terrible and beautiful, teachers, bosses, girlfriends, his time in the army in World War II, his early days in radio in other cities. When he talked about being a kid, well, nobody I've ever heard before or since, got the precise special terrors and joys of childhood down the way Shepherd did. He was a live human being, a master teller of tales, in a medium since turned, with just a few exceptions, to a wasteland of superficial corporate shit.

Shepherd would never even get on commercial radio today. There's no place left in our chopped, diced, sound-byte world for a person to simply take his time with a thought or a feeling or a good old-fashioned story.

There were other good programs: leftover, old-time serials, later Bob & Ray, even some of the local DJs sounded human and personal, but it was Long-John and Shepherd—those strong, soothing voices, pouring from that little warm plastic box next to my bed—that kept me sane.

That radio was both father *and* mother to me. There were times I'd sit up in bed, reach over, and put my hands on it, feeling the warmth and the vibrations of the voices, talking on and on into the night.

CHAPTER SIX

By the time I was thirteen, I had become silent and withdrawn, one of those kids in the last row who slouches far down in the seat. To a teacher, I must have looked something like an alligator: a snout and a pair of hostile eyes, glaring over the top of a desk.

I was always pissed-off, depressed, and had effortlessly slipped into the role of supreme underachiever of the SP (Special Progress class) of the eighth grade of JHS 59 in Springfield Gardens, Queens. I never volunteered, and when called on by the teacher I'd say nothing or mumble, "I don't know."

The time came for the English final, the winter term. The teacher handed out the question sheet and the little blue books, looked at the clock, and said: "Go." But I was not going anywhere. I caught the teacher's eye and slowly but surely folded the question sheet into a paper airplane, got up, walked over to the window, opened it, and sailed the final exam out into the street.

The teacher told the principal, and they called my mother, who was in one of her relatively sane periods. She came to school and they told her that I *might* be emotionally disturbed. They recommended that she take me to a therapist. "OK," said my mother, "I'll take him to mine!"

My mother's shrink was a gynecologist—and my mother was his entire psychiatric caseload.

After my mother had been through her third psychiatrist, the family had decided to send her to see an old family friend, Charles Grauber, a guy my mother had grown up with in East New York. He was about five years older than she was, and had an obstectric practice in Brooklyn. Since Charles had taken neurology and psychology classes in medical school, he decided that he was more than qualified to treat my mother. I knew him simply as Charles. He'd been coming to my house off and on since I was born.

One Saturday afternoon, my mother and I got in my grandfather's dark green Chevy. Off to Brooklyn to see Charles, my shrink.

Brooklyn was foreign territory for me. It seemed very far away and vaguely frightening—even a little disgusting. It was one of those places from the past, where the *old people* lived; gnarled grandparents and fat aunts; people who ate strange food and spoke with accents. When I went to the old neighborhood for visits, and this was true of the Bronx and Manhattan too, I saw crumbling concrete and worn marble, apartment buildings with white tiled hallways and green painted plaster walls. These places smelled funny—not clean and new like Queens.

Places in Brooklyn had weird scary names. In Queens, there were towns like *Laurel*ton, *Fresh* Meadows, *Spring*field Gardens. In Brooklyn there was *Sheepshead* Bay, *Red Hook*, *Graves*end....

After about an hour of driving, we pulled up in front of Charles's office—on the first floor of a fairly modern-looking tan-brick apartment building. My mother and I got out and my grandfather said, as he always did, "I'll wait in the car." He was always waiting in the car while my grandmother or my aunt went into stores to shop or my mother was in some doctor's office. That was one of his jobs, chauffeur. My grandfather was a good man, but like the rest of the men in my family, he just worked there.

Charles stood in the foyer of his office. As soon as my mother saw him, she collapsed against his chest and burst into wracking sobs. He put his arm around her and led her into his office and I was left alone in his empty waiting room. Of course there were no other patients there because he had come in on a Saturday exclusively to see my mother, and now me.

I paced around for a bit, then decided to see if I could hear anything going on in the office. I went over and put my ear right up against the door. I heard my mother crying and caught parts of some of her sentences. *...and then he...oh God!...they had no right....* I didn't want to hear anymore of *that* so I snuck back and sat down on one of the couches in the waiting room.

There was nothing to do but look at the magazines on the coffee table. In 1958 the only magazine doctors had in their offices—except maybe *Life* or *Look*—was the monthly magazine of the American Medical Association. It routinely featured hundreds of pages of articles on diseases and treatments, and advertisements for drugs and medical paraphernalia.

There I sat, skinny and understandably more nervous than usual with my mother inside crying. By this time in my life I was riddled with constant psychosomatic ailments, and here I was reading articles on every vicious disease in the Western Hemisphere, and a few from the exotic East as well. The articles were illustrated with graphic color drawings, all extremely realistic; heart surgery, veins, lungs, stomachs. There were also close-up photographs, sparing the reader nothing, of people with horrible goiters, knees splintered to pieces in accidents, gangrene. There was a special article in the magazine I was reading that morning about elephantiasis, a disease I'd never heard of before. There were pictures of skinny little foreign guys, their eyes dull and hopeless, with legs the size of tree trunks.

Fifteen minutes, a half hour, my mother was shouting and weeping behind the door. My breathing was getting ragged, my skin was starting to break out; I was biting my lip and my foot was tapping out of control against the coffee table. I looked down and I saw—yes! my right leg had gotten thicker! It was pressing against my dungarees, growing, I could feel it growing bigger by the minute, it was, it had to be—elephantiasis! Oh no! My heart was beating out of control, my brain whirling in terror.

At that moment, my mother came out of Charles's office. She looked terrible, like she had just seen a train wreck. She smiled weakly at me and said, "It's your turn, sweetheart."

I walked into the office and saw Charles standing just inside the door, wearing his white doctor jacket. He shook my hand and said, "Sit down,

Mike." I sat, slouched actually, down in the chair in front of his desk and looked at him.

Charles was easily six feet tall, ramrod straight with a military-style haircut and a small dark mustache. He'd been a captain in the Army in World War II—the Big One. And, like a lot of men of his generation, it was one of the defining experiences of his life. There was, among the framed degrees and graduating class pictures on his office walls, a picture of him in his uniform, smiling, standing amidst the ruins of some French town— and in the background, a smashed German armored vehicle with a body hanging half out of the hatch.

In fact, Charles hadn't been just any army captain. He had been a Beach Master at Normandy, *directing traffic*, yelling at men to get up off their terrified asses and charge the Germans.

The first thing Charles said to me was, "Sit up straight, son." So I did. I sat up straight—therapy was working already! Or rather, not therapy but simply fathering. Here was a man who was not a wimp, not a toady for my mother or my grandmother, not even a half-ass junior high school teacher—he was a tough guy, a World War II combat veteran, a doctor with a white coat and a gold watch. I thought, *Well, here's something. Here's somebody who can maybe help me.* I sat up straight and waited for my next order, but then, as fast as they had shot up, my hopes came crashing down. "You know, Mike," Charles told me, "your mother is very upset."

I collapsed back in the chair, eyebrows raised, and said sarcastically, "My mother is upset?! Oh no! What happened? She was her usual cheery self when we got here."

Charles didn't appreciate that kind of talk. "You know, Mike," he said, "nobody likes sarcasm, and I told you to sit up straight." A direct order, as it were. Even though I did sit up straight again, I was already going AWOL from Charles's army. I said a little about what I thought was bothering me and he kept telling me not to be a crybaby and to be nice to my mother.

I continued to go each Saturday with my mother and my grandfather, hoping, probably, that Charles would finally see that I needed him and side with me against all the unfairness and oppression. After all, he was the closest thing to a real man in my life. Alas, Charles never did sympathize with me during the six months I saw him.

THE TALKING CURE / 53

At seventeen, when I was a senior in high school, it came time to take the state Regents exam. If you did well, you could get what amounted to, in those days, a pretty good chunk of money from the state of New York for the first year of college. I took the test along with the rest of my school, not expecting anything, not really caring. My grade average was so low that I was not qualified to get into a free city college like Queens or Hunter (this was before open admissions). None of my family's concerns about my future and college meant anything to me. I was just treading water, hostile and depressed most of the time and wondering when, or if, this odd phenomenon, my life, was going to change for the better or simply end.

They posted the test "winners" on a list in the main hallway. There they were, the names of about thirty or so kids, well-known for being the best students in school—the most likely to succeed—and then my name, *third* from the top of the list. The very next day I was called out of class to the dean's office.

I was not a stranger to the dean's office. I was always being sent there for talking too much in class, skipping class altogether, or "causing a disturbance."

I went into the dean's outer office on the first floor, across from the principal's office, and as I walked in, Susan Feinberg, one of the smartest students in the school, passed by me on the way out. Her eyes were all red and she was honking vigorously into a hanky. I took a seat and waited. In a minute or two the office door opened and Mr. Bloomberg, the dean, motioned me to come in. I slouched down in the chair in front of his desk. He looked across his desk at me with undisguised contempt, but not only for my various provocations and screwups. I'm sure he had also decided that I was a discredit to the Jewish race, a blight on the great record of intellectual and scholastic achievement that Jews were supposed to display to the rest of the world.

He picked up a copy of the Regents winners list, sort of shook it at me at eye level, and said: "Very funny, Feder." I grinned at him, playing the game. But I wondered, did he think I had scored high on the test purely out of contrariness and malice? Well, that was partially true, of course, but really, he didn't know me. After all, I hadn't cheated, I really *did* know the answers to the questions on the test, and I wanted to show them all in that school that I had value, that I was smart. No matter; I acted out my part, smiling at him in my best punk manner. "I know," the dean said, "that you don't care about college, but that girl," referring, no doubt to Susan the honker, "really does care. She wants a good education and she is capable of doing something with it." In other words, Susan was something that I most definitely was not...an *achiever*.

The dean wanted me to withdraw, give back my scholarship. That would somehow allow Susan to get onto the list since she had just missed by one point. It didn't make any difference to me that he was basically right and the scholarship was really wasted on me. The dean had just marched right into my maximum hostility minefield and he had to pay the price. I smiled at him. "No. Uh-uh." He was disgusted, threw the paper down on the desk and said, "You know, Feder, you're *sick*—you are a mentally disturbed individual."

Bloomberg told me that he was recommending I be sent to the Bureau of Child Guidance for counseling. To him, of course, this was punishment, not a desire to help. My mother and my aunt were summoned to school, and I was officially referred.

About a week later I was told to report to a room in the basement of the school. I left class and went all the way down the stairs to where the locker rooms were, underneath the gyms. The note said, "Room B-141, Mrs. Rosenzweig." I had never heard of her. She wasn't in the dean's office, not in the principal's office, she wasn't a teacher. This was mysterious and more than a little worrisome. Pulled abruptly out of class and sent to a nameless, faceless room somewhere, I started to sweat. I had read *1984*. I knew what the authorities were capable of. Also, I lived in the constant fear of being *punished*.

At the bottom of the stairs, just opposite the door to the boys' locker room, I looked up at the room numbers posted above the doors. I took a few steps, then stopped. I was two feet from some large swinging doors that said "To Girls' Locker Room." I stood rooted to the spot. I had never, of course, gone through these doors. I had never heard of *any* boy going through them. I looked through the glass windows in the door and I saw, just twenty feet or so down the hall, the actual door to the girls' locker room. Right next to that door, off to the side, was room B-141—Mrs. Rosenzweig.

How could I go down that hall? What if the door swung open when I was there and I saw into the girls' locker room? I was assailed by visions of screaming girls, pointing fingers, shouts, running feet. I am clubbed down by the authorities, jerked to my feet, surrounded by angry female faces screaming: "Hang him!" "Kill him!" "He looked into the girls' locker room! Cut off his dick!"

I was terrified of women. My mother used to walk around in her madness half-naked; she wore sheer nightgowns, left over from when she had a husband and a sex life. I could see her breasts and the dark triangle between her legs, just before my grandmother would grab her and hustle her back into her room. And my mother had a habit of sitting with her legs wide open when she was wearing dresses. I never knew if this was from living too long without a man or something intended directly for me.

In the summer when I was eight, I slept in her room, on a mattress at the foot of her bed, my sister in the bed next to her since my mother had the only air conditioner. I had to be there not only because it was so stifling up in my attic room but because I had allergies and asthma, so the air-conditioner was a medical necessity. I would lie at the foot of the bed, a couple of feet from where my mother lay, under a thin cotton blanket. I don't know what she was wearing and I was always very careful not to look. It was very hard to go to sleep.

At night, even when I was sleeping up in my own room, I would wake up once, sometimes twice a night and wander downstairs to the bathroom to pee. Her door was open. And that was the problem. Her door was open. With my father gone and me the only "man" in the house, I felt a powerful pull from her. My mother had no decorum, no sense. There was no boundary line drawn between her as an adult and a mother and me as a child and her son. I was certain that anytime I wanted, I could crawl right into that bed with her. I knew she wanted me to. She was up half the night anyway, lying there in the dark, needing someone to console her, soothe her fears. And what did I want? All alone up there in the attic, bursting to touch and be touched by a girl. There were brief, aching, crazy moments when I thought I'd do it, go into her bedroom, but rage and fear and sheer willpower chased these thoughts away. I kept to my side of the boundary line.

By the time I was ten, it occurred to the rest of the family to buy me my own air-conditioner and get me out of her room. Still, especially when I was in my teens, I could feel her down there waiting for me.

As I stood, frozen outside the swinging doors, I suddenly felt a hand tap me on the shoulder and a girl's voice say, "excuse me." I jumped and moved aside to let her go past me and through the doors to the locker room. She looked back over her shoulder at me and I felt my heart thump. Standing there sweating and looking demented was clearly a very bad idea, so I pushed through the doors and walked the twenty feet to B-141. Over the door, in gold lettering, it said BUREAU OF CHILD GUIDANCE. I looked through the window in the door and a woman sitting behind a big wooden desk gestured for me to come in.

I was in that office for about three hours. Mrs. Rosenzweig, a matronly woman in her late forties, dressed in expensive clothes, gave me a bunch of tests: an IQ test, a Rorschach test, and something called the Thematic Apperception Test. The IQ test wasn't much trouble, and the Rorschach pictures, as the old joke always goes, looked basically like a bunch of moths or butterflies reflected in a mirror. The Thematic Apperception Test was something different—a series of realistic drawings that could mean anything. Each scene, a house with a sun shining on it, a window with a face looking out of it, a street with people talking to each other, was designed to be ambiguous, leaving all sense of meaning up to the beholder.

One drawing made me particularly nervous.

There was a small, simple, forties-looking bedroom with a single nightstand, a rug, a picture on the wall—very Edward Hopperish. The evening—or, if I preferred, morning sun—was coming in the open window. In a double bed was a woman: long hair, attractive, with a sheet drawn halfway over her breasts. She was staring at something in a part of the room you couldn't see. Sitting on the edge of the bed, facing away from the woman was a man, half-dressed, just his pants and a T-shirt, who was either getting ready to take off his clothes and get into bed with the woman or had just gotten out of bed and was putting on his clothes.

This picture stopped me cold. At that point in my life I had never touched a girl, never even seen a copy of *Playboy*! The picture she was showing me was like pornography.

Finally, looking down at the floor, I managed to tell the Mrs. Rosenzweig what I thought. "The man feels bad because of something he just did, and he's feeling guilty that he has to leave now."

"What did he just do?"

I turned red. "Something bad."

"What?"

"I don't know—something bad."

"Why does he feel guilty?"

"Because of what he did...and because he is leaving her alone." What I had said set her scribbling on a pad for a few moments. We went through a few more pictures; all of them seemed upsetting, sad, or ominous. Then, after a few more questions, I was out of there.

A couple of days later, I got a note to come to the dean's office. The dean, without a word, handed me a sealed envelope jointly addressed to me and my mother and told me to go back to class. In the boys' bathroom on the first floor I opened it—I could always tell my mother I didn't see her name written on it. I was requested to report to the Queens headquarters of the Bureau of Child Guidance that coming Wednesday afternoon after school for "further evaluation and treatment."

So, that was that. I was now an official mental patient, a registered nut like my mother. I felt like I had just been permanently joined to her whether I liked it or not. All those years struggling to keep out of her clutches and I run full speed into her, traveling in the other direction.

That Wednesday after school, everybody got on the regular bus back to the neighborhood; I got on a bus to the opposite side of Queens—to the Bureau of Child Guidance. "Where you goin'?" my friends wanted to know. "The allergist," I think, was the excuse I gave them.

As the bus went through neighborhoods I had never seen before, I calmed down, watching everyday humanity out the window. We arrived in a very quiet, clean neighborhood with small houses a lot like mine, but it had a different feel—more compulsively neat, more severe looking. Even though it felt a little uncomfortable there, I still had the feeling I've had so often in my life when taking a trip—no matter the distance—to a place I've never been before. It was a sense of sudden comfort, a kind of serenity. I think it was the knowledge that I was only drifting through, that I was, for a little while, blessedly anonymous, traveling in a duty-free zone of responsibility. There have been times when I felt so jammed, so overwhelmed where I lived that I would jump in a car or even go down to the bus station and go—travel for an hour or two, then get out and walk the streets of a strange town, sit and have lunch, have a cup of coffee on a bench in the town square. Something inside me would straighten out, and after a while I'd return home.

Three blocks walking and I was at my destination, an elementary school. It was after three so there wasn't much activity in the schoolyard, just one little kid launching a basketball at the hoop. Inside, it was library quiet. A janitor looked at the paper I brought and told me the room I wanted was downstairs. Why are all therapists in the basement?

Downstairs, some doors were open and there were a few people writing at their desks or talking on the phone. I got to the room typed on my piece of paper and the door was open. I looked at the big school clock down the end of the hall—three forty-five, right on time, of course. I was never late. I'm still that way. In fact, I'm usually early. It gives me some time to reconnoiter, see if there are any hostiles near the perimeter, machine-gun emplacements or traps I should know about, or good escape routes in case I need them.

The room was very small, maybe ten by twelve, a chest-high wooden bookcase filled with books against one wall and a regulation board of education gray metal desk in the middle of the room. The walls were painted standard city green and gray. Up in one corner was a small dust-covered window that looked just like an ant farm; since we were in the basement you could actually see the dirt and the roots of the grass at the bottom half of the window, and above it the grass and a little bit of pale late afternoon sky. Hanging by a long black cord from the high ceiling was a gray metal shade with a low-watt board of education lightbulb.

A man, a very unusual-looking man, stood behind the desk. He was tall, a couple of inches over six feet, and wore a dark blue suit. He was completely bald, with a round smiling face like a Happy Halloween jack-o'-lantern. And he had a funny shape: narrow shoulders and big hips. In fact, he looked very much like a Schmoo—originally a creature in an old comic strip by Al Capp and later a plastic blow-up toy that tipped over but swung right back up again, swaying and smiling. The Schmoo extended his hand across the desk. "Dr. White," he said. I sort of touched his outstretched hand and slid down into the chair in front of his desk. He sat down, smiling his moonfaced smile, and said: "Well, Michael, you and I will be talking with each other."

I stared at him. He continued: "I understand that you've been having some problems." I stared. He said nothing, continuing to look right at me, smiling. We were in suspended Bureau of Child Guidance animation.

The black second hand on the office clock moved slowly around. On Dr. White's upper right forehead, just below the beginning of his curved domed head, was a big red wart. As he sat and smiled, every half minute or so he rubbed his right hand up over his brow, over the wart, and halfway across the top of his head. The wart and his head were constantly being polished. The wart was very red and his head was very shiny in the light of the overhead bulb.

For the next hour, he said nothing and I said nothing. I watched him polish his wart. Finally, after what seemed like years, he glanced at his watch, stood up, still smiling, put his hand across to me, and said, "Thank you very much for coming. I'll see you again next week." I touched his hand and left.

Next week, I boarded the bus, journeyed across Queens, and arrived at his office at three forty-five. He said hello, we sat down and stared at each other in silence for another hour.

This went on, in exactly the same manner, for the next seven months, right to the end of the school year. In my life, I've heard of various kinds of therapy: behavior therapy, Gestalt therapy, nondirective therapy. I would call my treatment with Dr. White nonexistent therapy.

What's interesting, thinking back on it, was the absolute regularity of my attendance. Here was a man you could probably hit with a five-pound sledge and he would keep smiling. He could bore a snail. Yet I never failed to keep my appointments with him.

Chapter Seven

I escaped from high school with a seventy-two-percent average —just enough to win a berth in the freshman class at Long Island's Hofstra University—a place populated by mostly middle-class, spoiled Long Island kids with—it seemed to me—not a lot of brains. Almost all of them drove new cars: Corvettes, Mustangs, and the like. It was a universe of football, basketball, and fraternities; crew cuts, loafers, sweaters, and beer.

Hofstra was a commuter college. Sleepaway school just wasn't in the cards. I belonged at home and that was that. Not only did my relatives deem my presence necessary to my mother's sanity (or what passed for it), but, more sadly to the point, by the time I was seventeen, I was afraid for my *own* sake to go away to school. By that point in my life, I was part emotional cripple, given to migraine headaches, heart palpitations, fainting spells, and states of helpless panic. So I wound up at Hofstra, a college no more than half an hour's drive from my house. I left in the morning and came home in the afternoon, not much different from elementary school except I had a driver's license.

The week college started, I began seeing my third therapist, Mr. Leo Bernstein, in an upper-middle-class town in Nassau County about twenty minutes from my house. The counseling service at Hofstra had found Mr. Bernstein for me. He was in his mid-forties, a handsome man, slightly stocky, with a confident, almost vain bearing. Bernstein had what seemed to me a very European face. He was actually a German Jew and had bright green eyes and a thick, straight mass of dark black hair swept up and back on his head. He had a slight German accent, a bright, charming smile, and the civilized and courteous manners of an upper-class European gentleman, which is just what he had been until the Nazis killed his entire family and stole all their money. He had come to the United States in 1946 after being bounced around various refugee camps.

Bernstein hated America; he hated the people, the customs, and the culture (or lack of it). He hated American politics, which he thought were much too liberal. He hated the way Americans dressed, they way they talked, and practically everything else Americans did—except the cars. He liked big American cars and owned a brand-new Pontiac. Aside from that, everything he had was foreign. His apartment was like a museum of French, Austrian, and Italian antiques—armoires, crystal chandeliers, beaded lamps, huge red velvet chairs. He was getting reparations checks from the German government. Every time I came to his place for an appointment he showed me some new antique he had acquired—a Louis the Sixteenth settee or something.

Why did Bernstein hate America, the country that gave him refuge? It was no secret, he was glad to tell you. Right after he arrived here, penniless, in his late twenties, not yet receiving reparations checks, he immediately, of course, had to go out and earn a living. He got a job selling ties in a fancy department store. Even fifteen years after the experience, remembering it, his very expressive face showed humiliation and disgust. He, Leo Bernstein, the son and heir to what had been a significant fortune in Germany, a kind of prince, had been forced to cater to the whims of what he referred to as "lumpen" American men—praising their "nauseating" taste and "absurd" clothes just to earn a few pennies. And even worse treatment was in store for him in the land of the free. In Berlin, he had completed his undergraduate degree in psychology and had been scheduled to go into the doctorate program. When he applied to Columbia here after the war, they didn't have his records, and he didn't speak English that well, so they made him repeat all his undergraduate courses again. Leo Bernstein, who had graduated from one of the finest universities in

Europe, a man of exquisite breeding and culture, was forced to sit next to pimply faced American undergraduates taking Psychology 101. He was more bitter about this than he could say, and he said plenty.

On my first visit, Mr. Bernstein opened the door and greeted me with a smile and a firm handshake. He waved me into the living room, which was also his office, and once I was seated took his place on a red velvet throne behind a two-hundred-year-old desk that might have once belonged to a duke.

He wore a white linen suit with a blue silk monogrammed shirt, a monogrammed tie, and large sapphire cufflinks on monogrammed cuffs. He smiled at me, a complicated smile that immediately drew me to him; it was part shark, part gigolo, part salesman, and part gracious nobleman. Bernstein seemed to be perpetually amused; he certainly seemed to find *me* amusing. I thought he was strange but I also thought he was cool. Why cool? Because he was exotic, the first European fellow I had ever run into. It wasn't just his physical appearance or the polished antique store-museum where he lived. His manner was so completely self-assured, so smooth, so utterly confident. He was not servile, or self-effacing, or nervous. *He* could never be mistaken for any woman's servant.

Within a couple of minutes of polite conversation, he told me he had met my mother. He laughed. "My dear boy," he said, "we have to get you out of that house. If you don't get away from that woman, you will be either dead or crazy in a few years."

Not only did Bernstein tell me he wanted me out of my mother's house, he told me he had lied to her to plan my escape. When he had spoken to her, about a week before, she told him that I was causing her a lot of trouble because I was "rebellious" and that she wanted Bernstein to calm me down—disabuse me of any silly notions of leaving home. He assured her he would do just that, and now he was telling me he wanted me out. I was in awe of his blatant disregard for the laws of my world.

Having survived one of the worst crimes in history, the man had nothing but contempt for intellectualized shilly-shallying, for long, drawn-out analytic cures. He believed in getting right to the point, identifying the illness, and fixing it by severe and immediate measures. He had no patience, as I mentioned before, for Americans, who in his opinion had never known true suffering. Neurotics bored him; they should just hold their heads up, take the bull by the horns and get on with things. Here was another World War II guy, like my first therapist, Charles. Twenty minutes into my first session, after he announced his liberation plan for me, I was telling him my problems. *My mother is crazy, I get sick all the time, I'm afraid of girls, I grew up without my father....* He frowned and held up his hand. "Stop!" He took off his suit jacket, rolled up his left shirt sleeve, and showed me a blue tattooed number on his arm. It was the first concentration camp tattoo I had ever seen. He said, "Come closer, take a good look." I looked at it, the faded blue numbers on white skin. Bernstein regarded me for a moment. "My dear boy," he said, "you think you have problems? ...you don't have any problems. This," he said, pointing at the tattoo with his right forefinger, "this is a problem." He rolled down his shirt sleeve, cuffed up his cufflink, and put his jacket back on. "Now," he said, "let's talk."

His behavior seemed harsh, unsympathetic even, but he was now my designated savior, so I was willing to do what he said.

The second time I saw him, he got a call in the middle of our session. Naturally I only heard his side of the conversation, but I heard enough of the squawking from the phone receiver to know that his caller was in dire straits. Bernstein listened for a few seconds.

"Hm-hmn, hm-hmn—look, Louis, I have a patient now and I can't really—Louis, don't be hysterical...oh, is that right? Please don't joke with me—I don't have time for jokes...oh, really?" Bernstein smiled, a cold, frightening smile. He looked across the desk at me and repeated the other side of the conversation almost as if he were doing it for my entertainment. "Hello, yes I'm listening...hmnnn...hmnn...so, I see, you're threatening me? Hm-hmn. Oh, I'm not taking you seriously, eh? Hmn—you're going to kill yourself right now? ...well, Louis, I don't like to be threatened and I don't think you're serious. Call me later please." And he hung up.

I stared at him, wide-eyed. He smiled at me. "A hysteric," he said, waving his hand contemptuously at the phone. "I have no time for hysterics."

I saw Bernstein for eight years, right through college and up until I was twenty-five. He brought me safely through my late teens, liberated me from my mother's house, and oversaw my first contacts with an alien race—women. I think he was right that first day; if he hadn't helped get me away from my mother—at first emotionally, then physically—I might have wound up dead or locked up. Murder and suicide were certainly on the original menu in Laurelton. His approach usually worked for me.

Things that baffled experienced therapists, problems that perplexed whole staffs of psychiatric clinics were nothing to Bernstein. I remember the time—I was twenty-three and living on my own in a small apartment in Brooklyn Heights—that I decided I was homosexual. How did I come to this conclusion? Was I sexually attracted to men? Not especially. Was I finding myself drifting toward gay bars and other hangouts? I didn't even know there was such a thing as a gay bar when I was twenty-three. Was I reading gay literature or pornography? Nope. It didn't matter—by a process of cancellation, I decided I must be a homosexual. I had had no sexual contact with a woman for the longest time, and I was obsessed with sex. And, to top it off, there was a gay guy who sat two rows away from me at the welfare center where I was a caseworker and who liked to talk to me. So, it was all very clear to me.

I had no friends outside of work. Each day, I walked home to my lonely two-room apartment, shut the door behind me, sat in a chair in my living room, and stared through the blinds into the street. Everywhere, men and women, boys and girls were walking, laughing, touching, holding hands, kissing. The whole world was in love, or at least having sex, and I was in solitary confinement; no girl and no hope of one anywhere. I spent so much time masturbating, my vital member was turning into a raw frankfurter. I used to keep a big jar of Vaseline on the table next to my bed to keep from losing too much skin.

One night about midnight after a multiple jerk-off it dawned on me: I must be homosexual. It was still four days till my appointment with Bernstein and I was terribly confused and upset about this new turn my life had taken. What was I to do?

The next day at work, a woman I had a crush on (secretly, of course) and who lived in the Village told me about a showing that night of a documentary film on Fritz Perls, a famous psychoanalyst. The woman was in analysis and was always telling me what I really meant by what I said. I decided that I would go see the documentary. Any shrink, even one on film, was better than none, and I still had three days till I could confess my disturbing discovery to Bernstein.

I took a train into Manhattan and got off in the Village, which was strange territory to a hick from Queens. I had only lived on my own for two years, and most of that in Queens and Brooklyn. Manhattan (especially Greenwich Village) was still the Sodom and Gomorrah of my youth. The place where errant, lost souls disappeared to once they stopped eating Wonder Bread and watching Milton Berle. It was appropriate, I thought, that with my newly discovered sexual orientation I should place myself smack in the middle of this pit of iniquity.

I found the church, St. Something or Other, one of those churches that only exists in Manhattan, a building that was more a political coffeehouse and a theater than a place of worship. A screen had been set up—the roll-down kind they used in high school when they wanted to show you how cells multiplied or how an assembly line worked. There were about a hundred or so wooden folding chairs, half filled with twitchy types of various ages and a few dignified-looking older folks in their fifties and sixties with pads and fountain pens at the ready.

The lights went down and there was Fritz Perls, a disheveled, little old white-bearded man in his seventies, standing inside the living room of an apartment somewhere, speaking in a tiny voice with a thick German accent. And what did he talk about? Masturbation! I was amazed. Good thing I had picked a seat away from other people. This was my standard practice anyway in all public places, like movie theaters and classrooms. Getting too close to anyone made me jumpy, and now that I had reason to fear that I was even more of an "alien" than usual, I thought it was best to keep away from other citizens. I looked out of the corner of my eye. Was everyone staring at me once they heard the word "masturbation"? Fritz Perls, looking straight out at me from the screen, seemed to know, why not everyone else? I glanced quickly down at my lap—maybe my penis had jumped out of its hiding place to surrender to the authorities.

The camera zoomed in on Perls's cute little fuzzy face. "Yes," he says, "I vas vonce a cumpulsif mastabader. Und," continues Fritz, "how did I cure myzelf?" I was transfixed; what lucky conglomeration of stars had lined up and brought me to this place to learn this very secret? I leaned forward. "Vell," he says, "Vurst, I—" And at that precise moment the projector broke. The film slowed and Fritz faded from the screen in slow motion, his voice deepening to incomprehensibility and his image disappearing like a sad ghost in the light of dawn.

Three days later, I sat in Bernstein's office, more of a wreck than usual. He, with his usual grin, said, "So, how's my favorite neurotic?"

"There is something very serious I have to tell you."

"Oh-ho, something very serious, eh?"

"Yes."

"So?"

"I'm a homosexual."

Bernstein smiled. "You're a homosexual?"

"Yes, I am."

"And when did this happen?"

"Monday night—around midnight."

He composed his face, nodded his head up and down in contemplation. I wondered what he was going to ask me and what he would tell me to do now that I had drifted beyond the pale. After a heavy moment, he said: "Let me ask you something, do you want to kiss a man on the lips?"

"What?"

"You heard me, do you want to kiss a man on the lips?"

"Well, no, no I don't."

"Then you're not a homosexual!"

Case closed. No discussion about any fantasies I might have had. Had I had a homosexual experience; was there something from my past? No interpretation of why I even thought this. Just, "you're not a homosexual."

Naturally I was very relieved; I already had enough problems without having to deal with an entirely new sexual orientation, but the real problem still remained. I wanted to have sex with a girl, to be blessed with a real girlfriend, but I was terrified to even ask anybody to have so much as a cup of coffee after work. Bernstein, swiftly following up on my recent miracle cure, leaned across the desk and whispered to me. "You know that cute girl who sees me right after you?" I did, and she *was* very sexy; about nineteen and always very friendly, almost flirtatious, when I passed her on my way out of his office.

"Well," said Bernstein, "when you leave my office tonight, ask her out on a date."

"What?!"

"Ask her out—she's a hot ticket. She'll do anything." But I never did talk to her; I was too afraid.

Bernstein used to describe his girlfriends—and there were many of them—in loving, salacious detail. He was the supreme ladies' man. So I was surprised to hear him tell me, after I had been seeing him for six years (I was twenty-four), that he had met a "very rich woman" and was getting married.

I remember I felt somehow betrayed and he took pains to reassure me that even though he was now going to live "in style," as he put it, he would still be conducting his private practice. He told me he was going on a honeymoon trip, four weeks "on the continent," and he would set up an appointment for me after he returned.

The first time I went to see him at his new place in Manhattan, I was overwhelmed by its richness. He and his new wife, a woman whose grandfather was the founder of some huge corporation and whom I had even seen featured in *The New York Times* society pages, lived in a vast co-op on Sutton Place. After I was shown into the apartment by a maid, Bernstein introduced me to his wife, a small, thin, very pleasant woman, pretty, and about his age, around fifty. We talked for a while, then she said she had some shopping to do, kissed him on the cheek, and left.

He took me on a tour of his new castle. There were so many rooms I got dizzy, with furniture, paintings, statues everywhere. In their bedroom was a king-sized—no, *emperor*-sized—bed with a carved, painted set of royal eagles mounted on the bedstead. In the living room, which was about twice the size of my entire apartment, he showed me more acquisitions: a new, bigger desk, inlaid with several different kinds of wood, from the eighteenth century, he said, cost him twenty thousand dollars; a striped, multicolored, silk-upholstered couch he said was from a French palace; various bronze statues; and huge dark oil paintings in ornate carved frames.

We entered the tiled-floor dining room, silk brocade covering the walls, swirly marble counters and gold-plated taps over the sink. Bernstein stood, hands clasped behind his back, surveying the East River. I could see he felt that he had finally come into his own, that he was now living, once again, in the style to which he had been born. He seemed more baronial, grander than ever. I congratulated him on his ascension. He turned and draped his arm around my shoulders. "My boy," he said, "if you want real success in this world, do what I did, marry a rich woman who is crazy about you."

Bernstein was never quite the same after his nuptials. He seemed to be even less interested in the petty details of my life and sufferings. He talked endlessly about his new purchases, trips he was going to take, auctions he'd been to. Still, despite his lapses, Bernstein was still the closest thing I had to a father, and I was utterly faithful to him. Though I whined occasionally and was slow to follow his advice, at bottom I doted on his every word and look. Nothing would ever make me miss my appointment with him—not hell or high water, not even one of my sudden fevers or periodic fatal diseases. I was always there at the appointed hour.

In the fall of 1965, my junior year in college, there was a complete blackout in New York City. I was still living out in Queens with my mother and the power outage occurred sometime around dusk on a weekday evening. I had an appointment with Bernstein at seven P.M. and no puny blackout was going to interfere with it.

I jumped in my car at six—the sun was just about down—and headed into the city. It was a magical ride. Darkness everywhere, no lights on the parkway except the headlights and taillights of other cars. Everyone was driving at half-speed, which intensified the unreal feeling, the sense of gliding through outer space. Here and there, in the houses and apartment buildings off to the side of the parkway, there was an occasional sweep of a flashlight beam or the flicker of a candle in a window. My magic ship flew through the darkness into Manhattan.

The Triboro Bridge, because all the lights on the spans were out, seemed suspended in midair, a road across the sky. From this high vantage point one could usually see the entire Ozlike brilliance of Manhattan. Two hundred blocks, ten miles of towers, blazing with lights. It was always an awesome sight, but that night…nothing. The sky was overcast, so even the starlight had disappeared. The city was utterly inert, dormant, like the ruins of an ancient civilization stumbled upon in the jungle. You could only make out the tops of the biggest buildings, backlit by the lights from the New Jersey side of the Hudson. In skyscraper windows, twenty, fifty stories high, there were small pinpoints of light: candles.

I got off the bridge on the Manhattan side. There were no toll collectors, just a couple of cop cars with their roof lights on, reminding you that there was still law and order. I drove, very slowly, down the East River Drive, looking for the exit sign for Sixty-third Street. It came up suddenly and I pulled off the highway onto the streets.

Cars had slowed to a crawl—there were no traffic lights to regulate us, so we were all on our own. I rolled the windows down, since now it was necessary to communicate by voice—vision being reduced to a bare minimum.

It was a relatively mild night for that time of the year, and everyone in the city seemed to be out on the streets. People were holding candles and carrying flashlights and lanterns. I drove about three blocks and hit a traffic jam. It was a busy intersection, and since nobody could see, people were leaning half their bodies out of the driver's seat to navigate and yell out to other drivers. My car rolled to a standstill and I got out.

I instantly understood why things seemed so unfamiliar on the streets; it wasn't simply that all the lights were extinguished. The electricity was off. Of course! Something so simple but so profound, you could never know the effect of it till it was gone. No radios, no televisions, no fluorescent lights or bright-colored neon signs, no music blasting from storefronts, no pulsing, no flickering, no blaring. This sudden blessed silence had even affected the drivers. Not one horn blasted, no one was shouting or cursing. I got back in the car, pulled over to the curb, and got out again. I was about ten blocks from Bernstein's apartment. The air was light and warm and there was, hovering over and rising up from the crowds of people milling around and standing in the doorways, a feeling of complete benevolence. Here was, finally, out of the blue, as from heaven above, a cessation to the relentless movement of things. For a space and time, there was nothing to hear, nothing to buy or sell, nothing to rush to or get away from. I guess things could have gone completely the other way—fear, panic, madness, violence, but they didn't.

Some men with flashlights stepped into the street and were guiding drivers, an informal corps of civilian traffic cops. People talked and laughed lightly in the darkness. I had never before, and never since, felt such an air of calm and civility in the city.

I made my way through the lovely darkness to Bernstein's building. The doorman shined a flashlight in my face, recognized me, and waved my into the lobby. No elevator, of course, so it was twelve floors up the stairs. No problem for me at the age of twenty, but a big problem, I could immediately see, for the old folks that lived in the building. Here again, civility had blossomed. Since all activity had slowed down and essentially stopped, people were thrown on each other's mercy. Another man and I, slowly, step by step, resting for minutes on each landing, helped an old woman up to her fourth-floor apartment. Two floors later, I shook hands with my fellow rescue worker (he lived on six), and proceeded carefully upstairs to Bernstein's apartment. Apartment doors, usually locked and bolted as tight as bank vaults, were thrown open and the warmth of candles shone out into the hallways.

I got to the twelfth floor and knocked on Bernstein's door. He opened it, in his undershirt, beaming at me. He clapped me on the back and ushered me in. "I knew *you* wouldn't fail me," he laughed, "my most faithful patient." His apartment was blazing with candlelight from silver candlesticks and gold candelabra. The ivory-gold light reflected off the mirrors and polished wood surfaces of his old furniture.

Bernstein informed me that due to the "emergency," which word he pronounced with great irony, therapy was canceled for the evening. He had been invited to a party on the tenth floor and I was coming as his guest. He went into the bathroom to take a shower and get himself dandied up while I sat on his living-room couch, perusing his art books.

The party downstairs was all candlelight and brandy snifters, and everyone was about twenty years older, or more, than I was. Bernstein, in a dark-blue sport jacket with white silk shirt and maroon ascot, sashayed in and located the hostess. "Allow me," he said, "to introduce my protégé, Mr. Michael Feder," and he left me to mingle. I shook hands with the woman, who pointed to the sideboard and told me to help myself to a drink. A drink! I was alarmed. I had never before had anything more than a couple of glasses of Manischevitz grape wine at Passover or a half-glass of beer at a college pub. I walked over and checked out the bottles and various amber fluids in crystal decanters. I held one up to a candle and the whiskey inside shimmered like a genie in front of the flame. Pouring some into a glass, I walked over to the living room window and looked down at the street. There were car headlights and flashlights creating paths of light in which people appeared briefly and faded away again. More candles twinkled in the windows in the building across the way. I sipped my drink. In a few minutes I was half drunk and the room took on a warm glow—everybody was beautiful; they were all wonderful. The hostess walked over; I don't know what I said to her, but she laughed and guided me to a couch.

After a while, Bernstein appeared in front of me and announced that he was tired—we were going back up to his apartment. We sat there in his den office—more whiskey in my glass, brandy in his—and talked for a long, long time. Or rather, he talked, I listened. He leaned back in his red leather chair, gazed at the candelabra, and reminisced about his youth, his parents, his two older sisters, his school days, his friends. Riding horses, weekends at his country estate, the grand soirees in his father's mansion. "Ah, my poor deprived boy, my benighted American peasant, you have no conception...the beauty, the elegance, the women!" He talked about his studies at the university, the great and famous professors he studied with.

He poured himself more brandy, told more stories. Then the inevitable happened. The long somber pause, the deep furrows in the brow, the darkening of his eyes. He was remembering the slide, the fall, the destruction. He shook his head—this was not the night to talk about such things, and maybe he never would, anyway. He shook himself and clapped his hands together. "But that is all in the past, and the past is dead. It's also too late and not safe for you to be driving home, so, you are my guest tonight." He winked at me. "Call your dear mother and tell her you are staying at the Bernstein Grand Hotel for the night—four-star accommodations." He went out and brought back a sheet, some blankets, and a pillow, tossed them onto the couch, and then made up the bed for me. I was on the phone with my mother, telling her I'd be home tomorrow. She started to protest but I just said good-bye and hung up. Bernstein stood in the doorway to the room, smiling. "Good night, good night, my boy... tomorrow is another day."

More than a little drunk, and floating on a cloud of happiness and security, I got under the blanket and drifted off to sleep.

I got up the next morning, slightly sick to my stomach and with a headache. Bernstein, dressed and smiling down at me benignly, told me to get up and get myself some coffee. "Laziness will never get you anywhere." He was all business, had to get to his job at the clinic where he worked in Lower Manhattan. I looked out the kitchen window. Everything, I was sad to see, was back to normal: rushed, loud, and crazy. I gulped some coffee, put my shoes on, and we went down in the elevator together. The daylight was a brilliant glare; cars everywhere, people walking too fast. He and I parted company at the end of the block; he was headed the other way to a garage for his car. He slapped me on the back and told me he would see me for our appointment the next Thursday, and off he went down the block, cocky and confident, meeting another day head-on. I finally found my car. There was a parking ticket stuck in the windshield.

As I neared the exit to Laurelton and my mother's house, the magic images slowly disappeared, like Prospero's fantastic creations. The only thing that stayed in my mind was the image of Bernstein making up my bed: the sheet had been light blue, the blanket dark red, and the pillow bright white.

PART TWO

BROOKLYN HEIGHTS

CHAPTER EIGHT

When I was twenty-four years old, three years after I moved out of my mother's house, I found my first serious girlfriend. Carol came from an upper-middle-class family in New Hampshire and was going to Columbia to get her master's in psychology. I met her in the supermarket a couple of blocks from my building. I was coming around an aisle, and before I cleared the corner, I heard someone crying. There, down on her knees, tears in her eyes, was a pretty blond girl, standing over a bunch of cereal boxes that had toppled off a display. I was immediately drawn to her.

If I had had any experience of the world, I might have known that someone (someone like me, for instance) who is so violently frustrated over such a small thing is probably a good person to avoid, but at that moment all I saw was a princess in dire straits, and I was there to save the day. I helped her pick up the boxes. We checked out together and discovered—obviously more proof that our meeting was destined to be—that we lived on the same block, only two buildings away from each other.

Within a couple of weeks Carol and I were sleeping together and we had discovered that we were deeply and hopelessly in love. After a few months of sex and movies and weekend bicycle trips, we decided that this was forever and we decided to plan on getting married. Well, to be accurate, *she* decided to plan on our getting married. Carol had a very clear idea of what the rest of her life was going to be; her grand plan included marriage and a family, a big house in New England, and a good amount of money as a foundation. When I heard her talk about weddings, marriage, and "Our Future," I felt helpless and full of dread, as if I were trapped in a mine. Carol got angry at me, told me that if I really loved her I would see that her plan was the only real way for us to live. I always convinced myself that she was right, but obviously I had as much business getting married then as a two-year-old would have had bungee-jumping off the Brooklyn Bridge.

Nevertheless, I *had* to have her. My future was clear, and whatever my hesitation, I would damn well just get over it for her sake, for our sake.

I met her folks; we went up for a long weekend to New Hampshire. Dad was a pipe-smoking tweed-jacketed English lit professor at a well-known college, and Mother came from a lot of money. They were thoroughbreds, a WASP lord and lady of the manor. I don't know what they thought of me, but they were unfailingly polite. I think the word used in their world is "decent."

What was I to do in return? The wedding was only about eight weeks away (we didn't see any need to wait very long. We were practically living together as it was). I was in a serious bind. I had met her folks, but I didn't have any real "folks" for her to meet. Though my father had moved back to Long Island a few years before, he was still often traveling. In fact, at that very moment he was in Paraguay, working on a fertilizer plant.

My father had actually met Carol once when he stopped over to see my apartment in Brooklyn. They only spent a few minutes together, but he seemed to like her. Several weeks earlier, when she first started pushing me toward marriage, I had driven out to Long Island to consult him.

I sat in his kitchen and told him I wasn't sure about getting married. In fact, I flat-out told him I didn't want to. I hoped he'd tell me that I was making a mistake, that I should think it over some more. He had no patience with my doubts. He got angry, gave me a big—for him—impassioned speech, about loneliness and *what is life for, anyway!*

My father had remarried when I was about nine years old—then divorced again several years later. He had been alone and bitter for a long time. "What's the point?" he said, pacing back and forth and pointing his finger at me. "What's the fucking point of working hard all your life if you have nobody to come home to!? You want to be selfish all your life?! Just marry her, or you'll regret it—I'm telling you." So there wasn't much sense in bringing Carol out for my father's review. I already knew where he stood.

Of course, I was not going to bring my bride-to-be around to meet my mother. All Carol knew about her was that she was a "little" crazy and probably wouldn't like any girl I brought out to see her—*ha, ha, you know how mothers can be, don't want to lose their only son.*

So, lacking a presentable set of parents, I did the only thing I could do: I took my girlfriend to meet my shrink, Mr. Leo Bernstein.

Bernstein was as gracious and debonair as he could be, but I could see right away that things were not going well. Carol wasn't a feminist particularly. Actually, she never needed any women's movement to take offense at macho behavior; she was macho herself. She had a determined, aggressive, sometimes almost bullish personality, and she was not buying Bernstein's continental charm.

There were danger signs from both of them. Carol's brow was furrowed, she had a nasty glint in her eye; and Bernstein's smile was growing wider, more amused, and sarcastic. They were going mano a mano, and I felt caught between them like a piece of white bread in an industrial-strength toaster. I was struggling to think of something to say, something to bring peace to the table, but then it was too late. "You know, my dear," said Bernstein, "Freud says that women were made to be vessels of pleasure for men." I have no idea if Freud ever said that, but it didn't matter. The damage was done. It was like triggering a nuclear device; Carol turned red in the face, leaned forward, stared him right in the eye, and said, "Who are you, some fucking sheik?"

Back in my apartment in Brooklyn Heights she was still fuming: "I don't know why you see that man. I have never met such a sleazy bastard."

"Well," I said, "I'm not sure what he meant by that comment about Freud, but—"

"I'll tell you what he meant! He meant that women are just sex toys for men, and if you agree with him—well I just hope you don't agree with him."

Of course I didn't agree with him. Well...maybe a little, but at that instant I wasn't about to tell her anything she didn't want to hear. I did tell her that he wasn't usually so obnoxious, and after all, he had helped me a lot so maybe she could just let it go, please? I hated being caught between the two most powerful people in my life. I didn't want to have to choose between them.

At my regular appointment with him, two days later, I told Bernstein that he had really upset my girlfriend. I was distraught, confused, and angry at him for insulting her. On the other hand I was fishing around, dying to know if he thought I was making a mistake by marrying her. Bernstein wasn't paying any attention to the nuances of my feelings that day. He had a proclamation to make. He raised his hand, index finger up in the air, and said: "I make a prediction! Inside of a month after you get married, you will come to me and tell me that since you are now a big married man, you don't need to see me anymore."

"No, no!" I wanted to cry. I would never do that. The truth was I would much rather have Bernstein adopt me than marry my girlfriend— but the man wasn't offering. I had the definite feeling he was getting ready to cast me off—a sort of preventive strike. Could he have been jealous? After all, I never asked his permission to get married. On the other hand, why should I? He never asked *my* permission when he got married. All this, I thought, was petty and immature. I assured Bernstein, "I have no intention of not seeing you anymore. *I* am very capable of making my own decisions about this."

"Sure, sure," he said, nodding his head gravely, mocking me.

I continued to see Bernstein, but by unspoken mutual agreement, we didn't talk about my upcoming marriage. In August he was off for a month's vacation to Shrink Island, a hidden, fabled land somewhere to the north where all therapists go each summer to participate in dark, cabalistic rites. By the time he returned, I was married.

CHAPTER NINE

Carol and I moved into a larger apartment in Brooklyn Heights. We were partners now on the true road of life.

She was entering the second year of her master's program, and I was taking English literature courses at Queens College. The plan was for me to get a master's in English, buy a pipe and a sports jacket—to become, more or less, her father. We scooped up thousands of dollars in wedding presents, a lot of cash and expensive gifts we converted to more cash. I had a part-time job as a file clerk at a law firm in Manhattan. We bought old furniture at secondhand shops and Carol, not a bad cook, rustled up dinner each night. On weekends we walked around, looking in antique shops and imagining what kind of house we would have up in New Hampshire after I got a job in the English department.

It didn't take long for it to become quite clear to me that I had passed some special test, reached a plateau unknown to the young and single. I was officially a grown-up. Who could deny it? The evidence was there for all to see.

Despite all my pleas, my brand-new wife relentlessly chiseled away at my relationship with Bernstein. She pointed out that I was doing fine. I had a job, a solid, respectable future, and, more than anything, I had her. Why, then, did I need to hang on to some twisted old roué who hated women? Wasn't it time for me to declare myself a free man? Between her ceaseless propaganda and my own new high opinion of myself, I decided I could make it on my own.

I went to Bernstein and told him. Immediately he was laughing at me—actually more of a sneer.

"What's wrong?" I asked. No reply at first, then, as he had done several weeks earlier, he raised his forefinger in the air and prophesied. "I wish you the best of luck," he said, "and I predict that in one year you will be crazy and in a mental hospital." I stuck around for the rest of the session, but there wasn't much to say.

As I approached the door of his apartment, I reached out to shake his hand. He touched my palm briefly and sort of waved at me as he shut the door behind me. I never saw him again.

In my new apartment with my new wife we went about our new lives. We worked at our part-time jobs, went to school, and planned our future. We set up a joint checking account, paid our bills, went grocery shopping, and bought a new welcome mat for the front door. On weekends we had other couples over for dinner and walked our puppy in the park. We had sex, now legal, in our new bed, on wedding-present sheets, and we dropped off to sleep under our wedding-present comforter. We cooked dinner in our new pots and pans and washed and dried our new dishes.

At Christmas, only ten weeks after our wedding, we bought presents, wrapped them, and drove up to New Hampshire for a white Christmas with the folks.

We were married, and our whole lives were before us; yet I knew, though I tried not to give it conscious breathing room, that something was wrong. I was living in a state of discomfort, tipping into dis-ease, and every effort to combat my growing anxiety was just making it worse.

One morning, about three weeks after the wedding, Carol said we had to go to Bloomingdales to pick out the perfect notepaper to write thank-you notes to the people who had given us presents. This seemed unneccesary to me; "Why not just call them up and say thank-you?" I asked. She was pained by my lack of breeding. "Nobody does that!"

Off we went to Bloomingdales. We had to go anyway to exchange some unsuitable wedding gifts: brass trivets; monogrammed, peach-colored towels; the usual crap people get when they don't know you or didn't want to get you a present in the first place. We made our way through this palace of conspicuous consumption. Growing up in the lower-middle-class fringes of the city, I had never been in such a place before. Ladies of all ages cruised around like sharks, their eyes sharp, their hands jeweled, hair dyed, lips curled, reeking of perfume. There were some unfamiliar species of men, too; one type was older, jaded, and bored, and the other was young, effeminate, and hysterical. This crowd made me nervous, even a little scared. They seemed to be in a kind of grasping, hungry trance; predatory, carnivorous. I felt like I had been thrown into the midst of a vampire picnic.

I was struggling to keep my equilibrium amid all the pillows and fumes. No matter where I cast my eye, I couldn't find a spot to steady myself. I've always had trouble in department stores—actually any kind of big, crowded space. People rushed in all directions and stuff was piled up everywhere. There were no windows, no doors; incomprehensible announcements came from hidden loudspeakers; elevator doors slid open and dozens of people burst out, looking, touching, buying!

Within five minutes of arriving in the stationery department, standing next to my wife as she had the salesman bring out boxes and samples, I got dizzy, then nauseous; then my head started to pound. I felt like I was going to fall over. I sat down on a chair near the escalator. By the time we got home to Brooklyn, I was in the clutches of a monster migraine headache, the worst one I'd had in years.

I lay in bed with the blinds drawn and a cold towel on my face. Carol, always healthy as a horse, administered some pain medication and stood over me, shaking her head in wonder at this bizarre outbreak of Victorian vapors. She went out, telling me she was going to look at paint charts to figure out what color we should paint the kitchen cabinets and then think about what curtains we wanted to buy.

About two hours later, I resurfaced in the land of the living, dragged myself out of bed and slouched into the living room. I sat down on a chair in one corner of the room. God, our living room was huge! It looked as big as a football stadium. Carol, off in the other corner on a stepladder, tape-measuring windows, seemed very, very far away, as if viewed from the wrong end of a telescope. It seemed to me that we were only *impersonating* a real husband and wife, like little children who had found some grown-up clothes in an attic and were pretending to be married.

I desperately wanted to ask her if she felt the way I did. I thought I sensed the same confusion, the same awkward tension in her that was in me. Maybe if we talked about it, we could figure out how to fix it, but then again, I thought, I might be wrong about how she felt, and I didn't want her to think I was bailing out, less than a month after our wedding, at the very beginning of Our Life Together.

Truth is, my sudden anxiety wasn't all that sudden....

A few weeks before, as we drove back from our honeymoon weekend at a fancy inn in Vermont, Carol was talking about the kind of house she wanted to buy after her father got me my teaching position up at the college. "The house has to be old," she said, "I think that's obvious. And, of course it has to have a pond in the back or at least a stream running though the property, don't you think? Also, I don't want it to be more than a mile or so from Mother and Father's place...." As she rattled on and on about our future domesticity, I had a frightening vision. I perceived that the highway we were on had no exits, that we would never get off, driving on it forever, the car loaded with wedding gifts and flowers, my wife talking without ever stopping. Then, floating on the other side of the windshield, I imagined I saw Bernstein's smiling, sneering face, his finger pointing like one of the ghosts in Dickens's *A Christmas Carol*. "I warned you, Michael Feder, I warned you not to get married... repent, repennnttt!" I spoke to the apparition. "Hey, did I ever want to get married? No, I did not. I got married because I had to or I would have lost the woman I thought I loved. She told me herself: 'You better marry me or somebody else will.' She knew other men, medical students, lawyers—*real* men. The whole world, apparently, was lining up to marry her—I had to act fast. And now look! What have I done? Oh, forgive me, ghost—forgive me!"

I broke into a sweat and had to pull off to the side of the highway. I told Carol it was probably too much alcohol. We had been celebrating all weekend and I wasn't used to it. She told me to snap out of it, that we had a long drive ahead of us.

As I sat there breathing hard, I was overcome by self-loathing. This was the same hysterical, whining bullshit I had to put up with my whole life from my mother. I was determined not to act like her. I would fight it or die in the attempt. My wife was right, I just had to snap out of it. So, I shook myself straight and pulled back onto the highway.

When I got my wife, she came complete with everything, like a toy doll set you might buy in a store. She had clothes, furniture, a family, friends, a career, a future; she had what appeared to be a completely developed personality and a full set of opinions, the right and wrong way to do everything.

The few friends I had from my old job at Brooklyn Family Court I let drift away. My oldest friends, some of whom I knew since childhood, I dumped, without a word of explanation. It wasn't conscious and calculated. I just figured: I have a real wife now and she knows what's best.

Not only had Carol lobbied relentlessly to get me to ditch Bernstein, she also found it strange that I had so many women friends from my high school and college days. She thought maybe that was an unhealthy thing and I should think about it. I thought about it for a couple of hours, then stopped seeing, calling, or writing all of them.

I never did speak much to my sister, and she was upstate in college anyway. I never called my mother, of course, and immediately got off the phone with her if she ever called me.

I did talk to my father, but with him I was boxed in. Anytime I expressed the slightest doubt about the new life I was leading, he would make it very clear that I should shut up and soldier on. He was willing to spend time with me if I didn't complain. We went to a Knicks game once in a while or I drove out to his house and we worked in his backyard garden. Sometimes I saw him for lunch in downtown Manhattan near his office. I wanted desperately to tell him how I was worried about the way things were going—that I was feeling more and more that I had made a mistake—but I couldn't. He didn't want to hear and I understood, too, that *my* marriage was a redemption for his two failed ones. I didn't want to let him down.

Aside from these times with my father, I had no life except my life with my wife. Her life. I borrowed her friends, her family, her taste, her opinions, and her future. And after almost a half year of trying with all my willpower to make this life work, I was falling apart.

I was always irritable. I worried all the time about something, but I wasn't sure what. I had trouble getting to sleep and staying asleep. Food was losing its taste. I was cold all the time, wore flannel shirts to bed and jackets and hats when I was walking around in the apartment. It was winter. New York was freezing all the time and I was freezing too.

I began to develop, despite the fact that I was sure it was my own problem, a growing distaste for my wife. I noticed imperfections in her I had never seen before; her hips were too square, her teeth were too big, she had coarse skin. Her laugh was too sharp. Her voice was grating. I didn't like her hair, it was too thin and straight, and her eyes were steely and hard blue like marbles. She had dozens of little habits that irritated me. The way she cleared her throat, the way she clomped around instead of walking softly. She brushed her teeth too much and too hard, jerked her legs and flung her arms around in her sleep, slammed the door when she left the apartment, threw her keys on the table when she came in, made too much noise.

I was also sick of Carol's opinions and her plans for us. I had no interest in drapes or furniture or dinner parties or anything she wanted to do. Half the time, I didn't want to talk to her or touch her. She, naturally, was increasingly irritated with me. I was a stiff, a pain, a drag—she was at a loss to understand my metamorphosis into a surly pain in the ass. Where was the funny, sexy, talkative guy she had married?

I struggled like Hercules against my sick and unworthy feelings. This woman went, in just a few short months, from being so desirable and so smart, the woman of my dreams, to being an irritating, boring hag. I felt deranged, selfish, and ungrateful. I tried to ignore all my degraded, petty feelings, but I couldn't avoid the fact that I just didn't want to be with her anymore.

At the end of each day, when I drove back from Queens College, where I was taking my master's courses, I began to feel a sense of dread. I pictured my wife in our apartment and I felt a strong urge to turn the car around and head out to Long Island to my father's house. As I approached home, the feelings of dread and avoidance increased. And when I finally saw the lights of our apartment on the fifth floor of our building, I stopped dead in the street.

Things finally got so bad, I asked Carol for a referral to a shrink. She thought it would be a good idea, considering what I was turning into.

Carol got the name of someone from NYU. I called and made an appointment for a consultation.

My new shrink, Dr. Jose Gold, was on the Upper East Side of Manhattan. He was a South American Jew, a very tall, dark-eyed, dark-haired, somber-looking man in his late thirties who was just beginning his practice. He probably came from money, because his new office, in an old luxury building, was very expensively done up with thick drapes, big new leather chairs, and a thick expensive oriental carpet.

Gold was a very serious fellow. He wore dark-blue suits and black, conservative shoes. Though he spoke with a fairly thick Hispanic accent and had not totally mastered the nuances of English, he was obviously very intelligent. He had an MD from Harvard and was attached to the Downstate Medical Center in Brooklyn, a prestigious hospital.

Dr. Gold asked me what brought me to him. Shrinks call this initial explanation the "presenting problem"—the simple recitation of what it was that was bothering you the most, right there and then. My presenting problem was this: I didn't want to be married anymore, but I felt like a murderer for even saying it. As good a place to start as any.

So we were off and running (or at least stumbling). Offices like Gold's, on Park Avenue, come with a pretty high overhead, so I could only afford one fifty-minute session per week.

Gold was a decent fellow. He meant well and he was certainly well-trained, but he really wasn't the right guy for me. He was a classically trained, psychoanalytically oriented psychiatrist. He expected his patients, most of them, no doubt, upper-middle-class ladies and gentlemen with a fairly reasonable purchase on reality, to show up a couple of times a week and slowly but surely, over a period of years, get to the root of their problems. In his dark, comfortable office, a decent neurotic could find a temporary oasis, a safe harbor from internal and external troubles.

What I needed—ironically enough—considering my previous experience with shrinks—was a tough, no-nonsense man with training in triage and crisis prevention, a combat shrink on the order of Charles, my first shrink, but one who was on *my* side. If I walked into an emergency room with the problems I had, any astute doctor would have shouted, "Code blue! Get this man to surgery at once—he needs an immediate wifectomy!"

Gold could only take the slow approach. I saw him every week that spring and into the summer, and as I carefully went over my troubles with him in the cozy seclusion of his office, I went slowly, but surely, crazy. I lost more weight, couldn't concentrate on my work, acquired all kinds of serious nervous tics, and developed an incessant cough.

I stopped wanting to have sex with Carol: she seemed completely unattractive to me, even repellent at times. Naturally, we had bad arguments, mostly her telling me to shape up, *what the hell was wrong with me, anyway*? I tried to tell her to take it easy, it was hard for someone like me to get used to this new life of ours, but I wasn't being honest with her—I couldn't tell her I didn't want to be married to her anymore, period.

There was a deeper dishonesty, too. She had never really known, and of course I had never told her, how scared and sick and crazy I had been before she met me—or, for that matter, exactly what kind of disturbed family I came from. I never told her all of that because I wanted to start fresh. Well, obviously it wasn't working. I apologized to her for the way I was acting. It seemed like I was always apologizing.

Gold urged me to tell my wife how deeply troubled I was, not just in terms of my interior fears and worries but also in my anger at her for what he thought were legitimate grievances. "After all," he said, proposing a startling new theory to me, "everything can't be all your fault."

When I told Gold how awful I felt about what I perceived to be her constant insensitivities and vulgarities, he advised me, his English not always the best, "Why not telling her? Why not telling her how you feel?" Easy for him to say. I was scared of her. She could be really scathing. And besides, I didn't want to hurt her feelings—she seemed to be working so hard on this marriage thing. I pointed to the phone on Gold's desk. "Why not *you* telling her." He frowned and shook his head. I didn't have to ask him what his prognosis for me was.

The situation degenerated. I was thinking of quitting school. I was even having vague but frightening thoughts of disappearing, just taking the car and driving off out west someplace. Or, not finding the nerve to drive off and start a new life, just driving the thing eighty miles an hour into the back of a tractor-trailer.

In June, pursuing the dominant fiction of my future, Carol gave me, for my birthday, a wool tweed sports jacket, just like her dad used when he was teaching, and a very expensive pipe, also like her father's. She figured these would get me off on the right foot when I joined the English department up at her father's college. There was no doubt I would get a job there, since he was the chairman of the department and his wife one of the trustees of the school. Since I was still trying to do the right thing, still trying as best I could to impersonate a husband, I put on the jacket and put some tobacco she bought into the pipe. I lit up, took a deep puff.

Coughing like a dying diva, I staggered into the living room, grasping blindly for the couch. I felt like throwing up. I lay there for a few minutes, then started to scratch. I felt like the temperature had suddenly risen fifty degrees. I yanked the tweed jacket off—I had been wearing a T-shirt underneath it—my neck, arms, and hands were covered in a bright-red, boiling rash. I finally lost my temper. I was shouting at her. "Get this fucking thing away from me!" I kicked the jacket across the room. "What stupid, brainless idiot would get me a pipe!? Did I ever say I wanted a goddamn pipe!? Did I?" Carol was mortified. She had never seen me like this. She dissolved in tears and ran out of the apartment.

I sat there scratching like a fiend and muttering. An hour went by, two hours, three. It got dark and Carol still hadn't returned. I felt the rankest, most stomach-wrenching guilt.

CHAPTER TEN

I had been seeing my shrink, Dr. Gold, for three months, but his cautious ways and my innate passivity were a hopeless combination. I was a mess. In this perilous state, around mid-June, when school ended, I went out into the cruel world to get a job. Carol and I had dipped pretty deep into the wedding money and, after all, there was just so much the families were willing to do to support two twenty-five-year-old children. The job was just supposed to be for the summer, but it was likely to be permanent until one or both of us finished our degrees and got a real job.

I didn't want to go back to the civil service, in any case it wasn't so easy to reenter after quitting less than a year before. I finally wound up working at an employment agency near Times Square.

People say these employment agencies—the ones that put ads in the paper like: MUSEUM JOB WORK WITH CURATORS. MEET ARTISTS! TV—ENTRY LEVEL. WORK WITH EXECS AS YOU CLIMB THE LADDER TO MEDIA SUCCESS!—are all flimflam, fake and phony, that the jobs don't exist and the agencies just take your money or try to steer you into crummy low-paying jobs. People who say this are right.

I worked for a con man who called himself Ron Manly, though that wasn't his real name. He had changed it on his own. Manly, the former Ronald Mazlusky, was a Polish guy from somewhere in New Jersey who was looking to get even with the world. He called his agency Fieldbrook Personnel. It had been Brookfield Personnel, but there was a bit of unpleasantness with some state licensing agency.

There were six "employment counselors" (assistant con men), though the turnover was heavy. Mazlusky liked me. He had a soft spot for me, he said, because I'd once been a social worker, a caseworker in the welfare department. To him this was a big joke. The whole idea of welfare, or, for that matter, of helping anybody for any reason, was ridiculous to him. He explained: "Fucking welfare degenerate fucks, Feder. Just a bunch of fucking junkie spics and niggers sucking up money, that's all they are."

I'd been hearing that same bigoted ignorance for years from people when they found out I had been a welfare worker. I didn't bother to argue about it anymore, but I was out of luck; Mazlusky *wanted* me to argue: "C'mon, Mr. Bleeding Heart, tell us all why you love the niggers so much!"

"I don't want to talk about it."

"No, I want to hear this, Feder—I want to hear why you felt it necessary to piss away all my tax dollars on whores and drunks."

"They're not whores and drunks, Ron."

"Oh, pardon *me*, Mr. Social Worker—I must be wrong—they're probably all angels, poor fucks down on their luck 'cause their great-great-grandfathers were slaves. Am I right?"

"C'mon, Ron, life is hard for everybody."

"You're fuckin'-A right it is, Feder—you simple minded, communist fuck! That's why you got to look out for yourself in this world—you know what I mean? No, I don't think you have a fuckin' clue what I mean." And so on. Every day, the same tired harangue.

I called personnel departments of companies to see if I could get listings for positions they were looking to fill. Then I interviewed the poor fools who came into our office with ads in their hands that Mazlusky had made up out of thin air. Girls, fresh out of college, high school graduates out with their diplomas and their new suits—all looking to start their exciting lives in the big city.

We actually did have some jobs available, usually the same crummy jobs every other agency had: file and shipping clerks, typists, the occasional personal assistant (read, slave) to some nasty manager someplace. We never had the "DREAM JOBS!" that the kids came in looking for.

Somebody's darling son or daughter, some new husband, a proud high school breadwinner sat there at your desk, trying to be grown-up and responsible. In their hands they have the Sunday *Times* classified section with Mazlusky's fictitious job circled. You read the forms they filled out, checked their perfectly typed résumés that no doubt they had carefully worked on the night before with their moms and dads or wives or husbands. You pretended to look it over carefully. Then you said, "Well, this is a very impressive résumé, and I see you had a really good grade point average, but I'm afraid our company is looking for somebody with a little more experience in—" Then you name whatever it was the poor victim *hadn't* listed on his résumé. Disappointment all over their faces, they'd complain, "But the ad doesn't say anything about needing to speak French."

"Oh, that's something we take for granted," I'd say, "a working knowledge of a foreign language." Anything they couldn't do or hadn't studied, you seized on as a disqualification. And if, by chance, as you did once in a while, you ran across a kid who could type a hundred words a minute and speak three languages, somebody who was probably qualified to be the *director* of a museum, let alone an assistant, you just lamented their bad luck. "Oh, I'm *really* sorry, we just filled that job no more than half an hour ago."

Then, after the bad news, the true sadism began. You had to convince the applicants that despite whatever they thought their qualifications were, they were hopelessly inadequate, unrealistic about their expectations, and completely unprepared for the real demands of business. You let them know that this was the *real* world they were in now. You had to convince them, in fact, that they were just lucky, for Christ's sake, that you were going to help them at all, poor benighted assholes that they were.

If someone came in without a *Times* ad, we started off with plain fairy tales, looking at a phony index card in a gray file box. We'd say, "Oh, here's one. This is a great job; you'll be working with really nice people, the hours are terrific and the chances for promotion...well! Last year alone, four applicants we placed with this company were promoted to executive level!

And the offices!—the offices are *beautiful*. The benefits package? Let me check that for you…[consulting the fake card again] Oh yes! The benefits are absolutely industry standard." All utter lies. There was no possible way we could've known what the working conditions were like at these companies, or what the people were like, or anything else except the starting salary, *because we didn't care what they were like.* We had never been to these places, never met the people to whom we were referring the applicants. The personnel at these companies could've been out-and-out baby rapers for all we knew, or the offices crawling with rats and roaches.

Mazlusky saw the world as one giant chicken coop with himself as fox-in-residence. He was never doubtful or ambivalent about his desire to plunder and pillage his way through the world, but he could tell right away that I hated doing all the things the job required. In fact, I hated it so much that at the end of the first week I went into his office and told him I had to quit, that I couldn't stand doing this to people anymore. "Ahhh, poor baby," he said, "can't stand to do it to them, eh?"

"No."

"Who the fuck do you think you are? I do it, Sal does it, Marilyn does it, are you better than them? *I* been doing this for ten years—are you better than *me*?"

"It's not that, Ron."

He stared at me, completely exasperated by my incomprehensible attitude. He waved his hands, shouted at the top of his lungs: "What? What then, you maniac bleeding-heart bastard? What is the FUCKING PROBLEM WITH YOU!!?" I could feel the whole office outside go quiet. He shook his head, then peered at me intently. "Oh, yeah, hmn-hmn, I know what's wrong with you, Feder. You *do*, you actually *do* think you're better than me! Well, let me tell you somethin', pal—you're not. Nobody ever gave me anything. I worked for every nickel I got. What are you, some kind of prince?" He pushed his chair back, stood up. He was a big guy, tall, thick, and menacing. I thought he was going to walk around the desk and punch me in the mouth. I just stood there, hopeless and helpless.

He must have seen something in my face. I was so naked then, so utterly depressed and confused about everything that I didn't even have the heart to argue with him or to judge him for the sleazy world he had created.

He lowered his voice, "Look, Mike, I like you, God knows why—you little commie prick—but I see something in you, kid. You have a way with people—they trust you. You could make real money at this business if you would only put some effort into it." Trying to help me, he pulled the top card out of his pack. Putting his hand on my shoulder, he said, with genuine awe and reverence in his voice, "Mike, you don't know what life is really like until you pay cash for your first Cadillac!"

I was moved. Here he was, really telling me something. From his heart to mine. Mazlusky was twisted and sadistic, but that was beside the point. He was, in his way, trying to be kind to me. And just like every time before and after, when a man was kind to me, no matter what manner of self-serving son-of-a-bitch he might be, I had no defense. He was right: I did think I was better than he was, and I was ashamed of myself for it. I told him I would stay.

He moved me to a desk in his office and I sat there in the corner of the room, doing the occasional interview and cold-calling companies from the phone book—speaking to personnel people, trying to get listings. He sat at his desk, wheeling and dealing on the phone, sweet-talking, cajoling, yelling, threatening, closing deals, and collecting payments from people he had suckered or bullied in some way.

Most of the people in the office were Jewish or Italian, and most of the personnel people at companies were WASPs. Mazlusky took it for granted that they were bigots. He was probably more right than wrong. So, to blend in, Marilyn Scheinbaum became Mary Schmidt, and Salvatore Balducci became Steve Barnes, and so on.

"Feder," Mazlusky tells me one day, "your name is no good." My name is no good? I could believe it. My whole life was already no good—what's in a name? Mazlusky sat at his desk, thinking...."Let's see. What's your middle name, Feder?"

"Robert."

"Robert, Robert—OK, from now on you're Mike Roberts."

At first, I had trouble being Mike Roberts, Personnel Counselor, so I wrote my new name down on a pad in front of me. I practiced it in my head, so that I would have it right when I got somebody on the phone:

"Hi, this is Mike Roberts of Fieldbrook Personnel...Hi, Mike Roberts here." Increasingly, as I sat there under his eagle eye, my face next to the clouded office window, my sweating hand on the phone, I lost touch with reality: Mike Roberts..."This is Mike Roberts, reporting to you direct from Saigon...Mike Roberts, Private Eye...Lieutenant-Colonel Michael Robertson, late of Her Majesty's Cold Stream Fusiliers...Bob Roberts, Mike Floberts, Rob Fleder."

Every Thursday morning, Mazlusky placed his ads. The same phony job descriptions he had been using for the last ten years; occasionally he'd change the salaries to adjust for inflation. He took a big scrapbook out of his top drawer, opened to a page of yellowed old clippings and dialed up the *New York Times* classifieds. "Hey, how you doin'? It's Fieldbrook Personnel—yeah, not bad...you? Good, good—OK, this week—what? Let's do...number sixteen, right—'Fabulous Opportunity', blah blah blah, and...let's go for twelve and twenty-one—right—'media giant needs go-getter,' et cetera, et cetera. Yeah, OK." He hung up, saw me looking at him. "What?"

"Nothing."

"Better be nothing—get back on the phone."

"OK, sorry."

At the end of the day, tired, degraded, and deranged from talking total trash and misleading poor souls for eight hours, I jammed into the subway with the rest of the leached-out lemmings and headed for home. I opened the apartment door with my key and peered in to see if Carol was home yet. I was happy if she wasn't; I didn't want to see her. I didn't want to see anybody. I sat in the living room and stared out the window.

When she got home, I was still sitting there. She told me I should change my clothes and asked me what I wanted for supper. By now I was seeing things: speedy, green and black bugs in my peripheral vision, so real that I jumped or felt the urge to swat them with my hand. I heard things: high-pitched tones and odd humming noises. Everything seemed to be alive and unfriendly, even threatening; the sidewalk felt hard and hurt my feet.

I was afraid to go into the shower, the water seemed dangerous. I was afraid to use my razor to shave, I thought there might be an accident. I couldn't think of anything to say to Carol, and so there were long empty silences in the apartment.

At Gold's office, the subject of hospitalization came up. He tried to tell me the hospital was an honorable option. I could get away from my problems, get some time and space, not to mention drugs, to give some relief. It sounded appealing the way he put it—I had been in combat so long that I desperately needed to be evacuated to an aid station, but still the very idea was so humiliating to me: it was a total capitulation to every bad thing I'd ever known, so I fought against it.

On weekends, Carol, seeing I was a basket case, did the shopping and spent time with her friends, no doubt trying to figure out what to do about me. I went out for short walks—only a block or two, afraid to go too far. I looked down at the ground, bending down now and then to pick up rubber bands and string, pieces of wire. I was making a really thick ball of these things at home. It seemed to give me some relief for a few minutes here and there—the idea of tying all these loose pieces into a tight big ball made perfect sense to me.

When Carol talked to me, sometimes I couldn't quite get the meaning of what she was saying. All my symptoms danced on top of one constant, growing fear—that everything was coming to an end, that I was near death.

Gold prescribed some tranquilizers and that helped a little, but I couldn't seem to find my way out of the twitchy-scared fog that enveloped me.

By midsummer I could hardly get out of bed to go to work. I dressed in a dream and walked in a trance to the subway. People bumped me out of the way. I felt a strong pull down on the subway platform to throw myself in front of the train. I often thought of jumping out the window at work. We were twelve floors up. I told Gold I wanted to die. He upped the dose of my tranquilizer and recommended I seriously consider the hospital. Again I resisted the idea.

I saw more bugs, heard more noises. At work, I dialed up personnel directors, spoke words to them, listened to what they said, but I was losing my ability to retain information. Sometimes I dialed the same person twice in two minutes. Mazlusky's face floated in front of me. He yelled and cursed, but his voice came from a distance. I drank a couple of cups of coffee at lunch, no food—I couldn't stomach it. I lost a lot of weight.

That summer, the prisoners at Attica, in upstate New York, rioted and took over the prison, taking a lot of guards as hostages. I sat at my desk in Mazlusky's office and listened to WBAI, one of the local public stations, on the portable radio as the drama played itself out. Mazlusky told me to turn it off and get to work: "Mike, gimme a break with those murdering nigger fucks!"

I couldn't stop listening to the radio. When I got home, I immediately switched it on and sat there for hours listening to news conferences, lawyers, commentators, prisoners, the governor. I was obsessed with these prisoners. I felt like a prisoner myself, and I knew in my heart that they were going to die, just like I knew that I was going to die: the end was coming closer and closer.

Sure enough, in late August, after ten days of siege, state troopers stormed the prison, indiscriminately slaughtering prisoners and guards.

That was it for me. I couldn't go back to work. I called Mazlusky and told him I wasn't coming in anymore. He was yelling at me over the phone as I hung up on him. I sat in the kitchen staring out the window at people walking across the street. They looked like aliens to me—how did they manage to do astonishing things like get dressed, go to work, laugh, talk, hold hands, have sex, *live* with each other? Who were these people? If I had ever been one of them, I wasn't anymore.

I paced around the apartment, checked the doors and windows; waited for each minute to get used up. I couldn't read or listen to music. I lived completely inside my head, in a storm, in a rage, in a paralysis of fear. I didn't want my wife to leave me alone, didn't want her to leave even to go to work or to get food. Sometimes, when I lay down in bed, the whole room started to shift and turn; I had to open my eyes. I never really slept anymore. I ate a couple of tasteless bites of food once or twice a day. I tensed my muscles, legs, arms, stomach, neck, keeping myself rigid, as if that would keep me in one piece. I was wracked with muscle aches, strains, spasms. I felt like one of those little cartoon creatures who are jabbed in a thousand places by tiny cartoon devils. A week went by like a month, two weeks like years....

The few times I did go out, the world looked like a jungle to me. Once, on a bus going to downtown Brooklyn, everybody's eyes turned red—people looked like wolves, and they were all staring at me: they wanted to eat me. I was terrified. I made my way up to the front of the bus and made the driver let me off between stops. I leaned against the wall of a building. I looked up and saw the light pole bending down to the ground, and the light was all different colors, purple and red and green. I sat down on the sidewalk. People came over to me but went away when I looked up at them.

Somehow, I managed to calm down enough to get up. I walked back home, about fifty blocks. It was late September and the light was starting to go—winter, dead awful, cold, gray winter, the time of the carnivore, was coming. I lay in the bed with all my clothes on, rigid, sweating. Carol came back from work, took one look at me, and called Gold. He agreed to see me for an emergency appointment. We drove to Manhattan, me wrapped up in a winter coat, huddled against the passenger door; I was shivering, though it was seventy degrees out.

Carol saw him first. Then I went in. I felt safe in there: I didn't want to leave. Gold asked me if I wanted to go to the hospital. I didn't. I didn't want to be my mother, crazy and scary like she was, but I didn't want to go back home with my wife, either. I wished I could just disappear or die. Something had to put an end to this misery. He prescribed another, stronger kind of pill. We drove back to Brooklyn. Carol was trying to get me to talk. She was saying that she should have been listening to me more—Gold must have been talking to her. I could hardly hear what she was saying. I just wanted to be gone, oblivious, away from everything. We drove over the Brooklyn Bridge. The water underneath looked black and cold.

The next day was Saturday. I lay in bed all day, trying to stop the room from spinning around. Carol was on the phone with Gold, with my father, whispering, crying. I didn't care what she was going through. I once thought I did, but no longer. My whole being was focused now on one thing. I wanted relief. I wanted to go away, to be taken away, I wanted someone to shoot me full of some massive tranquilizer and help me slip into unconsciousness.

The hours crept on. Around six, I staggered off the bed, holding on to the walls, and went into the kitchen. Carol was standing in front of the sink. Over her head was a wooden knife rack. I looked at her back, at her neck, at her long blond hair. The knives, just inches above her, were bright and shiny. And it came to me—the perfect solution to all our problems— I would stab her in the heart, kill her, then kill myself. I started to tremble as if I had a high fever. She turned and looked at me with terror in her eyes. I gripped the refrigerator to keep from falling over. My throat was constricted, my tendons and muscles were stretched to breaking. I managed to say: "I think I better go to the hospital."

She called Gold. She called my father. I sat, bundled up in my coat, in the living room, in the dark, waiting. My father showed up and together they guided me down to the car and drove me out to Kings County Hospital. It was a clear night, with a bright, bone-white full moon. In the front seat my father talked quietly to my wife as she drove. From the back seat, looking into the rearview mirror, I could see her face. Her eyes were filled with tears. It was September 26, our wedding anniversary.

CHAPTER ELEVEN

Saturday night, a full moon, the emergency room of Kings County Hospital. People are bouncing off walls. And I don't just mean figuratively. The cops were hauling them in and throwing them down on benches; if there was any back talk or trouble they smacked them up against the walls to quiet them down.

Carol and my father navigated me through the chaos in the emergency room. I was sitting on a bench, watching people bleed, cry, scream, or suffer in silence. I was in a state approximating rigor mortis, but I knew I was still alive because in my head I felt terror, and throughout my body I felt pain.

Carol talked to some nurses at the desk. A psychiatrist was to see me as soon as he got through seeing some other poor lunatic. Carol sat on the bench next to me, telling me it was going to be OK, but she knew, and I knew, that I was certainly *not* going to be OK. I was at the beginning of a very bad journey.

I looked around for my father. He'd already gone out to the lobby or the car, waiting for me to be put away. What went on in his mind while he lingered outside this loony bin on a bad Saturday night? He had seen this before with my mother. Now he was seeing it again. Did he ask himself if he had any hand in causing such misery? Did he regret the fate that had tied him to such crazy people?

Minutes passed very slowly, then a nurse came over and brought me and Carol into a small office. I sat at a scarred wooden desk across from a child. No, that couldn't be, why would a child be wearing a white coat and stethoscope? Was it Halloween? I focused my eyes; it wasn't a child, it was a psychiatrist. A baby psychiatrist, a resident; he couldn't have been much older than I was, but he looked like a teenager. Who else is going to get the shit detail, the Saturday night massacre? Give it to the rookie; it's good for his training.

The doctor's name was Jerkowitz; it was on his name tag. He was a short skinny Jewish guy with a big nose and thick frizzy hair—a Jewish Afro that made him look like Clarabel the Clown or one of the three stooges.

Carol sat in a chair off to the side, supplying whatever details I couldn't remember: medication I was on, when the symptoms first started. My muscles were so tight, my throat so constricted that I could hardly speak. I felt that it would be dangerous, even fatal, to speak.

Dr. Jerkowitz wrote all the relevant details down on a form, then asked me the standard questions. The process is called, at least it used to be called, "Orientation as to Time and Place." He asked me what day it was. I knew that. He asked me where I was. I knew that too. Then, he asked me who the governor was. Well, of course I knew who the governor was. Governor Rockefeller, the son-of-a-bitch who had just murdered everybody up at Attica. I was still sane enough to be insulted by having to answer such simple questions.

I managed to get some answers past my lips. The doctor asked me some more questions, but I had nothing left to say to him; his words started to congeal in the air in front of me. The world around me had narrowed to a small, vague area about two feet from my eyes and ears. Everything else dissolved into a meaningless white fog. There could have been a herd of stampeding buffalo ten feet away and I wouldn't have noticed. I believed my death might be moments away. Everyone around me, including Dr. Jerkowitz and my wife, were enemies, ready to strangle me, rip out my heart, cut my head off. I feared and hated everybody.

I was taken into a curtained-off area and put on a high, rolling bed. I stared at the fluorescent ceiling light, my eyes wide open, waiting for my life to continue or not continue. Carol came through the white curtains and stood by my side. She put her hand on my shoulder. I could feel it, and now that I knew I was going away from her, I was able to experience again the warm memory, her loving touch that I remembered from the first time we sat next to each other on her couch and touched, the first kiss, her soft lips. It had been so thrilling then, such a great adventure. I remembered thinking: *I am delivered from emptiness, now a woman loves me.*

I turned my head and looked at her; she was crying, big tears streaming from her eyes. I wanted to be someone who could love her, to be her husband, but I knew at the same time I just wanted her to leave my life forever.

Some orderlies came in to take me up to the psychiatric ward. Carol's hand fell off my shoulder. I turned my head as they wheeled me out and saw her face, receding into the white haze.

Upstairs, on the locked ward, I was wheeled into a room with several other men. The orderlies, big, mean-looking black guys, threw some hospital gowns at us and ordered us to change into them. I took off my clothes and folded them neatly, something I never did, but at that moment it seemed to me that I had to be very careful about my every movement. I lay back down on the rolling bed, with my clothes and shoes lying on top of my stomach. The man next to me, a short, pockmarked Latino man, was yelling, in Spanish and English: "Fucking faggots, maricóns—I keep my fucking clothes." The orderlies laughed. "*You* the fucking faggot."

I lay there and waited. An orderly came by and told me I would get a shot soon. He seemed to know that was all I wanted. I thought he was being so kind, so solicitous, but I was nothing special—the shot was what everybody there wanted; the chemical peace that passeth understanding.

We were told to come out of the room and line up for meds. I stood there, looking neither right nor left, just fixed my eyes ahead on the table where a nurse and a couple of orderlies were dispensing pills and giving injections. I got to the table; they looked at the plastic nametag on my wrist, "He gets thorazine." Right there on the spot, they lifted up my gown and jabbed a huge hypodermic needle into my ass. An orderly led me back to my bed. I got up on it; it was very high. "Don't get off that bed," he said and went out. I lay there staring at the green painted ceiling and the white light which soon blurred, then, thank God, faded into nothing.

I woke up not knowing where I was; someone was yelling. It was the man next to me, still in his street clothes, which, I noticed for the first time, were covered in crusted blood. He looked over and shouted at me—"I din't do it! I din't do it!!" He was screaming and cursing and banging his hands against the side of his bed, throwing his head around so much I thought his neck would break. The orderlies came in. "Shut the fuck up!" they told him. He didn't pay any attention to them. "I din't do it! I din't do it!"

"Oh, shit, get this asshole another shot." One of them held him down, and another one left and came back with a nurse. The two orderlies held onto him while they stuck a needle in his arm. He was howling now, like an animal. The orderlies were angry he wouldn't quiet down. "Shut *up*, man! Shit!" They held him for another minute or two, then he started to calm down, just mumbling now, half asleep but still in agony. His legs jerked, his head rolled, his lips moved."I din't do it."

I needed to take a piss. I started to sit up on my bed and get down. One of the orderlies turned to me, put his hand on my chest, and told me, "You jus' be good and don' move off that bed." I drifted again, then opened my eyes—it could have been minutes or hours later—my bladder was bursting. There was nobody around. I slipped down off the bed and went into a long empty hallway. It was hard to walk. I knew I was awake but felt as if I were asleep and moving in a dream.

I drifted off for a split second and found myself leaning against the cold tile wall. I kept shuffling, cold in my hospital gown, looking for the bathroom. I got to the door of the bathroom and almost fell asleep again. I was standing in front of the urinal, pissing, and my eyes closed again. Next thing, I'm being jerked off the floor by the orderlies. They were pissed. I was pissed—literally. My hospital gown was soaked. They got me on my feet, disgusted, cursing: "Shit, I don't need this trouble. I tol' you, stay in your fuckin' bed!" They half dragged, half carried me out of the bathroom down the hall, then picked me up and slammed me down on a cold steel metal gurney. "Stay there!" Blam—my foot twisted, my head smacked the gurney. I passed out.

When I woke up again, the drug was wearing off. I was lying on the gurney, directly under a glaring overhead light. I heard voices behind me, twisted my head and saw the orderlies sitting at a table, playing cards, laughing, drinking from plastic cups. I was cold. My gown, thin, half off, was damp with piss, and the steel table underneath me was freezing. I felt a vague throbbing in my left foot and I noticed one of my toes was purple and swollen. The back of my head hurt; there was a big lump where they had slammed me onto the gurney.

I lay back; there was no pillow; I kept my eyes closed because the light was so strong. I wanted to get another gown, get a blanket, move away from the light, but I was afraid to bother the orderlies. The minutes went by. It was dead quiet in the place. With my eyes closed, I saw my father's eyes, puzzled, my wife's eyes, helpless.

Morning. I got another shot, a lower dose, and was directed into a huge common room for breakfast. I had no interest in eating and hung back against the wall. Wild-eyed men cursed, laughed, and talked to themselves, pacing back and forth or circling.

Too long in this place, I thought, and I would be dead meat. I was concentrating on the promise Dr. Gold had made when he sent me to Kings County, that he would get me a bed at Downstate Medical Center, right across the street. This was supposed to be a smaller, quieter place, with better treatment and only one or two patients to a room. Gold was on staff there. I imagined the clean white beds.

I was startled out of this mini-fantasy by a commotion right in front of me. A man shoved another man, who stumbled, got up from the floor, and ripped his own gown off. Naked, he ran at the other man, screaming that he was the devil and he was going to kill him. The orderlies ran down the hall and dragged him off. Jeez! I thought *I* was crazy. Until I got put into this place, I didn't know the meaning of crazy. These people saw things, spoke to unseen presences, tore at their faces and arms and legs till they bled. They laughed hysterically at unheard jokes or shook with fear from the threats of invisible demons.

Scared and sad as I was, I had never been as sick as these men. Hunched against the wall, I began to return to myself. To think, very dimly, that maybe I had a future and that I needed to protect myself to ensure the possibility of living to see it.

Breakfast passed. Lunch came and went. I was getting apprehensive, waiting for Gold to show up. I didn't want to spend another night in Kings County. I stared at the clock. One o'clock, two o'clock, three o'clock. The shadows stretched across the common-room floor, dusk wasn't too far off. I was panicking. Then an orderly called my name.

"Here," I said, waving my hand like a second-grader. He told me to follow him. "C'mon, you gettin' released." I grabbed my clothes from my room.

I was buzzed into a glass antechamber, a small room where there was a doctor and receptionist with some forms to fill out. And my father. God, I was so happy to see him. I didn't want to act too excited: maybe they would take that for agitation and drag me back to the ward. I was as calm as I could possibly be. The doctor asked me if I felt like leaving, if I was in control of myself. My father was watching me, as if wondering the same thing. I was very careful to assure them all that I was doing OK. I needed to sell this proposition to them—it was a matter of life or death.

Everyone seemed satisfied that I was dischargeable. I signed a bunch of forms and my father and I were buzzed out through two locked doors. I was out. He told me that Gold had secured a bed for me across the street at Downstate.

We walked slowly down the hospital corridor side by side, descended in the elevator, and emerged outside—incredibly, into a beautiful garden! I could see the other hospital, Downstate Medical Center, across the street through the metal gates of the garden. The air was still and the sun was out, a perfect early fall day. Some flowers still bloomed and the leaves had started to change. Men and women, mostly hospital employees, were walking around, or talking quietly to each other on benches. My father and I found an old stone bench. It was beautiful there in the garden, so peaceful.

"How're you doing, Mike?" he asked. He hardly ever called me Mike. No more than I ever called him Dad. All my life we had been strangers. He was big and tough, I was skinny and sick. He talked and laughed too loud; he was rough and ready, a doer. After he left my mother, sister, and me, I had become more internal, a watcher, a thinker—especially when I was around him.

My father and I sat in silence. The sun was beginning to go down. "Well," he said finally, "we should get you checked in." We got up and started to walk. I stopped. I didn't want to go to the hospital. I wanted to go home with him. I looked at him. He was nervous, looking up at the trees, rubbing some gravel under his shoe.

I wanted him to look me in the eyes, put his hand on my shoulder and say, "Fuck it, Mike. You're not crazy. You're coming home with me." *Say it! Oh, say the word and I will shed my fears, toss my problems into the trash for you. Just say the word, Dad.* I felt my whole life pivoting on this moment.

He didn't do it. He looked at his watch, glanced up at the sky for a second, and told me we better get going, that I had to check in. He started to walk toward the gate and I followed, out of the garden and across the street into Downstate Hospital.

My father asked at the main desk where the psychiatric ward was. We waited in front of the elevator doors in the lobby. "Do what the doctors tell you," he said. I nodded—the muscles around my mouth had gotten tight and my throat had started to constrict again. The elevator doors opened. I got in and turned around to see my father's face disappear behind the closing doors.

The first two days in Downstate I was put in a private room and placed on a suicide watch, checked on every half hour by an orderly or nurse. I was given powerful tranquilizers during the day and massive knockout drops at night. I had my blood pressure and temperature taken twice a day, was awakened and fed breakfast, and was given lunch and dinner on a tray. I had a night-light in my room. As I drifted off to sleep, the door was open and men and women patrolled the lighted halls outside. I was safe and secure, protected.

For the first time in months, I was able to sleep more than an hour at a time. My need to be taken care of and escape even the slightest adult responsibility was so great that I gave no thought to what I'd left behind. My father and my wife, my apartment, my job were forgotten in those two days.

On the third day, they decided I could be taken off suicide watch. This upset me; I *wanted* somebody to check on me every half hour; even though I found it shameful, I wanted some grown person to watch over me at all times.

Toward the end of my first week in the hospital, I awoke to discover I had a roommate: a gigantic baby in a crib. I was still dazed and shaken enough to believe I was dreaming or having a hallucination, but I wasn't. In the depth of night, they had wheeled in what looked like a crib but was actually a reinforced hospital bed with sidebars. In it was a man of indeterminate age who was completely naked except for a white T-shirt and a large diaper. He was huge and soft and must have weighed at least two hundred and fifty pounds. He lay there in the giant crib, hardly moving, never speaking a word, only smiling. This monstrous baby was probably getting frequent shots of something really strong, because he spent most of his time dozing or sleeping.

Every day, in the afternoon, his mother visited him, a tiny old Jewish lady. She came into the room, said hello to me, then bent over and kissed the giant baby right on his mouth. "How's my little Sheldon?" she said, patting his head. "How's my little baby?" Her "baby" was delighted to see her. His smile turned up about two hundred watts and he began to coo and hum little ditties to her. She took a huge bottle of talcum powder out of her bag, got him to sit up, and powdered his back where he had bedsores, all the while kissing him and singing along with him. "Oh, my little baby...such a sweet little Sheldon...."

Visiting time over, she packed up her powder and kissed him goodbye, her eyes a little misty. This went on for five days and it sobered me up plenty. Here I was, twenty-five years old, a veteran of four years as a working man, married, getting a master's degree, and I had the nerve, the narcissistic self-indulgence, to imagine *I* should be treated like a child.

On the fifth day, Sheldon's mother was there as usual, but something was different. She was much sadder, and though she powdered him as she always did, her voice was quivering as she sang to him; she was obviously trying to keep from bursting into tears. It depressed Sheldon too; he almost looked as if he were going to cry. When visiting time was up, she came over to me and said, "Don't you worry, darling, everything is going to be OK." And she left. When I woke up the next morning, Sheldon and his crib were gone. I asked the nurse what happened to him.

"They have him in the terminal ward," she told me. It turned out he had been suffering from a brain tumor. He died two days later.

CHAPTER TWELVE

In the middle of my second week at the hospital, I was asked who I wanted on my visitors' list. I hesitated, and the nurse told me I didn't have to have any visitors if I didn't want to. I felt guilty even considering such a thing, but I felt, also, that I'd been granted a strange new power—*I didn't have to do what I didn't want to do.*

I told them I didn't want any visitors, which meant my wife and my father. I felt positively gleeful hiding from them—and with official approval, too!

Three weeks went by; my drug dose was reduced, I saw a shrink twice a week and went to group therapy. I got a new roommate, Morty, an older Jewish man who always wore the same outfit: pressed slacks, loafers, a short-sleeved leisure shirt with an alligator on it, and a snappy straw hat. He was maybe sixty-five and had flashy big rings and a thick gold bracelet. He was a card player, a gambler. His hands shook badly and he was always telling me, "I don't really have to be in here, but I'm just a little confused." Whatever I said to him, whatever I asked him, he would tell me he was "just a little confused." When his wife came to visit him, he became *very* confused and she usually had to leave early.

I was getting used to life on the ward: rise at seven-thirty; line up at the nurses' station for meds; take your pills; make your bed—*nice and neat*. Then off to breakfast in the dayroom: delicious powdered scrambled eggs, white toast with scrumptious Welch's grape jelly, and a small, school-sized container of milk. Then ward activities: arts and crafts, music and singing, or dance therapy, a visit with your shrink, or maybe, when you were stable enough to participate, group therapy. Then we had lunch: another hospital taste treat on an orange plastic tray. Then more activities: ping-pong, cards, Parcheesi or Scrabble in the dayroom. At four you had snack—milk and cookies! That was to wash down twenty-five milligrams of Thorazine. Then later, dinnertime. After dinner: more activities, more cards and ping-pong, or you could read in your room. Then nine o'clock: meds at the nurses' station and off to bed. A cozy, neat child's life, while the doctors and nurses tried to convince you that you were getting better.

Sometimes we took field trips to refamiliarize us with the world.

We went to the aquarium at Coney Island. Crossing at the green and not in between, holding our buddies' hands. The nurses and orderlies got us on the train, a very scary proposition for most of us, and we made it out to the beach.

We wandered through the place, pressing our noses up against the glass tanks, watching the sharks and whales swim around. I felt sorry for the fish, who seemed very human to me, not like a separate species at all. They seemed trapped like I was, doomed to circle a boring small space for eternity, trapped in the locked ward of a glass fish tank for life.

By the time we took this trip, I'd been in the hospital for four weeks. I was a lot better, whether I liked it or not, and I didn't like it because it meant I was closer to going home. I was, at that point, considered one of the more responsible patients on the ward.

I was placed in charge of my buddy, Mandy. She'd been there much longer than me, going on three months, but she wasn't doing very well. Mandy was about seventeen, a little chunky, and average looking. Mandy took feminine to the point of burlesque. She wore rings on every single finger, sometimes two to a finger. She had a dozen pairs of earrings, necklaces, toe rings, armbands. She had boxes of lipsticks, eyeshadows, blushes, and she hung all sorts of ribbons and shells in her long hair, which she sometimes brushed for hours, sitting in front of the mirror in her room.

She changed her dress and her jewelry at least three times a day, also her makeup and her hairstyle. She was a one-girl fashion show that never stopped. You got the impression there were several of her and you never knew which one you would see next.

Mandy was an LSD casualty—she had taken far too much of the stuff and the word on the ward was that she was probably never going to come back from her last bad trip.

She was the daughter of a lawyer—a senior partner at some huge Wall Street law firm. This pillar of society came on the weekends to visit her, upright and correct in his expensive suit and tie. He sat straight in the chair in her room, his legs crossed and his hands folded in his lap. You could hear his voice all the way down the hall, deep and censorious. Mandy introduced us all to him. Sometimes she brought him out into the common room. He sat there, shaking our hands and being polite, but you could tell he thought we were all freaks.

We disliked him on sight. Once a patient tried to throw a pitcher of water at him; another time someone spat on his shoes. Maybe they were trying to melt him, like the Wicked Witch of the West.

When her father showed up, Mandy, who during the week could almost approximate normal behavior, went right off the deep end. She giggled, made no sense, blushed, and ran around, chattering like a bird. She hurried off to change her jewelry, clothes, and her hair ten times in the two hours he was there. She seemed to revel in provoking him, knowing that the crazier she acted the more irritated he would get. And the more irritated and judgmental he became, the crazier she acted. A couple of times she sat on his lap and rested her head on his shoulder. It was sweet, I thought, and sad, and it painfully embarrassed him. Mandy's mother never came.

Mandy and I walked through the dark, twisting halls of the aquarium. Fantastic-colored fish darted and swooped through the clear water behind the glass, gliding over the beds of seaweed, exotic shells, and pink and white sand. The aquarium was very soothing, no doubt the reason we were brought there. Mandy was all jangly and colorful with her bracelets and ribbons; she probably looked familiar to the fish, who hovered at the glass, staring at us with their dark, blank eyes.

We held hands. She was quiet, utterly entranced with the dreamlike quality of the place. We opened a door and we were in the penguin habitat. Little tuxedoed Charlie Chaplin birds, absurd and shrewd-looking, waddled around, jumped into the water and out again onto the smooth rocks. They swam in quick long sweeps, as if through blue air. Mandy put her face right up against the glass. Two penguins swam up and hovered right in front of her, regarding her with great interest.

"Hello, Penguins," she said, "remember me?" Maybe they did. They gave her a second or two of their time, then swam off a few feet to check out a family standing near us, a father, a mother, and two little girls. Mandy let go of my hand and darted over to the family, squeezing herself right in. "Hey, penguins," she said, "where are you going?"

The family was alarmed. Mandy pretended not to notice that she had intruded so deeply into their little circle. She became strange and agitated in her inimitable fashion; she tapped on the glass with her long, blue-painted fingernails. "Hi, penguins, don't you want to talk to me?" The father reached out and took his kids' hands and hustled them toward the door. He threw a look in my direction, as if to say, "Hey, I got kids here—can't you control this girl?"

As they went out the door, Mandy called to them, angrily. "Hey, where are you going?" I grabbed her hand. "Mandy, c'mon, you're scaring those people." She pulled her hand away and addressed herself to her bird pals. "Well, penguins, some people are *very* unfriendly!" I took her hand again and led her out the other way. She was crying. "People can be really mean, Michael."

"Yeah, I know."

One night on the ward, late, I couldn't sleep, but I didn't want to take some mind-numbing drug to achieve unconsciousness. The halls were half dark. I wasn't supposed to be up, but since I was a veteran now, going on five weeks, they gave me the freedom to walk the halls till I tired myself out.

The ward was shaped like a big, long horseshoe. I walked, sometimes quickly, sometimes slowly, a half hour, an hour, completing a hundred circuits of the ward. People waved at me from their rooms as I walked. In four weeks I might have walked half the distance to Canada.

After patrolling the semidark hallways in my slipper-socks for about twenty minutes, I got a little weary but still not tired enough to sleep. I had a lot on my mind, now that my mind was mine again. What had settled on me, like a huge black bird, was the Great Guilt: *What a stupid, shameful, worthless asshole you are for going crazy, letting everyone on the outside down and scaring them half to death.*

After three weeks, after Carol had called every day, I changed my visitor status so that she could come and see me for a couple of hours.

When she walked through the doorway of the ward, I was overcome with the realization of what I had done. There I was, her *husband*, locked up with a bunch of maniacs and half-wits; I was a baby, a fool, a pathetic loser. She was polite and solicitous, but I could tell she was ashamed to be there with me. After about fifteen minutes, I told her I had to take a nap. I couldn't stand her being there, knowing so surely what she must think of me.

She came two more times, staying a little longer each time. On her last visit, she told me she missed me and was hoping I would be home soon. What could I say to her but that I hoped the same thing.

At night I paced the halls, picked at my cuticles till they bled. Tired, finally, I stumbled into the dayroom and slumped onto one of the couches. It was dark and very quiet, even a little peaceful. I chewed on myself in the dark, trying to figure a way out of my predicament. As always, being dead, killing myself, seemed like the best way; throwing myself out a window, jumping in front of a train, or stabbing myself with a scissors seemed like a real solution. Yet if I did that, I knew I would be hurting other people even worse than I already had. You have to be more vengeful than I was to commit suicide. I wasn't ready to do that—so what *could* I do?

As I sat there in the dark, the door opened and the old black janitor came into the room with his pail and utensils. He was gray, bent, and he moved very slowly. I was reminded of an old fairy tale: the elves and the shoemaker. While we all slept soundly in our rooms, this old man toiled from midnight till dawn, like a magic elf, cleaning our little world, disappearing before we opened our eyes to discover the bright shiny floors and walls.

The old man went to the corner, turned on a lamp, then tossed some foul-smelling disinfectant chips on the floor. Carefully, he dipped his mop into the pail and commenced to swab the floor in wide circular strokes. Five minutes into it, he noticed me sitting there in the half-dark. He stopped, holding the mop upright in his hand.

"How you doin'?" he asked.

"Not too good."

"Well, you got to know you goin' to be alright."

"I do?"

"Yes, it's just some trouble you have now, but it won't always be."

My troubles were, after all, in my head. What *real* troubles, I wondered, has this man seen? What kind of life has he come through to be here in this place of eternal misery, mopping this floor? Something about his radiant smile penetrated me to the bone. I felt as if a great burden had been taken off my shoulders. I stood up. He put his hand on my shoulder. "Now you get some sleep, you feel better in the morning." I went to my room, slipped under the sheets, pulled the covers up, and fell right to sleep, undrugged.

Anybody who has ever been on a psychiatric ward will tell you the same thing: the doctors are useless. The real healers are the orderlies, the nurses, and, once in a while, a psychologist or a social worker. Of course, you have your Nurse Ratcheds, your sadistic prison-camp guards, but on every ward there are always a couple of nurses and orderlies who are miracles of sympathy.

One night, only about two weeks in, I had awoken sweating and terrified, and with the usual plunging despair, and immediately realized where I was. I was sick to death of myself. Truly, I wanted to end my life, putting myself and everyone who had the misfortune to know me out of our combined misery. I was shaking with fear. I went to the nurses' station and, thank God, Head Nurse Kathleen Reilly was there: a big, sexy, motherly blond woman in her early thirties. She was as beautiful as the sun, the mother everyone dreams of having. Even the mean nurses mellowed, or at least shut their mouths, when she was around.

I walked over to where she was sitting, in a bright circle of desk-lamp light, writing up reports. "Hi, Mike," she smiled, and I felt a little better already, but my problem remained—I still wanted to end my life. "What's wrong?" she asked.

"I feel like killing myself. I don't want to live," I told her. She smiled at me and said, "Oh, Mike, you're just having a hard time now, but believe me, it won't last forever. Why don't you go into the kitchen," she told me, "have some milk and cookies—that will make you feel better."

So I did. I went into the kitchen, got the milk out of the refrigerator, opened a box of vanilla wafers, and sat there having my little snack. And I did feel better.

A couple of years after I was out of the hospital, I ran into Kathleen Reilly on the street in Brooklyn. She was as beautiful, as radiant as ever. I asked her if she remembered me, and I was thrilled to see that she did. Functioning normally now, just a man encountering a woman on the street, I felt sexually attracted to her, then I noticed she had a wedding ring on. "Were you married when I knew you in the hospital?" I asked.

She laughed. "Oh, yes, but you weren't noticing things like that then."

CHAPTER THIRTEEN

When I first came into the hospital I wouldn't or couldn't talk. I was so resolutely silent, they sent me for tests in the ear, nose, and throat department to see if there was something wrong with my throat or my vocal cords. After the first couple of days, I managed to squeeze out a couple of words. Yes, no. As the days and weeks went by I began to loosen up, and I was able to carry on short conversations. I realized later what had kept my lips sealed and my mouth shut. Rage. If I had said anything then, it would have been a volcanic eruption of violent shouting and cursing, a foaming-at-the-mouth diatribe against everyone and anyone in my life past, present, and future.

My refusal to speak also may have been revenge.... everyone, including my wife, liked my stories, my sense of humor, my way of describing some experience I'd just had or person I'd just met. My father, too. He used to tell me I should be a comedy writer or maybe a comedian—he imagined a good talker made money. My grandmother, my aunts and uncles, even my shrinks liked to hear me talk. Talk talk talk—all the way back to the source, my mother, who liked to hear me talk more than anybody. It was the one and only thing I was really good at. I was a fair athlete, but I ran out of wind after a few minutes. I had brains but not the patience or willpower to get good marks in class. I wasn't ugly, but I wasn't any movie star. The one thing I could do for sure was talk.

I talked my way into passing grades in classes where I didn't do the homework or failed tests. I talked my way out of being beaten up by Neanderthals in the schoolyard, and I talked my way into having girl-friends when I had nothing much else to recommend me. When I worked in the welfare department I managed to persuade my supervisors to come up with more money for my clients. My father once told me I should go into sales because people would buy anything from me.

So when the time had come for me to cave in, to strike the phony set I had used for so long as the backdrop for my acting, the first thing that went was my talking. It was my only gift, and withholding it was my only weapon.

Near the end of my hospital stay, my conversation, then finally my sense of humor —my other saving grace—returned. I was surrounded by the most exquisite and relentless misery. Aged twenty-five, I walked the halls in my bathrobe and slippers, eating milk and cookies and asking a nurse if I could go down to the lobby to get a candy bar from the vending machine. I played ping-pong in the recreation room with people who quacked like ducks, who were as likely to throw the paddle at your head as knock the ball back over the net. Now that's funny.

After six weeks, I went home on a day pass. I could have had a weekend pass, but I hadn't wanted one. Carol picked me up, drove me back to our apartment. I was nervous the whole time, thinking of my safe little room at the hospital. We talked, mostly about—what else?—my condition. Then I couldn't take it anymore and asked her to drive me back. She was sad to see me so anxious to get away from her. After she dropped me off and said good-bye outside the hospital, I sighed with relief. When I final-ly got upstairs to the ward, I felt like I was truly home. My family was all there—the orderlies, the nurses, all the patients. There was my room and my little bed, with the radio on the nightstand.

It was depressing thinking that I would soon leave the hospital. Here I was, getting better, and my reward was to be a husband again, live with my wife, go back to school and work—all the things I had resisted so much in the first place.

Another day pass, then a weekend pass, then another. I was able to get through the weekends, aided by drugs, without debilitating terror. I sat in the kitchen having a quiet breakfast with my wife. I took walks in the neighborhood. The world was still disturbing to me but not as terrifying as it had been before. Fear was replaced by sadness. You can't exist in a constant state of fear, but you can get by feeling sadness.

The next week, almost two months to the day after I was taken to the Kings County Hospital emergency ward, I was discharged. My wife and my father were waiting outside. They loaded my suitcase, containing the wallet and belt I had made in arts and crafts and my good-bye-get-well card from Mandy, into the trunk and we drove home.

Outside the protective ring of the ward, I felt constantly unsafe, as if the same primitive evil were waiting—just around the corner—to grab me by the throat again.

I tried to do one little thing at a time. Get up, eat some cereal, listen to the radio. Say good-bye to Carol and get myself ready to go back to the hospital where I was a day patient from ten to three. I saw the shrink, played ping-pong, got my medication, had lunch in the dayroom. At three o'clock, just like leaving elementary school, I was let out and took the train back to my apartment in Brooklyn Heights.

I couldn't keep this half a life up forever, of course. I had to make the final leap back into adult life. I had to get a job. Carol worked, but what she earned wasn't really enough and I needed a job to feel like I had some worth in the world. I applied for my old job as a New York City probation officer. In February, three months out of the hospital, I was notified that I was hired. I called Queens College and they told me I could start taking courses again in the fall. My father came to visit as often as possible. Carol and I, once again, had long talks about the future—she didn't like to talk about the hospital. When I brought it up, she frowned and told me that was the past and we had to move on. Just like before, she rambled on about fixing up the apartment and a hundred other mundane subjects.

I started working back at Brooklyn Criminal Court, struggling mightily with my constant depression and the heavy drugs I took every day. Just out of the locked ward myself, I wound up interviewing "offenders" convicted of various small and large crimes—writing reports for judges and recommending how long somebody *else* was supposed to be locked up.

It was hard to pay attention to the bullshit excuses most of these guys (I saw mostly men) spewed out. *I didn't do it, I wasn't there, I never had a chance....* I knew all about excuses; I had spent my life making them. I had no pity for myself and very little to spare for them. Even if they were innocent and deserved a fair hearing, I had trouble concentrating on anyone else for more than a few minutes at a time. Sometimes, under the influence of Thorazine, I would almost nod off at my desk. But I played my part. I traveled out to Queens College to talk to my old department head about which courses to take for the fall, Renaissance Drama, Nineteenth Century English Poetry.

I went to Knicks games with my father. He asked how I was doing, but he only wanted to hear about good things—progress being made. So that's what I told him. We talked about sports and drank beer. The message I got was clear. I was on my own. We're all on our own, and the sooner we knew that, the better.

At home, I lay in bed next to my wife, trying to get up the courage, the self-confidence, to have sex with her, but it was hard, or, I should say, *it* was not very hard at all. Between my generalized fear of everyday life, my depression at being right back where I had started, and the heavy tranquilizers I was taking, my libido was down around zero. Viagra was just a gleam in Bob Dole's eye back then, so if I was interested in getting a hard-on, I was going to have to use splints and superglue. Day after day, Carol tried to make things right and normal. I admired her for that. I knew she seriously doubted we had a future, worried that I might remain a semi-invalid, not a real husband. Yet, she forged right ahead and tried to make the best of things.

And, to complete the picture, I had returned to therapy with my Park Avenue shrink, Dr. Jose Gold, the Freud of South America. I had not laid eyes on him for three months—since the moment I had gone into Kings County. While I was in the hospital, I wondered why he didn't call or visit me. After all, he was on the staff of the hospital, probably right down the hall some days, teaching other shrinks. Naturally, in my first session back,

I wanted to know what had happened to him. He sat there in his big leather chair, blue-suited and composed, waiting, as usual, for me to speak first. If I didn't speak, he wouldn't. Finally, I was too irritated to continue the game. "Where the hell were *you* when I was in the hospital?" I asked. He considered this, then said, "It is our policy, when one of our patients has been committed to the hospital, not to visit them on the ward…we see them again when they are discharged." I took in this formal spiel and suddenly it dawned on me: he was *afraid* to come on to the ward. He didn't want to get his hands dirty up there in darkest loonyland. He liked it much better sitting here in his leather and mahogany hideout, writing Valium prescriptions for nervous ladies on Fifth Avenue.

"You know," I said, feeling some righteous anger now for the first time in months—and liking it. "I think you're just afraid. In fact, I think you're a goddamn coward!"

He was insulted; I could tell by the way he raised his eyebrows. "Do you feel that we did not want to visit you on the ward?"

I leaned forward in my chair: "Oh, do me a fucking favor!" I yelled. "Stop with this *we* bullshit, will you?"

"I see you're angry," he said.

I sat back in my chair, and suddenly, the stupidity of it all hit me. After everything I've been through, do I really need to sit here and listen to this undertaker? We talked for a while and I calmed down. As narrow and inhibited as he was, he was still the only one I could talk to, and, to give him his due, he *was* always advising me to tell my wife off when she was being stupid or thoughtless. He once even suggested I might not want to be married. At the end of the session we agreed that I would continue to see him as before.

In April I experienced a violent case of spring fever. I couldn't stand pretending to be a husband, working at a place I hated, planning a future that meant nothing to me. Carol felt it too. We began, finally, to discuss the possibility that our marriage was in trouble. Naturally, in my perpetually self-involved trance, I had hardly noticed that she too was depressed about the sad state of our relationship. Despite her understanding that we were in trouble, I could tell that Carol still wanted us to be married and to carry on with her cherished plans. I didn't want to hurt her, so I slogged ahead, but I was about done in by combat fatigue.

One cold, wet day, I was sitting quietly in Gold's office, having exhausted my usual sad menu of complaints. I slumped forward in the chair, my head in my hands, too glum to continue. Finally, he took pity on me and said something completely out of character. "Cheer up," he said, "things will get better." Better? I just didn't see it happening. I gave him a check for the session, sixty dollars, and shuffled out the door.

I walked out onto the street; it was about four in the afternoon, and a slow, steady drizzle was misting down from the gray sky. I was supposed to head home, but I couldn't bring myself to do it. I walked over to the subway, dragged myself onto the train bound for Brooklyn. When the doors opened at Centre Street in Manhattan, a couple of blocks from Chinatown, I jumped off. I walked through the rain, dreariness inside and out. I was thinking, maybe if I just keep walking, I'll disappear: there are such cases in the annals of the paranormal.

I was staring in the window of a restaurant, when I realized I was only a few doors away from one of my old favorite spots, a trashy, silly tourist attraction called the Chinese Museum. They sold "original" Chinese statues and "authentic" antique swords, all of which were no doubt delivered in job lots, straight through the basement next door. The main feature of the Chinese Museum was Clara the Talking Chicken. Who knew where they got "Clara" from? It wasn't a very Chinese name.

There she was, a scrawny, sick-looking bird pecking around inside a glass-enclosed cage. You put a quarter in a slot, it clanged down through some intricate mechanism, and one measly kernel of corn was deposited in a little metal plate inside Clara's see-through henhouse. She pecked it up, the vibration of the peck set in motion some other arcane mechanism, and a fortune popped out of another slot. What the fuck, I thought, what do I have to lose? I took out a quarter, dropped it in—clankety clank, ker-*ping*, plip. Peck, clank, pat-*ting*! and out came my paper fortune. "Cheer up," it said, "things will get better."

Saturday morning, I was sitting at the kitchen table, listening to the radio, drinking coffee, and wondering what to do with the next ten minutes of my life. Carol came in, sat down opposite me. We looked at each other. And, suddenly, it's over. We're both crying, holding hands across the table. "I'm sorry," she said. Jesus Christ, *she's* sorry. "I'm the one who needs to apologize," I said. "I fucked this up from the beginning."

We talked and talked, the first honest conversation we had had in more than a year. Was it possible that we could turn this around, build a marriage on a sadder but wiser foundation? No. It really was over. That afternoon, I called my father and told him I was coming out to stay. He had been expecting something like this for weeks and he seemed resigned to it. Actually, I think he was looking forward to it. He was lonely out there and wanted my company.

I packed two suitcases. At the door to the apartment, the last kiss: soft, loving, real.

"Good-bye," I said.

She held on to my hand. "I'll see you soon?"

"Yes, of course." It was what we had to say at that moment. But we were not going to be seeing each other soon.

Face in the doorway. Tears. The sad history of the world in a few seconds. The elevator arrives. I'm down, out, and in the car, driving to Long Island.

The next week, I'm in Gold's office. Though still shaky from my last year's trek through the wilderness, and still taking heavy mood-stabilizing drugs, I'm feeling that hope has been restored to my life. And if not hope, the next best thing for somebody like me, the absence of pressure.

I have given notice at my job, having found a better one with the state probation department—more pay and autonomy. I've notified my advisor at Queens College that I'll be taking a couple of semesters off or quitting entirely. Ensconced in a small bedroom in the basement of my father's house, I play pool or watch TV with him at night. In the morning he cooks breakfast and we take the train together into the city to our jobs. We meet again at five-thirty and take the train back out to his house. I finally had a father.

As I sat in the shrink's office for my next session, I realized that I didn't want, or need, to be there anymore. The prime cause of my misery, my ill-fated marriage, had ended. Nevertheless, I felt funny about quitting. It seemed impulsive. And, like Bernstein, maybe Gold would feel bad if I just up and left. Or would he be happy to get rid of a loose cannon like me? Either way, I had trouble breaking it off clean. We were smiling at each other. "You know," I said, "last week, when I left here, I went down to Chinatown and had my fortune told by a talking chicken." His smile grew a little wider.

"Yes?"

"Yes," I said, "and you know what the chicken told me? She said, 'Cheer up, things will get better.'" I held up the little fortune paper for him to see.

"And?…"

"Well, I was thinking, the chicken told me the same thing you did. I had to give you sixty dollars—all I had to give *her* was twenty-five cents."

He laughed. I laughed. We regarded each other benevolently for a minute or two, but in the end I had to say it. "I don't think I want to continue coming here anymore."

We talked for the rest of the session about my leaving, but it was a closed issue as far as I was concerned. I could see, too, that he was not falling into deep grief over it. At the end, I got up. We shook hands—and I was on the street again.

The May sun illuminated everything in sight—one of the few times in the year when New York City can look beautiful. I walked two blocks over to Central Park and found a bench a little way in. I sat there, watching the parade of humanity passing by.

I thought of Carol, crying on the phone just a few days earlier. She was feeling lonely and angry and accused me of hiding the lunacy that ran in my family from her. I should have told her, she said, how crazy I was.

I thought of Bernstein, my old lord and master, tossing me out like trash into the garbage can. I thought of my father not knowing exactly what to do with a brooding neurotic son living in his house. I thought of my mother, who never learned I had been committed, or that anything was wrong with me. I hadn't wanted her to know because I was sure she would take it as her final triumph—sonny boy follows in Mom's footsteps.

I got up, walked over to the carousel. I bought some Cracker Jacks, gooed up my hands searching for the plastic prize. I could *never* wait to get to the prize. I watched the kids on the ride, shrieking and laughing. Pigeons came around begging, a couple of squirrels. I tossed Cracker Jacks at them. A kid waved to me from one of the carousel horses. I waved back.

PART THREE

LONG ISLAND

CHAPTER FOURTEEN

I began, very slowly, to recover from my breakdown. But I still couldn't think clearly and felt like sleeping all the time. I was about twenty pounds underweight, riddled with doubts and fears, and consumed with guilt about the way I had treated Carol.

As an engineer my father was used to tackling real problems and coming up with real solutions. He let me in on his theory of mental illness and the solution to it: "Mike," he told me, pouring me out a glass of beer, "this whole problem of yours is very simple. It's the same as if you had a broken arm. Your *mind* was broken, like a fracture, and now it's in a cast, healing itself."

I liked that image, my cracked mind, resting lightly in a sling. It comforted me.

After due consideration, my father had obviously come to the conclusion that vigorous life activities were the only way to get me going again, what you might call the Teddy Roosevelt approach: cold showers, brisk long walks, big hearty meals. *Never say die!* Every morning, he got up about 6:30 A.M., came to the door of my room and sicced his eccentric mutt, Bismarck, on me. The dog jumped onto the bed, right on my chest, and commenced licking me like a maniac till I had to sit up and throw him off the bed.

I sat in my father's kitchen while he rustled up breakfast—my face pale, my hands cold and trembling. Everything, the dishes and silverware in front of me, the headlines in the morning paper, seemed overwhelming, or meaningless and sad. He grabbed some eggs from the fridge, slammed the door shut, and banged a big iron frying pan down onto the stove. I winced with every noise he made.

He beat up the eggs in a bowl, threw some butter and sliced onions in the pan, and fried the whole mess up. Then he dished it out and dropped the plate onto the table in front of me. Blap! He sat down, lit up a cigar, and then scooped up his eggs and onions. "C'mon," he said, his mouth full. "Dig in! It's good for you."

The smell made me sick to my stomach. "What's the matter?" he asked. I didn't know what to tell him. We were, after all, virtual strangers. We talked sports, one of his favorite topics, but after a while that bored me. He tried to stir up political arguments—we had once gone at it hot and heavy over Vietnam—but now I didn't give a shit what happened to the world. He told me the latest dirty jokes; I winced. Out in the garden, he tossed me a shovel—I dropped it. He bought us some beers at a local pub, but I could never drink more than half a glass and wanted to leave after a couple of minutes.

After three months, despite my contrariness, my father's no-nonsense healing program began to take effect. I slowly began to let him cheer me up. The old man and I, with the dog running ahead of us, took rambling walks in the morning and evening. We planted roses and tomatoes in his garden. We caught flounder off the docks at Freeport and cooked them on his backyard grill. We had fun. Fun was a new concept to me; this is how it worked: you went to a place you wanted to go and did things you wanted to do. And you didn't worry about it. Amazing.

My father was like a big kid. He liked to just *do* things—jump in the car, drive out on the back roads, buy a homemade pie, come back and eat the whole thing washed down with a big glass of milk. He loved to cook, and he was good at it, frying up masses of chicken, barbecuing ham, steaks, burgers, and sausages. We went to basketball games and ate bags of popcorn, cheered the Knicks on to victory. We went for long hikes on the beach, my father pointing out the various kinds of shells, telling me the uses of silicon, explaining how certain clouds were formed, how weather patterns developed.

We talked politics, law, government, history. I liked doing all this, but, of course, the real treatment here was getting a daily dose of the medicine I had needed for twenty years now—an IV, straight into my veins, every day, five hundred cc's of pure father. I slept like a baby in his house, just knowing he was there.

Over a period of months I "grew up" all over again, this time with my father present. As I progressed from early childhood through puberty to adolescence and beyond, I got to know my father as I had never known him before.

One thing I discovered, my father was very competitive. So competitive that it didn't matter who the competition was, a total stranger or his own kid. He had to win. A simple conversation often turned into a heated debate. Any game, like pool, cards, or checkers, was like a sudden death match in professional hockey. When he won at something he would boast and point out all the foolish moves I'd made. If he lost, there could be real trouble.

For instance, soon after I moved in, he bought a used pool table and we lugged it down to his finished basement. We had long, marathon tournaments. It's so true that you can tell a lot about somebody's personality by seeing how they play a game. My father carefully gauged the angles and all the possible trajectories with his engineer's eye, then carefully grasped his cue stick and executed his shots. The balls should have dropped perfectly, but the table was warped.

After the first couple of games, he became frustrated, agitated in the extreme about the eccentric little journeys the balls were making across the table. He got out his level, his slide rule, and a few other implements and determined that what he suspected was true: the pool table had a surface like a chocolate cream pie. He made some adjustments to his shooting, but essentially he continued to shoot straight and he continued to miss.

For *me*, warped was not a problem. In fact, I was better off with a bent table: it conformed to my extensive interior warping. I played like a pro, making all kinds of impossible shots without even trying. My father sensed this perverse harmony. "Well," he said, "I guess this is a good table for somebody like *you*." That didn't faze me. It was only the truth. He kept it up: "You wouldn't stand a chance against me if this was a real pool table." He missed a shot, cursed, banged his fist into the wall. When I took a shot, he talked or coughed. He "accidentally" banged his stick against the side of the table.

He kept on trying, I kept on winning. Finally, he'd say: "Alright, enough of this shit—let's play a game where some brains are required!" And we'd go into the kitchen to play checkers—a game he never lost. He triple-jumped me. "You didn't see *that* coming did you, Mr. Smartass!" "C'mon, you gonna sit there all day? Make a move, you're gonna lose anyway."

My father could be a tyrant if you disagreed with him. He'd turn red in the face, throw a fit, yell, break things, ridicule and curse anybody who dared to question him. He had been that way when I was little, but I guess I had forgotten, unintentionally or deliberately.

To be charitable, you could say he was just an overgrown child who threw an occasional bad tantrum. Most of the time he meant well; he often went out of his way to help people in need. His neighbors on the block liked and respected him.

His neighborhood was mostly black; the whites had run out a couple of years before when black people started moving in. My father had, at least on political and social issues, a fierce sense of right and wrong. He remained where he was and joined the new block association, the only white member. There were some threats to the black homeowners at first, some drive-by rudeness and pranks perpetrated by the local rednecks. My father was right there on the front lawn, shoulder to shoulder with his neighbors, armed with a crowbar—the only white man in the neighborhood ready to kick ass in the name of equality. He saw himself as a kind of lone knight, an avenger of the oppressed, and if anyone attempted to thwart his do-good urges, the results could be calamitous.

There was the incident of my sister's birthday cake.

When I was twenty years old, my cousin Russell got married. My sister and I were invited to the ceremony and the party afterward, held at a large

Jewish center out on Long Island. Coincidentally, it was also my sister's birthday.

We were all downstairs, sitting at the table. The band was playing, the main course had been served, and dessert was on the way. My father said mysteriously, "You kids just wait here, I'm gonna get something from the car." He got up and went out. My sister and I looked at each other—we had no idea what was going on. A couple of minutes later, there was a huge commotion over at the door. I looked up and I saw my father, arguing with the rabbi and some other men who were blocking his way into the room. In my father's hand was a big white cake box. He was working himself into, as the Irish say, a fine lather; red-faced and shouting, you could hear him loud and clear over "Hava Negila," "What the hell do you mean I can't bring this cake in here?!"

The whole room, two hundred people, looked at the door. The Rabbi, a little old man, seventy-five if he was a day, yelled right back at my father. "I told you before, sir. It's not Kosher; you cannot bring that cake in here!"

"Well, goddamnit," yelled my father, "it's my daughter's birthday and this is her goddamn cake! I damn well *am* gonna bring it in!"

"Sir, I—"

"Get the hell out of my way, you little runt!" My father stepped forward, cake in hand. A couple of guys reached out to stop him, and he dropped the cake, smush! onto the floor. With his left hand he grabbed one of the men by the shirt front. He drew his right arm across his chest, ready to backhand the little rabbi into the next world. My cousin Russell and his two brothers—they were floor waxers—big, burly guys, jumped off the dais, rushed over to the door, and grabbed my father. They were laughing themselves sick, and so was I.

My sister, however, did not see the humor in the situation. She was so embarrassed she had literally gone under the table. I moved the tablecloth aside and looked down at her. She was crying. "What's happening now," she whispered. I could hardly talk for laughing. Finally I told her, "It's OK, you can come out now, they got him calmed down."

The poor girl was so mortified by my father's behavior she wouldn't talk to him for the rest of the wedding. The entire drive home, he ranted on about stinking little hypocritical jerks and their phony-baloney religious rules that were meant to keep the common man down. The flattened cake was on the back seat.

By September, about five months after I had gone out to live with my father, I was much improved. I had reduced the amount of drugs I was taking and life didn't seem so black to me. I felt strength flowing back into my body.

I began to consider the possibility of getting my own apartment again, in Brooklyn. I had been working for a while back in the probation department and had made a couple of new friends. There was even a girl or two interested in me. I got itchy; a social life, even sex, beckoned.

Some nights, instead of meeting my father at the train station for the ride back out to his house, I stayed late in the city and went over to my friends' apartments or took in a movie.

When I got home, my father was seated in his usual place, on a couch downstairs in the den, watching television. It's what we did almost every night. After dinner we went downstairs to the den, flipped on the TV, and watched sitcoms, comedy specials, or ball games. He lay on his couch, propped up on some big pillows, and I sat in a leather easy chair a few feet away.

It was dark in that room. The only light other than the TV was from a lamp way off in the opposite corner. I watched the television and I watched my father. And what did I see, now that I had regained my mind and confidence? I saw a father I had never known before. In his unlit corner, illuminated only by the artificial light of the television screen, he seemed worried and sad, almost empty. When a commercial came on or it was time to go to bed, he just sort of folded up and collapsed in on himself.

At first I thought it was just me. Maybe he didn't feel comfortable in my presence. I knew sometimes he didn't seem to know what to say to me. And I knew he was upset that I wasn't coming home with him every night, like I'd been doing for months. After a while, I realized it wasn't me; it was him. He was essentially a lonely, isolated man. At meals he read the paper, throwing an occasional look at the dog, who sat next to him waiting for table scraps. On the train he read the paper or did the crossword puzzle.

And when he finished the paper, he stared out the window, silent for long stretches at a time.

It wasn't that he didn't *want* to talk, or that he had nothing in his brain. There was plenty brewing there, but some powerful inner censor kept his mouth shut. He actually seemed apprehensive about talking, as if he were unsure about the reception he would get.

I wasn't used to this lack of free-flowing dialogue. In our house when I was growing up, my mother never shut up unless she was drugged. She ranted, raved, talked a blue manic streak all the time. My sister cried and yelled, and chattered endlessly in her vain attempt to get one of us to pay attention to her. And then there was me, of course, who, even after my verbal shutdown in my early teens, was still prone to the odd raconteur-ial burst. Sometimes it seemed like there was a perverse contest going on in my house. Whoever stopped talking first, lost.

Having grown up in my own personal Tower of Babel in Laurelton, I was always surprised by and secretly admired people who were quiet. Not passive scared bunnies like my uncle and my grandfather, but hard, strong types like most of the men in my neighborhood: cops, plumbers, guys who didn't waste words. Even the women were like that; they'd gossip, of course, but they had a quiet shrewdness about them. They knew when to shut up. Nobody talked half as much as we did in our house. In the movies, tough guys were famously tight-lipped. Hemingway guys. Real men didn't run off at the mouth. Take John Wayne, for example. He never said anything unless damn it! it needed saying. Gary Cooper, Humphrey Bogart, Marlon Brando—they never wasted a word.

I looked at my father lying there in the TV room, picking at his cuticles, staring tight-lipped and gloomy at some foolish commercial on the tube. This was not strong and silent; this was something else. He looked more like a big kid who had been sent to his room for breaking some grown-up rule.

My father had no friends; the only calls he got were from my sister and my aunts, checking to see how he was. He was awkward around women. His jokes were corny and he never seemed to know the right thing to say. He meant well yet tended to ignore the feelings of those around him.

Later on, after my father died, I spoke to my aunts, his sisters, about him. One of them told me that though she thought the world of my grandfather, he was often mean to my father while they were growing up. My father was his mother's favorite. She dressed him in precious little suits and patent leather shoes. She made him take violin lessons. I saw a picture of my father in one of my aunt's albums. He was maybe five years old, all dressed up in his velvet suit with a fancy lace collar, his hair long and curly. This was how he looked when my grandfather ridiculed his son, told him he was a klutz, a bumbler, an awkward lump of a boy.

CHAPTER FIFTEEN

I n the fall, almost a year to the day since being committed to Kings County Hospital, I told my father I was moving back to Brooklyn—I'd found a small two-room apartment. I expected my father's blessing. After all, it was he who had helped me back into life. What I couldn't see—or didn't want to—was that he had come to really count on my being there. I was the only friend he had. And he was getting a rare chance to bury the guilt of having abandoned me and my crazy mother all those years ago.

My father was angry when he heard my news. He told me that in his considered opinion I wasn't ready to move out.

"I know I'm taking a chance," I said. "But I want to try it. And besides, if I run into trouble, I can always come back out here, right?"

"This isn't a hotel," he said. "You can't just come back and forth whenever the mood strikes you." I just couldn't understand what was making him so nasty.

"What are you talking about?" I asked him. "You'll be here, won't you?"

"Maybe I will, maybe I won't."

"What's that supposed to mean?"

"Goddamnit! I've been living with you every day and I'm telling you you're not ready!" He was working up to a full-blown rage, something I hadn't seen in a while. I *was* ready to move out and I just couldn't get why he didn't see it as clearly as I did. Now *I* was angry: "Well, you know, I can't stay here forever."

He was on his feet, his face red, pointing his finger at me. "I'm warning you, Mike, if you move out on your own now, you'll crack up again and have to go right back into the hospital."

We stood there in his kitchen, staring at each other—a sudden, terribly familiar gulf opening between us.

The next day, in Brooklyn, I gave the landlord one month's rent and the security deposit. That Saturday, my father drove me to the train station. He had retreated into a grim, angry silence. He dropped me off in the parking lot. I got my suitcases out of the trunk and walked around to the driver's side of the car. He looked at me, cigar firmly clamped in his mouth, his eyes hard. "Well," I said, "I'll call you when I get in."

"Yeah," he said, "you do that." I walked up the stairs and looked over the rail of the elevated platform to wave to him, but he had already driven out of the lot.

I called him as soon as I got to the city, but there was no answer. That really worried me. Here was a man who used to travel at a moment's notice to all ends of the earth. Maybe he had driven straight from the railroad parking lot to the airport. Maybe he was halfway across the Atlantic by now. I called him all evening until he picked up the phone around ten o'clock.

"Where were you?" I asked.

"Out."

The first few weeks in my new place, I called my father every day, but he was distant and had practically nothing to say to me. I resented this because I could really have used his help. It was scary, being on my own for the first time in two years, but it was exhilarating, too: doing what I wanted, when I wanted. I bought furniture, a big stereo unit with a record player and headphones. Every day, I went to work at Brooklyn Criminal Court. Increasingly undrugged, I worked hard on my cases, made friends at the office. I even went on a few dates. I felt human again, as if maybe I had a chance to make my life something more than a bad joke, a gloomy ride to nowhere. I talked to people on my block, got invited to a couple of parties. Late at night, I sat in the window seat of my apartment, a drink in my hand, watching people walk up and down the quiet lamp-lit street. I was *living*! And, amazingly, I was doing it without a shrink!

Two months after I moved out of my father's house, right before Thanksgiving, he called and told me he had something he wanted to tell me. I should come out to his house. I was alarmed, since my father wasn't given to such formal rituals. I took the train out to the Island, and he met me at the station. We had lunch, made meaningless small talk, then he cleared his throat to tell me his news: "I'm taking a job in Turkey."

At first I could hardly understand what he was saying.

"You mean, you're going to...where?—the *country* Turkey?"

"Hmn-hnn."

"When?"

"This Friday."

"What?!"

"I'm flying out Friday afternoon."

"Wait, wait. You're going there for a visit? A project?"

"Nope. I'm heading up an office for Foster-Wheeler. It's a permanent job."

I was stunned. He was going halfway around the earth. Leaving me behind. *Again*. I couldn't believe he would do such a thing. I couldn't even speak.

"Look," he said, getting right to the point, "you made your choice, you have to live with it." I was mad, tears in my eyes. "You know what you're doing?" I said. "You're stealing yourself from me again!" He was very smug and self-righteous, "Let me tell you something, Mike, you're never going to grow up if you don't stop feeling sorry for yourself."

My father told me I could meet him at the airport to see him off on Friday afternoon. I didn't go. For all I cared, he could fly to the moon and stay there.

More than a year went by. I was living in a studio apartment in an old brownstone on a beautiful tree-lined street in Park Slope. My wife—now ex-wife—had moved back to New Hampshire, and now Brooklyn seemed free of bad memories. I was shrink-free and had stopped taking drugs to calm me down. I worked as a state probation officer, splitting my time between an office in downtown Brooklyn and state supreme court in lower Manhattan.

In the last year, my personality had undergone something of a change. When I surfaced in Brooklyn again, after surviving two years of misery and near-insanity, I no longer felt required to be everyone's good little boy, doing and saying the right thing, worrying about everyone else all the time, rescuing people. I felt that I, even I, general in command of the Guilt Division, had earned the right to take some real R&R, bust out a little.

For instance, I decided, for the first time in my relatively shy, repressed life, that I was a tough guy, a man who took no guff from anyone—man, woman, or beast. My grandfather, who had been a boxer and a union organizer, my father, the brawler—their spirits rose up in me: don't mess with Mike!

The state probation office conferred on its officers a nifty gold and blue badge that looked exactly like a New York City detective's badge. I loved that badge. Since I was a little kid I'd wanted to be a cop—specifically, a homicide detective, tracking down murderous felons and seeing they got their just deserts. I would be relentless—have no mercy—always get my man.

My first job right out of college, when everybody else I knew was joining corporations or becoming a teacher or going to law school, was as a Pinkerton guard. I had a uniform, a night stick and badge. In fact, I was never much more than a glorified night watchman, but I always had my imagination to fill in the missing parts.

My wish to be a real cop lay somewhere between a daydream and an actual desire. In the end, though, I never seriously tried to get on the force; I didn't even take the test. When it came right down to it, I didn't really like wearing a uniform and I knew you had to be a beat cop—uniform, arrest reports, midnight shifts, and all—for years before you could be a detective. I was too lazy and perverse to consider such discipline and hard work. Besides—and this was a real drawback to police work—I couldn't really imagine hitting somebody over the head with a nightstick. I had enough bad stuff on my conscience already.

Then came Vietnam, welfare protests, black voter registration; the cops always seemed to come down on the wrong side. By the time I was in my mid-twenties, 1971-72, the possibility of being one of the boys in blue was completely out of the question.

Do deep-seated fantasies ever die? I don't think so. The minute I was handed my probation officer's badge, I pinned it inside my wallet, so that when I—coolly—swung it open, it was right there in all its official glory for the whole world to see. I was a man of power, of respect, a man to be feared.

And guns. I loved guns too. All my life I had some kind of gun. Water guns, cap guns, BB guns, CO2 pellet guns. I had fired real guns, pistols and rifles, when I was visiting a cousin who lived in Phoenix. I loved hearing the bang! and feeling the sharp kickback.

During our training period as probation officers, we were told that we were legally allowed to buy and carry a gun. That's all I needed to hear. The second week into my job, I went to a police equipment store and bought a terrific little detective's special, a snub-nosed .38 Smith and Wesson revolver with grained walnut grip. I got myself a box of bullets and a brand-new leather clip-on holster. And, shazzam! There I was, an honest-to-god law enforcement officer. Evildoers the world over were no doubt shaking in their evil boots.

I didn't want to wait till I got home to load my gun, so I walked around the corner to a coffee shop, went into the men's room and into a stall. I took my new gun out of its wax-paper wrapper, opened the box of shiny new copper-jacketed bullets, and loaded the pistol. I rotated the cylinder slowly, loving each little click as the chambers lined up with the hammer. I clipped on my belt holster, slipped in my new gun, and zipped my jacket over it. I was tough; I was cool.

It seemed, suddenly, undignified to be standing in a toilet stall, so I walked into the restaurant, sat at the counter, and ordered a cup of coffee. Did everyone know now that I was one serious hombre? I believe they did. *Detective Sergeant Mike Feder. A decent guy, an honest cop, but don't cross him—it could get ugly.* I looked slowly around the place, squint-eyed, tight-lipped. I hoped, for their sakes, there were no felons around.

Back at my apartment, I stood in front of my big color movie poster of Al Pacino as Serpico. We looked in each other's eyes, me and Serpico. It was there alright, the deadly knowledge, the blood camaraderie of men on the street. I practiced pulling my pistol out of the holster. Freeze! Drop it! You're coming with me, motherfucker!

Unfortunately for me, but fortunately for society at large, the probation department did not like its officers to actually *carry* guns, especially the kind of probation officer I was: my job was mostly writing up presentence reports for judges and recommending sentences for convicted felons. I worked out of a small office in the State Supreme Court Building on Centre Street in downtown Manhattan, interviewing "offenders" and doing paper work. Sometimes, not too often, I had to supervise these guys, monitor their progress while they were out on bail, waiting to be sentenced. They had to report to me once a week and tell me whether they had found a job, how they were doing in their rehab programs, if they were keeping out of trouble. It was an ironic situation. Not too long before, *I* was on a kind of probation, living, freshly de-institutionalized, like a lost teenager in my father's house. Now *I* was the father, dispensing justice and setting limits for a lot of big wayward children.

I remember one case I had, a doctor in his early sixties who had been arrested by an undercover narcotics officer. The man was handing out prescriptions for diet pills—speed—in huge quantities to people with no discernible medical problems. They busted him in his office, right in front of his patients. Because he had been a doctor for thirty years and had no prior record, they let him plead to an E-felony, the least of the serious crimes they could have pinned on him. It was up to me to recommend either a five-year sentence or five years' probation. The doctor sat, dressed in a suit, in my small, cramped courthouse office. He was a big man, tall and heavy, with iron-gray hair. He reminded me of my father a little, but he looked rumpled and crushed, as if some essential fluid had recently leaked out of him.

After he was arrested, he'd been handcuffed, kept overnight in jail. Then, of course, he lost his license to practice medicine. His life was in ruins. I felt sorry for him. Obviously he had been a person of power and substance and now he was reduced to telling his story, pleading for his freedom to a twenty-seven-year-old civil servant. The tears poured down his face as he asked me to keep him out of jail. What was I gonna do? Put this poor guy in with rapists and murderers? In the end I recommended probation.

Well, so much for two-gun (or even one-gun) Mike. In my office, we were supposed to be investigators, almost caseworkers—not really cops at all.

But even if I wasn't Serpico I was at least free and unencumbered. My mother never called me, and I had no intention of calling her. My father had taken himself twelve thousand miles away, and my ex-wife was just a bad memory. Who was around to say I was ungrateful and inconsiderate? That anything I wanted was only to be had at somebody else's expense?

In my studio, I blasted rock music all the time. I bought bottles of Southern Comfort and jumped around my apartment with the headphones on, getting drunk, singing, in my terrible voice, at the top of my lungs.

On warm nights, I sat out on the front stoop of the brownstone, talking to whomever passed by or chose to stop and sit with me. I was lonely sometimes, and a little scared. Nothing new about that. But I was living a simple life and I was more content than I had ever been before.

CHAPTER SIXTEEN

I had been living the high bachelor life for more than a year when I ran into the second serious woman in my life, on the one and only blind date I ever had.

I had conceived a heated passion for the sexy girlfriend of some guy from the neighborhood. They asked me to go to a movie with them in Manhattan, and I agreed. I figured I could sit on one side of her and rub up against her. Her boyfriend was a nice guy, but I didn't care. When I got to the theater—it was a freezing-cold day in February—I was unpleasantly surprised to see they had invited a woman to be my "date." They had set me up—and with an obvious message: here's *your* woman, Mr. Hard-on, stop sniffing around someone who's already taken.

I was pissed, and in the theater I didn't say one word to my "date" the whole time. After the movie, we went to have coffee, but I still didn't say anything to her. As far as I was concerned, she wasn't even there.

They all got up to leave and the woman looked at me. It was an open question—a direct appeal. I could see loneliness there, real need. If I wanted her to stay and have coffee, if I wanted her to come home with me right then and there, all I had to do was ask, but I didn't.

A couple of weeks later, I got a call. It was my forgotten date from the movie fiasco. She asked me if I remembered her. I didn't but said I did. She invited me over to her apartment for dinner.

Susan lived in a wretched basement studio in a rundown brownstone on the edge of Brooklyn Heights. She met me at the door, obviously ill at ease. We sat in her room and she served me a simple dinner she had cooked. I was polite, biding my time, waiting to see what developed. She didn't have much to say; just stared at me a lot and seemed to be waiting herself. She had clearly taken pains to straighten and dust the place—she wanted it spotless for her big dinner. I was touched that she had gone to so much trouble.

We talked about our jobs. Susan was working as a secretary for a non profit organization, putting together statistical reports on elderly welfare clients. She was planning to go to NYU in the fall to get her doctorate in psychology. Jeez, I thought, *another* therapist.

After dinner, the evening crept slowly along. I was getting bored; she was so quiet. Shy or scared, I didn't know which, but really all I could think of, as usual, was: am I going to get any sex? And if so, when?

I had never gotten to the point where I could just put my arm around a woman or reach out, for no reason, and take her hand. Women still scared me. Generally, I preferred them to initiate physical contact. That way, whatever happened was not my "fault." A truly guilt-ridden attitude about sex, but what are you gonna do? Lenny Bruce once said: "The best thing about sex is, it's dirty."

This reticence of mine was always a problem, but there was one little trick I had come up with in those days. In the last few months I had conceived an interest—it was the going thing in Park Slope—in astrology and palm reading; I had a dozen books on both, but my specialty was palmreading. I had a natural talent for it. And besides, palm reading had an added benefit; it was a can't-lose way to get hold of a woman's hand without having to go through hours of polite drivel (on either side). The way it usually worked: *Oh, do you actually read palms? Yes, I do. Would you mind reading mine? If you really want me to.* It was just like Dracula; the victims had to enter the fiend's domain of their own free will, then he had power over them. Give me your hand...hmmnnn...*I see you have a passionate nature, but until now you haven't been able to express it*...right. And *now* is the time to express it.

I held Susan's upturned palm in my hand, looking at the lines, reading her past and her future. Susan's hand was long and a bit pale, with strong, bony fingers, a little cool to the touch at first but almost hot later on.

She was from Montana, tall, almost my height, and big-boned; pretty much what I imagined a Westerner to look like. She had black hair and intense dark-blue eyes. She wasn't absolutely pretty but she had a good figure and sent out a kind of magnetic, witchy signal.

Something huge was burning inside this woman yet at the same time she seemed remote, even calculating.

I traced the thin lines of her hand with my index finger. I looked into her eyes. She was staring at my face, almost, it seeemed, mesmerized; like a rabbit caught in the gaze of a snake. She was lonely, and I had the feeling she had been without sex for a good long time.

When I finally let her hand go, she sat utterly still and silent. I was waiting for her to come closer to me, to lean in and ask me if I wanted to sit on the couch—some prelude to sex—but she said nothing, obviously waiting for me to make the move. Receiving no explicit invitation, I didn't do anything. We were at an impasse. Who was going to be the aggressor? Who was in charge here?

All this silence and immobility was beginning to get on my nerves. In a few minutes, I stood up and told her I had to leave. She walked me to the door, still obviously waiting for some sign of further interest from me, but I was confused; her signals weren't clear. I was anxious to get back to my apartment, where it was safe. Where men were men and movie cops were movie cops.

A few days later, she called me again. Still nervous, still with that concealed sense of desperation and intense need in her voice, she asked me if I wanted to go to a movie. I didn't really want to. I had the sense she was more trouble than I needed, but she *was* sexy, and she was tapping some old feelings in me. A woman was in need, in need of *me*. How could I say no?

A couple more movies, another dinner. Finally, we were in my bed, and I was astounded by what was unleashed. This was a woman who loved sex—who wanted it and needed it like a tiger needs fresh meat.

Afterward, just like a big cat, she stretched every limb, every muscle in her body, yawned and smiled, a wide satisfied smile. She seemed to have metamorphosed, shape-shifted into a different creature than the one who had lain down next to me twenty minutes before. I had the funny feeling that something invisible but massive had changed in our relationship, that suddenly I was being sucked into something I didn't understand. "Enter of your own free will..." says Dracula, knowing damn well there is a lot more to a human being than just his puny will. Susan lay diagonally across my bed. I sat on the edge, watching her, absolutely fascinated.

We wound up in bed two nights a week and a couple of times each weekend. Susan was strong, so was I, and our sexual encounters seemed to be extra-driven, as if two huge magnets of opposite polls had been activated inside us, causing us to come together with tremendous power, until an orgasm or two, or three, temporarily cut the circuit.

We spent most of our time together now, going to museums, movies, taking trips up the Hudson, going for hikes. We talked about ourselves; the past, the present, what we imagined the next part of our lives might be.

That summer, we took our vacations together and spent two weeks up in the country at a friend's house. Surrounded by the quiet darkness, in the yellow-white light of a kerosene lantern on the kitchen table, Susan talked for hours.

Her father was a cop in a small city in the northern part of Montana. Her mother was a part-time nurse's aide. They lived way outside town because her father was something of a loner, and when he wasn't working he wanted to get as far away as he could from civilization. There were seven brothers and sisters; Susan was the second youngest. There wasn't a lot to go around—money, food, time, or attention—all were in short supply. Susan was a smart girl with big ideas, surrounded by hide-bound ignorance and small-town pettiness. She spent most of her time alone, walking around the hills. She developed a habit of confiding her secrets, her wishes and dreams, to inanimate objects. No tree or rock was going to tell her she was too big for her britches, that she was cracked, thinking she was going to be a success one day, making it in the big city.

Her bosom companions were the earth and the sky. The scale seemed to suit her internal geography—she had big dreams, grand plans. She couldn't wait to get away from that place and start her real life.

Up in the country, sitting on the porch in the late afternoon, we came to what seemed like an inevitable conclusion. We decided that when we returned to the city we would move in together. We found a small two-room apartment a few blocks from my studio in Park Slope, dragged our few pieces of furniture out of our bachelor dens. I was hitched again, but this time there were no promises exchanged. There were no rules of behavior or cast-iron future plans to bind me.

For the first couple of months, living with Susan was a breeze, especially compared to living with my ex-wife. We weren't married, there was none of that till-death-do-us-part pressure. There certainly was no problem with class differences. Susan, despite her intelligence, was less sophisticated than I was, and that's saying a lot. She came from some nameless town on the prairie and I came from outer Queens, not really that much of a difference. That she was such an untutored dreamer was part of her great charm for me.

We didn't have much money, but we didn't seem to miss it. Susan was used to getting by with little, living on meager rations and hand-me-downs as a kid, working her way through college and later, never so much as owning a car or more than a couple of changes of clothes. She was working part-time at her job and taking three courses in the afternoons and evenings at NYU. I never cared much about money anyway. My job at state probation had ended a few months before. The office closed down when they finished their original mandate, cleaning up the city's backed-up caseload. I was living on unemployment insurance and making extra money selling old and used books by mail. Collecting old books had always been a hobby of mine. I loved the heavy cloth covers, the thick old paper, the dark, stamped ink. There was real history, real wisdom in old books. And the best thing about them was that they weren't going anywhere. You didn't have to chase them. They just sat there, resting in the arms of the past, waiting to be discovered. I poked around the secondhand stores in Brooklyn, came up with out-of-print books and advertised them for sale in Bookman's Weekly.

That past spring, inspired by Susan's example, I contacted Queens College again, and re-upped for my masters in English. I had a vague notion that I might be a high school English teacher. I signed up for one course—no need to rush.

We worked and we studied, practically right on top of each other in our tiny apartment, and carried on a constant, flowing, seemingly endless dialogue. We took long walks through the streets and the park, talking about everything: books, ideas, movies, people, politics, experiences. We borrowed a friend's car and took drives up to the country, talking the miles away—with no destination, our intimate exchanges our only map. To paraphrase a couple of lines from Rilke, "Love is not two people sitting, staring at each other. It's two people sitting side by side, staring out at the same thing."

That's what Susan and I did. We sat, or walked, or drove, side by side. We walked and talked, we drove and talked, we had sex and talked, and talked and talked. She got to pour out all the pain and fury she had stored up for close to thirty years, all her dreams and great plans for the future. And I did the same, except the future never interested me much. I told her stories of my blitzkrieg childhood, entertained her with tales of strange jobs and crazy encounters—emptied out, for her, the treasure chest of my imagination. As far as I was concerned, this way of being with a woman was sublime. To this day, my greatest source of contentment is sitting on a porch, or walking in the quiet of the evening, or lying next to someone in bed, pouring out my mind and heart, exchanging stories, casting up dreams in the darkness.

One Sunday morning in January, I came back to our place with the paper. Susan was standing in the middle of the living room, agitated, pale. There was something she had to tell me. She blurted it out: "Your mother just called: your father died in a plane crash."

And that's how it goes sometimes. You suffer the great slips and falls of your life in a few short sentences—spoken by another person standing in a small room. She might have said, "You won the lottery," or "I have cancer."

Two seconds of speech, the course of a whole life turned.

I was devastated. My father was too young, too big, too blustery and healthy to be dead, and yet that was what I was being told. He was dead.

And, more specifically, he was gone. His plane, on a midnight flight, had plunged into the Black Sea just off the coast of Istanbul. Not a sound was heard, not a ripple was seen. There was never so much as a nut or bolt, a shoe or hat, much less a body, found from that plane or the fifty people who had been on it.

There was something terribly familiar about the news of his death and the way it happened, as if this final telegram had always been there waiting to be delivered. My father had never really been there to begin with. He was either away or brooding in the living room when I was growing up. Now he was on a much longer trip, and instead of waiting months or years to see him, I would have to wait my whole lifetime, again, before I might possibly see him.

For me, the special anguish of his death was in that ceaseless outward movement of his. I had never had him, and now I never would; as if all my life I had been grasping for a prize that was always beyond my reach. The closer I came, the further away it went. What haunted me especially was that he had disappeared, literally, without a trace. No body was ever found. I knew in the conscious, rational part of my brain that he was dead, that I would never see him again, but in a sad, distorted section of my mind, that special territory where hope mingles with the imagination, I allowed myself to think he might still be traveling. And maybe, one day— it could be years from now—the phone would ring and it would be him, telling me he was back.

CHAPTER SEVENTEEN

My father left a lot of money; not that he had so much, but since he died on company business, and since the airline was at fault in his death, my sister and I split a pretty large amount.

In the summer of 1975, after wandering around in a stupid daze for a couple of months, and pushed by Susan to get a hold of myself, I took some of the money and opened a used bookstore in Park Slope. It was something I had always thought I would do if I could. It was, also, a kind of monument to my father, who always had dreams of owning a business of some kind. I bought up most of the used books from the thrift and antique stores in my neighborhood, put up some rough metal shelves, and got myself a desk and a chair.

I sat in my bookstore, surrounded by thousands of old books, customers coming in and out, but I couldn't seem to shake the sadness of my father's death. I was in the grip of a life, not a death, a life of sadness, of loneliness and forlorn dreaming, now revived and replayed constantly in my mind by his sudden departure.

Susan and I moved to a bigger, nicer place across the street from our first apartment, and, since I could afford it, she quit her job to go to school full-time. She was absorbed in her studies and spent long hours every night reading and writing papers.

I had no interest in studying anymore. I had enough money, if I didn't waste it, to live for the rest of my life without having to work. The thought of getting a master's degree in English literature seemed comical to me. What the fuck did I care about the hidden meanings in seventeenth century religious poetry? Did I really want to be an English teacher? Dragging myself to some crumbling city high school to drive bits of unwanted knowledge into bored teenaged brains? I also felt robbed by my father's death. A hole opened inside me. English degrees, bookstores, other people, even the possibility of a happy future seemed to tumble down that hole and disappear. Naturally, that started some serious trouble between me and Susan.

She was zeroing in on her goals. Doctor Susan, PhD, Professor of Psychology, Chair of the Department of Psychology. She shed her old acquaintances at her nonprofit job, just as she had, in the last year, shed a lot of her old insecurity and awkwardness. As she saw the prize coming closer, she began, slowly but surely, to change. Her natural confidence in her ultimate success took on some extra weight and she became haughty. She returned each night to our apartment with some new grievance; some foolish professor or idiotic classmate had challenged her or committed some unforgivable gaffe.

I moved my store to a better location and had a steady flow of regular customers, but I was still haunted by my father's death; I imagined him trapped in the falling plane, surrounded by the black water of the ocean, drowning. I thought of him every possible way, pictured his face and body, replayed his voice. I recalled his every gesture and the nuance in his way of saying particular phrases. Since my original collection of memories was limited, I found myself revisiting the same ones time and again: our camping trip to Canada, when he almost tipped our boat over into the lake; or our visits to the zoo, where he seemed to know every species of animal, even the trees lining the walkways—as if he were a living natural-history encyclopedia.

His profile came to me—with his gray-black bristly beard—as he drove us fast up some country road, the ever-present cigar jutting from his mouth; his muscular hands, fiddling with some dial or machine setting; a frown, a joke, a word, a laugh. Sometimes, walking on the street, steeped in memories of him, I almost expected to see him appear in front of me, stride right up to me and say, "Well, pal, you fell for it—I was just hiding out to see who really cared about me—now I'm back!" Often I picked up my pace, convinced some big older man on the street just ahead of me might actually be my father. In the apartment, I pored over things I had retrieved from his apartment in Istanbul: a letter opener, a leather bookmark, an old pocket watch—just as I had pored over his things in the attic when I was kid.

Susan was growing increasingly irritated with my soppy behavior. She wasn't naturally patient or easy with other people's misery. The only way she knew to deal with someone else's grief and depression was the way she dealt with her own. Stop moping and do something. Grab your life and make it do what you want. My father, I thought, would have loved this woman. They were both forward-looking, hard working, nose-to-the-grindstone types.

What made matters infinitely worse was my loss of interest in sex—a sad repetition of the decay of my marriage to Carol. I was depressed and sex just doesn't grow in that soil. Susan had no patience with this. The less sex she got from me, the more pissed off she got. She was critical of most everything I said or did. I didn't have the heart to argue with her, nor did I have the will to shake myself out of my sad stupor. In short, Susan's energy was increasing and mine was decreasing, inexorably, like some math formula where distances expand rapidly outward at an increasing rate of speed. She spent more time with her friends at NYU, I spent more time alone.

The inevitable moment arrived. Susan confronted me in our bedroom one night, about a year to the day after my father had died. I was surprised, even grateful at the time, that she had given me even that much time to get over things. Now she told me she was through waiting. She said she was going to find a place in Manhattan to be closer to school. She was moving out. If I had any doubts as to what brought this on, well, I had only to go look in the mirror. Filled with contempt, she said: "You have no *ambition*. I can't stand living with someone who has no interest in making something of themselves. You're just giving up and I have no wish to sink with you."

I just stood there and listened to her little speech. Maybe there was a mute look of appeal on my face. "Look," I told her, "I just can't seem to get over what happened to my father." She didn't want to hear that. "You have had plenty of time to do that; the truth is you don't want to get over it."

"I do. I do want to."

"No, you don't, or you would!" She glared at me, daring me to contradict her. I had no response.

"I'm moving," she said with a dramatic flourish. "I am moving to Manhattan and I am going to find a *real* man."

Do people actually say things like that? Yeah, they do. Susan did. She was given to old-fashioned proclamations and operatic (soap-operatic) expressions. I once thought it was cute and funny, but I wasn't laughing now that I was on the receiving end. A *real* man, she said. To Susan, that meant a doctor, another shrink, a psychologist; better yet, a psychiatrist, a man with a title, with money and status.

Two weeks later, Susan returned home and announced she had found a studio apartment and was leaving that weekend. I could help her move or stay out of the way—whichever.

Sunday, she moved her things out—only a suitcase of clothes remained. In the end she stood in the doorway, tall, impressive, quivering with righteous indignation. I looked at her dumbly—my powers of speech, much less persuasion, had disappeared entirely. "Good-bye," I finally managed to say. "Hmph," she snorted with contempt. "You better pull yourself together or you are going to wind up back in the locked ward." Hearing that, I summoned up a flash of anger. Essentially, I thought, she was doing nothing less than leaving me when I was down. I moved toward her. "So go if you're going, get it the fuck over with!" She backed up a bit. "I am going," she said, turning to leave. Then she turned back, always determined to have the last word, the final pronouncement: "I'm glad I'm leaving. Brooklyn is for losers, anyway."

I lie on my side of the big double bed. You know how that works? You live with someone for a while, maybe for years, and then suddenly she's gone. Now you're a one who was once a two. The rest of the bed, viewed from your 'side,' looks as big as a football field. Loneliness is a matter of space, too much of it. Suddenly each room looks too big, the closets have too much room in them, the medicine cabinet looks like a looted storefront. The apartment is huge and empty. When you speak out loud all you hear are echoes.

I went through a period of heavy depression, near-lunacy. A guy I knew from the neighborhood was a fence, dealing in every manner of stolen merchandise, from silver teapots to Saturday-night specials. I placed an "order" for the largest color TV he could lay his hands on. Susan and I had never bought a TV. There didn't seem to be any need for one. Now there was.

Jimmie the Fence came around the next day with a brand-new emperor-sized RCA, right out of the box, a bargain at a third the retail price and no pesky warrantee to fill out. I paid him in cash—there was plenty of it in those days—and set the monster on a table right at the foot of my bed. I spent the next couple of weeks sitting in my darkened bedroom eating take-out food and staring at the TV, more often than not with the sound off. I watched anything and everything, no matter how stupid or trivial: cops, cowboys, models, sitcom jokesters, soap-opera weepers, grinning idiot reporters, weather maps. "Bedroom sets on sale now!" "Caribbean cruises for two!" "Tall buildings at a single bound!"

Watching the images flicker and flow meaninglessly in the dark room only increased the profound silence that filled the apartment. Loneliness fell on me like a mountain. I was buried underneath four million tons of inert matter, otherwise known as *me*. That I didn't go out and get (or order in) alcohol or drugs is surprising. I think what saved me from falling through the huge cracks in my ego to the bottom of nowhere was anger. I began to feel like I was getting a raw deal—abandoned by a selfish, self-righteous bitch—just when a little tender, loving care might have lifted me out of my excessive grieving.

I was really angry. Angry enough to get out of bed, turn off the TV, and move it into a closet. I thought of ways to get even. Susan told me once she thought I might be a good writer. I'll show her, I decided. *I'll become a world-famous writer, and when she comes begging to come back, to bask in my glory, I'll tell her to take a fucking walk.* Good idea! I went into Manhattan and found, at a used office furniture store, a good-quality IBM electric type-writer. I set it down in the middle of the desk in a small room in the apartment that had been *our* office and study. The machine was scary, sitting there like a great stone idol, waiting for me to make a move. I circled around it for a few days. I thought of Susan. She wouldn't let some stupid machine interfere with *her* desires. OK, I said to myself, I *will* write! I stood in front of the typewriter, flexing my wrists, cracking my knuckles, lighting the inner afterburners, getting ready to launch myself into the writo-sphere. Finally, I knew in my heart that the time had come. I could feel it.

I sat down, took off the plastic cover, rolled in some paper, and hit the first key of my great opus. The "*I* " key—naturally. Instantly, a huge roach appeared, crawled slowly out of the undercarriage, and perched right there on the key, staring at me. I was repulsed and broke out in a sweat. I whipped the plastic cover back on, pushed my chair back, and walked out of the room.

But wait, I couldn't let some filthy little bug stop me. My righteous creative anger reasserted itself, and the next day I tried again.

In three days I knocked out what I modestly thought was a pretty good short story, about an addled Holocaust survivor who haunts a cemetery out in Queens. I brought the story to my bookstore to show all my friends, but, surprisingly, they were very subdued in their responses. What was the problem? Jealousy, no doubt. That was it. They were plain jealous—especially the writers among them. I pushed them. "Tell me what you think...*really*." Finally, my friend Ralph, a believer in tough love, gave it to me as diplomatically as he could: "What you got there, Mike, is a really good Isaac Singer story." He asked, very politely, if I had been deliberately trying to copy Singer's style. I was deeply insulted. Genius is always misunderstood, attacked.

Later on, at my apartment, I took a good look at the story and realized, of course, that Ralph was right. My story was a perfect imitation of I. B. Singer. There was precious little originality in it. Still, I thought, though the content wasn't inspiring, the style wasn't all that bad. I decided to try again. However, when I sat down again to write, I found, after the first burst of words, that the experience was disturbing. Something was missing. What was it?

When I wrote, I hovered over the typewriter, banging away at a rapid pace, pouring out a river of ideas and descriptions, like a composer at a keyboard. Exhilarated, exhausted, I sat back and...nothing. Stillness, a silence surrounding me. Then I realized what the problem was. I had just told a great story, and *no one* was *listening*! I just couldn't stand to "speak" if there was no one to hear. Writing, I thought, was only a refinement of loneliness. No wonder writers drink. I needed somebody to *talk* to.

I realized it was way past time to get back to my bookstore.

CHAPTER EIGHTEEN

By this time, my bookstore was a known location in Park Slope where people came to talk poetry, writing, art, or just to gossip and flirt. I sat in an old leather swivel chair up at the front of the store and patched myself into the circuit. Just like Kim on the Grand Trunk Road in India, I let the waters of humanity swirl around me. Friends, customers (in the end a lot of customers became friends) came in all day and all night. Long conversations, short bursts of news, reminiscences, stories; it was an endless, wonderful orgy of conversation. I opened early and stayed late, milking the last word out of the last visitor.

I thought of Susan less and less. After a few weeks back at the store, my depression started to lift, and a good part of my anger seeped away.

Women came back into my life.

I immersed myself in a great warm pool of sex. Park Slope was full of single women, recuperating, just like the men out there—just like me—from wrecked relationships. This time around on the sexual carousel, it wasn't just skin hunger or the mean mania of a vengeful boy. Now the women I spent my time with had names, faces, and personalities. It was all so much easier, less driven and urgent.

I was half in love with three or four different women. One woman in particular, Mary, had just separated from a blow-hard Italian guy in the neighborhood. She was bright and good-hearted, from down south. She really cared for me and I had, for a change, the good sense to realize this. We spent a lot of time together, in bed, out of bed. We always seemed to be laughing.

This relatively blissful state would have gone on perfectly if it hadn't been for...my mother.

I'd been avoiding her successfully for a long time, something I had to do for my basic sanity. I don't think I had seen her in three years, and there couldn't have been more than a dozen phone calls from her in all that time. What news I had of her, not that I wanted any, came from my sister.

Now that my sister was older and on her own, she spent more time with my mother. She went shopping with her and had what she claimed to be intimate talks with her. This was inconceivable to me. I didn't think my mother was capable of it, but good for my sister if she thought she could get something from the woman.

The trouble for me was that my mother had lately developed the awful habit of calling me at my store, something I asked her from the beginning not to do. Of course, that was just *my* wish. Paying attention to anyone else's needs was not my mother's job in life. If she felt like calling me at the store, she did.

My mother was increasingly agitated because my aunt and uncle, who lived next door, were now old and tired. They were taking the next step to their final rest—Florida. All their friends had long ago escaped the city, and now they too were headed south.

And what was to become of my mother? Their ward. Their patient. It was a real problem. Surprisingly, my mother had the guts and independence to say she didn't want to go down there with the "old people." And in truth, she wasn't old, only fifty-five. She didn't want to become a moldy coconut hanging from the tree of retirement, but she was in a bind. She had never once in her life been on her own.

As her fears increased, my mother became more wild, her past mania coming back with a vengeance. She was seeing her ninth shrink, my sister said, and taking several different kinds of sedatives and mood stabilizers. So, over the top again, she bashed right through the wall I had built between her and me and started calling me in my private hideout, my little bookstore oasis. At least once a week she called me with her fears and complaints—never stopping till I practically hung up on her. I was reaching the boiling point.

One Saturday afternoon in mid-August she calls me. I'm in my store, talking to a friend, looking out my window at the flow of traffic on the avenue. The phone rings and I pick it up. "Hello, darling?" Christ! My mother. There were some customers browsing, sitting in chairs, reading. I didn't answer her at first.

"Hello, darling?" she says again. She has that old sickening dramatic tremor in her voice.

"Yeah."

"Oh, nothing special, sweetheart." She treats me to one of her fake laughs. "I just wanted to call you."

"Hm-hmn."

"So how are you, darling?"

"OK."

"Oh." My mother was always disappointed if I told her I was all right. She seemed to praying for me to tell her I was sick. Illness—any kind was OK—would reestablish our earlier connection. Maybe to her it was evidence that I still loved and needed her. Of course, even if I was *dying* I wouldn't tell her. My sufferings belonged to me.

Bravely recovering from my bad news (that I wasn't sick or sad), she launched into the usual nonstop riff about her various woes. "Well, sweetheart, the doctor says I'm doing a little better, but I don't think so. The new pills don't seem to be working, and I may get him to change them. Your sister says she thinks I'm doing better, but I don't think she really knows because—let's face it—she's not a professional and I don't—" And on and on…

I listened to the same tired rap for a couple of minutes, throwing the occasional "aha" or "hm-hmn," but then it was suddenly too much for me. I stopped her in mid-complaint: "Look," I said, "could you do me a favor?"

"Of course, sweetheart."

"I told you before, and I don't want you to get upset about this, but I wish you would call me at home—not here."

"Oh, why?"

"Well, I just have more time there." Now it starts....

"Oh, and you don't have any time for me right now?"

"No, since you ask, no I don't."

"Well, Michael, I don't believe I ever ask you for very much. In fact, I don't think it's asking a lot just for you to listen to your own mother for a couple of minutes. Do you?" No answer. "Michael? I am asking you a question—Michael!?" Nothing. She starts to cry and yell, both at once. "Alright, Michael, if that's the way you want to treat your mother, you go right ahead! I just want you to remember who's responsible if something happens to me."

I got furious. "Look," I said, my voice rising like a rocket, "don't threaten me!"

"I'm not threatening you, Michael, I'm telling the truth. I am very shaky now, and I can't be responsible for what might—"

"Now!? You're shaky *now*!!? You're always shaky! And you have never been fucking responsible for yourself, or me, or anyone else in the goddamn world!—ever!!" More crying, more yelling, I can see her crazy face, her bony finger shaking at me—a nightmare from the past. "You listen to me, Michael Feder. I'll have you know that I have just made out my will."

"Yeah, well, who cares!"

"Who cares?! Who cares!!? Michael, I am going to cut you out of my will. Do you hear me, Michael! I'm cutting you out of my will!!"

"Well, go ahead and do it, then! Cut me out of your fucking will. Just don't ever call me here again!"

I slam the phone down: red-hot—shaking with rage. There is utter silence in the store. I look up. The two customers over at the shelves are staring at me. I stare back at them. They hurry out of the store. I stand up and smack my fist into the back of the chair. "When," I practically shout out loud, "when is she going to die and leave me in peace?!"

About six weeks later, in late September, the phone ringing woke me up early on a Monday morning. It was my aunt. "Michael, you better come out here. Your mother killed herself. We tried holding a mirror up to her face, there's no breath. She's dead."

I threw on some clothes and drove out to Laurelton, parking directly in front of the house, next to a cop car. The cop was in the doorway and wouldn't let me in till I identified myself. I guess this was a crime scene now, till they ruled out homicide. *It was always a crime scene, officer—and where were you all that time?*

My aunt and uncle were sitting in the living room with another cop. They started to get up when I walked in, but I waved them down and walked back to my mother's bedroom. She was lying on her single bed, which was pushed into the corner of the room, her head right next to an open window. It was a warm day and the room smelled a little sickly sweet. There was a slight breeze rippling through the thin white curtains. On her bureau, there were several large plastic bottles of prescription pills —all of them empty.

I pulled a chair up and sat right next to the bed. My mother, the body of the person who was once my mother, was lying on her back, her eyes closed and her hands folded neatly over each other across her stomach. I can't say she looked exactly peaceful. And she didn't look like she was sleeping. What she looked like was...gone. Whatever life is—a spirit, a soul—it had just disappeared. Now there was only a body, its skin already turning a little yellow.

It was very peaceful in her room. It was a bright sunny day outside, and quiet save for a few birds chirping. One thing for sure, there would be no more trouble in *this* little room. No more terror or fury flying around like bats from hell. All that had obviously flown away, along with my mother's life.

I sat there for a long time, not moving. I can't say I felt nothing, but I wasn't immediately churning with the usual fear and rage that she always stirred up in me. I felt sadness. Not so much that she had done this to herself—it was almost overdue—but that she had had such an awful life. That she had lived in constant agitation, in outright terror for so many years. What an awful existence. So unbearably sad.

Unbearable. Would I have borne it? I don't know. I had to admit she had some courage. I couldn't have lived the way she did. To withstand all that battering for so long, with no one to really love her? I probably would have ended my life a lot more quickly than she did under the same relentless attack of demons. I also felt—strange to say—proud of her, that she had had the *guts* to do it. I *say* I would have killed myself quicker if I had suffered like her, that I wouldn't have endured such misery for so long, but I wonder. She took the law, *the* law, into her own hands. You couldn't help but be impressed by such ferocious daring.

I sat very still; it was probably just a few minutes, but it seemed like years, my knees touching the bed right next to her body. No tears. Crying was not something I did easily, and the lifelong fear and hatred she had inspired in me kept my emotions in check: maybe her spirit was hovering around somewhere near, and if it was, I didn't want her to have the satisfaction of seeing me cry.

Then, inevitably, there was another very familiar feeling. Anger. It was always *her*. Always *her* feelings, *her* fears, *her* nerves that had to be soothed, *her* happiness that had to be considered and the hell with everybody else. My mother had won *again*. She had taken center stage from the very beginning and never moved off the spot. She was center stage now, and she would be there forever. Who could possibly follow this act?

Forever I would be standing off to the side—the foil, the dupe, the straight man, second billing for eternity. Her suicide had sealed my awful life with her. They could just come right now and preserve us in this attitude forever; cover us both with thick clear plastic, or stuff us, make this room an exhibit in a museum, a diorama: *Son, Stuck Looking At His Mother*.

I hear some movement and talking in the hall, and I get up and poke my head through the door. The cop tells me it's the paramedics from the coroner's office. Suicides have to have autopsies to determine the cause of death. I come back into the room and look down at her. I notice she's wearing a thin gold necklace. I know enough, after having worked for the city for so long, that her necklace would get "lost" after they take her body away. I try to pick her head up to unclasp it, but she is too stiff and I just can't bring myself to roll her onto her side; it seems indecent. So I just loop my finger inside the necklace and tear it off. The paramedics lift her body onto the rolling stretcher and into a black rubber body bag. They zip it straight up and over her face. Then they roll her out.

My aunt is in the living room. She is crying and wringing her hands. My uncle is trying to comfort her.

"Where's the note?" I ask. My aunt looks up, nervous, scared. "There was no note, Michael." I don't believe that for a second. There is no way my mother would go out of this world quietly. She had to have the last word.

"Don't tell me that," I say. "I know there was a note, so just show it to me." My aunt looks at my uncle and he nods his head. She goes next door to her house and comes back with a wrinkled, square piece of notepaper. In pencil, in block letters: I CAN NO LONGER LIVE WITHOUT THE RESPECT OF MY CHILDREN.

I drive back to Brooklyn slowly, taking the back streets, seeing the road, the other cars, the people standing there, but more clearly seeing the past. So I am, finally (this time with my sister as accomplice), a murderer. It is true, all the things my mother had screamed at me all those years, all the warnings from relatives.... I had driven my mother crazy, and now I have killed her. It was my fault. What a rap. What a final judgment. Unappealable. She should have killed me first before killing herself, but that wasn't her way. She wanted to bequeath a legacy. A parting gift. *And now, for my last trick...*

For the next couple of days I hung around my house or walked the streets, frozen stiff. I could feel my lips compressed, my face all stony. I was in a quiet, deadly state of rage. I kept seeing her body, kept seeing the words on that note.

I lay on my bed, staring at the ceiling, with no real thoughts in my head. Soon I started having horrible nightmares, night after night. My mother, a skeleton, reaching up from under my bed, her hands, like claws, dragging me down underneath the bed. Her yellowed body, lying on her bed, sitting up, pointing her finger at me, laughing insanely, advancing on me. I wake up covered in sweat, trembling. I drink half a bottle of whiskey just to calm down, and even then, awake, I am convinced she is trying to kill me from beyond the grave.

CHAPTER NINETEEN

My mother wasn't dead more than a couple of weeks when I got a call from Susan. She was soft on the phone, uncertain, the way she was when I first met her. However, the old picture in my mind didn't fit the soundtrack. Her angry contemptuous face floated into my field of vision again. I could see her in my doorway, off to Manhattan to find a "real man."

"What do you want?" I asked her.

"I wanted to know," she said, almost like a child, "if I could see you again." This too was part of Susan's odd charm, at least for me. She was naked in her expressions—without shame. She may have been nervous, she might stumble over her words a bit, but she always knew what she wanted. Forget about the last six months—no problem. She wanted to see me again. "Well," I said, not being in a generous or forgiving mood, "what happened in Manhattan? Where are all the doctors?" She was unfazed. Ask a straight question, get a straight answer. "Well," she said, "I did go out with some doctors."

"Yeah, so?"

"They were boring."

"Boring?"

"Yes."

"Doctors? The great doctors, boring? I thought *I* was boring. I thought you told me I was a depressing jerk, a loser."

"Well, at least you know how to talk." Ahhh. I knew how to *talk*. My one and only saving grace. I was a pathetic bum, a depressed, aimless vagabond, but I knew how to talk. I suspected there was something else, too, that I was better at than the doctors, but I let that pass.

Susan patiently awaited for my verdict.

"Well," I said, "what do you want me to do?"

"Can I come out to see you?"

"Yeah, I guess."

She was coming out to Park Slope that Friday night after she got off work. I didn't tell any of my friends I was going to see her again. I don't know why. Probably I thought they might disapprove and try to get me to change my mind. None of them liked her—they were happy when she took off. On the other hand, I hadn't made any promises; I had no intention of moving in with her again, or even dropping any of the other women I was seeing. By Friday morning, I had gotten increasingly nervous. I wasn't sure if I was making a big mistake, letting her back into my life.

At five minutes to seven that evening, I walked out and stood at the top of my stoop, looking for her to come walking up the block. The atmosphere was strange. It seemed to me that the sky was very overcast, hazy and dark. The streetlights seemed a little dimmer than usual. Was there a power dip? There was a mean, twisted feeling coming off the streets. She was late, and now I started to worry. It was such an ominous night, maybe something had happened to her on the train or walking from the subway station. I pictured all kinds of destruction: assault, rape, murder. I decided I was going to walk over to the train stop to look for her. It seemed like a good idea to go armed. I went back into my apartment and got my pistol. I checked the clip, put it in my pocket, and went outside again. I walked toward the subway station, thinking that I would murder anyone who tried to do anything to her. And then I saw her, walking toward me in the gloom. "Hi," she said. "Hey." We went back to my place. I laid the gun on the night table next to my bed and offered her a drink. I had a big one myself. I told her about my mother. She seemed genuinely shocked and was unusually sympathetic.

One hour and several drinks later, we were having sex again. It was slower, very personal at first, then rapidly crescendoed into a thumping, heart-pounding assault, much the way I remembered from before. Then we fell away from each other, drenched in sweat, recovering our breath. Lying there, I told her about the awful nightmares I was having, how I was twisted up and crazy inside about my mother's suicide and the note she had left. Susan suggested—what else?—I should see a shrink.

Sometime around midnight I walked her back to the subway. She told me she'd call me in a couple of days with the names of some shrinks for me to consult.

I liked Dr. Ziegler the first time I laid eyes on her. She was in her late forties, small, wiry, almost like a tomboy but very mothering. There was real sympathy in her. My new shrink had the same first name as my mother, Ruth. Ruth had a good sense of humor—she appreciated, as long as I didn't overdo it, my tendency toward wisecracks and irony. She was an A1 listener and seemed to be genuinely fascinated—not to mention entertained—by the stories of my life. She pointed things out when they needed pointing out, my faults, my bullshit, but she was always tender at bottom. I wished I had had a mother like her.

Ruth oversaw, among my other struggles, the unfolding of my strange and multiform love life. And it needed overseeing, too. I was back with Susan, sleeping with her once or twice a week, but I was seeing other women too. By seeing I mean, mostly, having sex. And a lot of it. Women I had never met before would wander into my store and, if the spirit was moving me—and them—that day I would have another girlfriend. Some afternoons, I'd just flip the keys to one of my friends who was hanging around and walk home with a woman I'd met only a half hour before. I remember once having sex with three different women in one day—morning, noon, and night. Susan didn't ask what I was doing, but I think she had a good idea. I didn't question her either.

My life proceeded along these lines for close to two years, but after a time my random matings were starting to feel shallow to me, directionless. There were just too many emotional balls to juggle in the air at one time. And, adding to my distress, Susan was slowly but surely hinting to me that I was really wasting myself out there in my circumscribed little world. And I felt she was right. She thought we should try our lives together again, but she didn't want to move back to Brooklyn. If I wanted to live with her, I'd have to come to Manhattan, play in the "big leagues." So, after some fussing and fretting, and some half-assed soul-searching, I decided that I really needed to change my life. I left my tidy, untroubled oasis and ventured forth into a larger, unfamiliar world.

Now I was living in Manhattan, on the Upper West Side, but I kept my store in Brooklyn. I commuted out there a couple of days a week but generally left the business to be managed by a writer friend who needed the money. I rented desk space in a tiny office on Fifty-seventh Street with the idea that I would try writing again.

For real money, I lived off the income from the buildings I owned in Park Slope. Yes, I was a landlord. Before my father left for Turkey, when I was still living with him, he mentioned (perhaps seeing I was drifting back into the city) that he would maybe like to buy a brownstone in Brooklyn and that we could live in it together, he on the ground floor, me in an upstairs apartment. I don't know why he didn't follow through on it. Maybe he didn't have the money for a down payment. Maybe my moving out of his house abruptly, and so obviously wanting to be independent, caused him to drop the plan and head twelve thousand miles in the opposite direction.

After he died, one of the first things I did with the money he left was to find a real-estate agent, buy a building, and move into the garden apartment. I thought of this as a kind of memorial to him; I even considered putting a plaque up on the building with his name on it. Buying this building, and later two more on the same block, proved also—and I knew my father was watching me wherever he was—that I wasn't just a vagrant, a ne'er-do-well mental case. I was a man of substance, a property holder and taxpayer like he had been.

Of course, I had the same awful opinion of landlords that most people have. They are, with a few exceptions, the scum of the earth, part of what makes New York so difficult and miserable to live in for seventy-five percent of the population. Hadn't I seen how vicious and uncaring landlords were when I worked in the welfare department? And when I was paying rent myself and saw such a huge chunk of my monthly pay go to men who did nothing but simply *own* a building? Parasites.

And yet, such contradictions meant nothing to me then. My grief after my father died was immense and turned pretty quickly into a kind of permanent anger at the world. Fuck everybody else. Somebody had to own the building I lived in. Why shouldn't it be me?! The world was a tough place and you had to do what you had to do. Right?

So much for my principles. The real-estate broker's visions—millions to be made in real estate—were infectious. I was dazzled by greed. It was the one time in my life that I felt the way I imagine such pathological greed-heads as Donald Trump feel—a bottomless pit of need and anger that can be filled only by stepping on other people like ants and amassing more money than could ever be counted or used. More, more, more!

I was hypnotized by greed and, less maniacally, the simple desire to live my life without ever working for anyone again. I practiced denial. What, *me* a landlord? Half of the tenants sent their checks in weeks, even months late. I never said a word. One tenant, a painter, paid four straight months with paintings instead of rent. And one month I took a long epic poem from a tenant instead of money. If the tenants were cold in the winter, I told them to go down to the basement and turn up the building thermostat. One January, I advised a man to go out and by a couple of bottles of brandy and take it off his rent.

So that was my life. Living off my dead parents' money, pretending to be a writer, and walking the streets of Manhattan.

Susan was in the next to last year of her doctoral program. Her vision for the future was getting sharper and closer, but there was one thing left to complete her grand plan, something previously unrevealed to me.

Six months into our new life together, she announced that she wanted to have a child, and, of course, it went without saying—God knows I would never say it—that we would have to get married. This news was a one-two combination that knocked me right to the canvas. Although, being the new, grown-up me, the serious man, I didn't collapse right in front of her in a sniveling heap or blow up and threaten to move back to

Brooklyn. I said I wasn't sure about having children; it was something I hadn't really planned on. She told me that perhaps I wasn't listening or didn't want to hear it at the time, but having a 'family' had always been her great dream. Well, I *hadn't* heard it. Maybe that was because I hadn't wanted to, or maybe it was because she had never said it—knowing I wouldn't ever have left Brooklyn if I knew what was in her mind.

I pondered and worried and ran it by my shrink. I knew she had children and loved having them, but I trusted her to be objective. Ruth told me, in her enthusiastic, motherly way: "Little babies are great. I love little babies, but they're not for everybody. The question is, what do *you* want to do, Mike?" I sighed deeply: "You're asking me…what do I want to do? I want to do something impossible. I want to go back to my childhood, rerun the tape from the beginning, this time with a standard-issue mother and father. Failing that, I just want to be left alone to stumble through my life the best way I can."

"You can still do that."

"What's that supposed to mean?"

"You don't have to have a baby."

"But Susan wants one."

"Mike, what do *you* want?"

"I don't fucking *know*."

I drifted uptown from Ruth's office, back to my apartment, my mind whipping around like a kite in a storm.

Six months later I was married, and a year after that my daughter, Sarah, was born. She began talking very early. And she never stopped.

My wife would come home from her office. I'd greet her at the door, bursting with things to tell her about my day, but my daughter would push past me, station her pint-sized self between us, and start talking right over me, telling my wife about *her* day. "Mommy, I lost my doll and Kristy told me I was mean so I told her she—" I'm irritated by this rudeness, but, after all, I'm a grown man, a father, I can handle this maturely. "Excuse me, Sarah," I say, "Daddy is talking now." She looks at me for a split second, frowns, then continues where she left off. "So I told her she was dumb and then she took my dolly and—"

"Excuse me, Sarah," I say, more firmly now, "Daddy's talking to Mommy now, and when I'm done, you can have your turn." Forget about it. "No!" she says, glaring up at me. "*I'm* talking to Mommy!" Well, so much for maturity. Now we were into it: "No, *I'm* talking to Mommy!"

"No, *I'm* talking!!"

My wife is looking at the both of us, especially me, of course, like I'd lost my mind: "Kids, kids," she says, "calm down, there's enough of me to go around." Embarrassed now, humiliated, I tell my daughter to go ahead and talk. "OK," she says, and launches into a ten-minute monologue.

Feeling ignored, bereft, I walk into the living room and stare out the window. Mothers and children. Arguments, loneliness. All this seems sadly familiar. No doubt I should have stayed in Brooklyn and lived my unattached, unparental life. I wasn't hurting anybody there and my presence seemed to bring a lot of people some comfort—even, occasionally, joy. I was able to regulate the flow of company, conversation, and privacy in my life. Ah, but all that is gone now. I'm in Manhattan. I'm married. I'm a father and that's that. What's there for me now? Who'll listen to me? Well, there's my radio show....

PART FOUR
WBAI

CHAPTER TWENTY

Now I have to take you back five years—to the winter of 1977. I'm approaching thirty-three and have a burning desire to know what I'm going to *be* in the world. It can't be my only destiny, I thought, just to hang around my bookstore in Brooklyn, talking away the days and nights with my friends and jumping, trampoline style, from one woman's bed to another.

Look at Jesus. *He* was thirty-three when he found his calling. What if he had just putzed around Nazareth, making chairs and shooting the breeze with his pals? Where would the world be now?

The future is no laughing matter. It was time for me to determine the exact lineaments of my fate.

I knew I had to take action, but what? Aptitude tests, finish my degree, go on job interviews? I paced around my apartment, trying to figure out my next big step. Exhausted, after hours of fruitless strategizing, I turned to my old companion, the radio, specifically my favorite station, WBAI. And, lo and behold—as they say in fairy tales, a sign appeared. What did I hear? The program director was on the air, asking for applicants for the job of assistant program director! I had no doubt he was speaking directly to me.

The next morning, I went down to the station and filled out an application. They told me they'd get back to me in one week. What a thrilling prospect! I was going to have the chance to meet, to work with all the

181

people I had listened to so avidly for so many years, to possibly have a job at a place that was one of the foundations of my spiritual and intellectual life.

WBAI was—is—one of the five stations owned by the Pacifica Foundation of California, a nonprofit organization founded after World War II by a conscientious objector named Lew Hill. His idea was to put something on the air that would be an alternative to commercial radio. Something that would tell you, uninterrupted by soap and car commercials or the rigid censorship of big business, what was really going on in the world. News, music, the kinds of people and personalities that could never have made it onto the big commercial stations.

I first discovered WBAI during the summer of 1966, right after college. I was living by myself, out at Rockaway Beach in a small cottage, really a glorified shack, owned by my family. I was enjoying the freedom of my first solo flight. Out of my mother's control, doing things for myself. Like all things, of course, this freedom had a price tag. I was never *supposed* to exist on my own. That wasn't what I was born and bred for. What I was supposed to do was stay home with my mother. Living on my own was like taking a camping trip on the moon; I had to figure the simplest things out from scratch. How to buy my own groceries, how to fry eggs, how to sit in a house by myself and not have my identity unravel.

To make matters worse, the location was completely isolated. There was no phone, and I was far from my old neighborhood. I lost track of my friends, off on vacations or working at jobs in the city.

The days were all right. I had a part-time job and I ran for miles on the boardwalk. I made myself coffee and read books on the cool, shady front porch. I wrote long entries in a diary. It was the nights that were a problem.

When darkness descended, I got jumpy. I imagined dangers everywhere, tangible and intangible. Violent attacks from every quarter. I was constantly checking the locks on the windows and the doors. Getting to sleep was really a problem. I wasn't a drinker so I turned, in the great tradition of my mother, to pills: phenobarbital to calm me down, and Dristan to dry up my allergies and get me off to sleep.

But sleep, when it came, didn't last long. I woke up often from scary dreams, half off my bed, trembling and sweating. The only thing I had to comfort me was my old childhood friend, my little brown Zenith radio.

One night, about three in the morning, I woke up a complete mess. I turned on the radio, looking for a consoling voice or maybe some soothing classical music. I was spinning the dial when I heard a song—it was a kind of music I've always hated—a twangy-flat country coal-miner's lament: somebody dying before their time, coughing out their lungs from working in the mines. Of course, those people had all my sympathy—I just couldn't stand the music. This one was really bad, warbled by a woman with a thin, high-pitched voice.

One of the lines that kept repeating was: "The white dove is a pretty dove...." I don't know why I didn't turn it off immediately. Maybe it was because it *was* so sad. *I* was sad. Sad enough to listen to the song for a minute or two before I finally got sick of it and reached up to find something else. Just at that moment the song ended. I automatically waited for the announcer to say what it was, maybe do a commercial. But there was no announcement. The song started right up again from the beginning. Maybe this doesn't sound so startling to anybody now, but in those days it was very strange.

This was in the "old" days of FM radio. There was virtually nothing experimental on commercial radio, which was the only kind of radio I knew. One thing for sure, you never heard anybody play the same song twice in a row, especially with no announcement in between. I was curious to find out what station this was. More wailing and warbling. The song ended. I turned up the volume to catch the name of the station and... the song came on *again*! It was really irritating. Who would do such a strange thing? Play this scratchy, whiny song three times in a row without even announcing what it was, taking a station break, something, anything. I got up, went into the kitchen, and put my head under the cold-water faucet. I had a glass of orange juice. I sat at my kitchen table with the volume turned up now, waiting for the song to end. It didn't end. Or, rather, it ended and started right up again. I was amazed now. I thought, *Well, the announcer has had a nervous breakdown, maybe locked himself in the studio or something.* I'd read of such things. Disk-jockey madness in the small hours of the night, the radio equivalent of white line fever.

Meanwhile, the fucking song was driving me nuts. "The whaht duh-hve is purty duhhve...." Screechy West Virginia wailing, driving straight into my New York ear like a hot needle. It started up again! Now I was truly angry. I decided I was going to wait this lunatic announcer out, no matter how long it took. I brewed up some coffee, something I would never think of doing at three in the morning. This station, whatever it was, was driving me to it. I was going to go mano a mano with this guy, stay up until he gave in and stopped this song.

The song played thirteen more times, *eighteen* times in a row! Then a man's voice, one of the most beautiful voices I had ever heard, deep and mellow like dark honey, came on: "This is Bob Fass, and you're listening to WBAI, 99.5 FM in New York." He went on to speak, in a seemingly form-less, rambling manner but with that flowing, gorgeous voice, about a demonstration taking place the next day outside the draft induction center on White Street in Manhattan: "Let's show the murderers," he said, "that we don't want their filthy war." Then he played "Masters of War" by Bob Dylan—three times in a row. From that night on I didn't move the dial off that station. Everything and everybody turned up. Arlo Guthrie, live in the studio, singing "Alice's Restaurant" before it was even recorded; Bob Dylan insulting listeners; prisoners phoning in live from Riker's Island; people calling up on acid trips. One caller said he was a rock, so Fass let him express his "rockness" for a couple of minutes, which was, of course, absolute silence. Amazing. This was definitely the radio station for me.

In the summer of 1971, when I was going nuts, I used to get up and sit in the kitchen in the early morning, waiting for Larry Josephson to come on at 7:00 A.M. Josephson, who is a living legend of noncommercial radio, was the WBAI morning man, a brilliant, curmudgeonly type who played the radio game exclusively by his own rules.

He spent the first couple of minutes on the air grumbling and cursing everybody and everything: the malfunctioning equipment, his incompe-tent colleagues, the cab driver who had brought him down to the station, the streets, the cops, the whole city and the whole world. Then he ordered his breakfast, usually a bagel with everything on it—*on the air*. And he ate it on-the-air too, talking nonstop with a mouthful of bagel and cream cheese. After the bagel-cream cheese fuel reached his brain, he calmed down a little, but never so much that he was what you would call benev-olent. His sense of humor would kick in, and he'd be so entertained by the absurdities he saw in the paper, or by some joke of his own devise, that he would burst into a compulsive laughing-giggling fit.

There was one thing above all that really defined Larry's show: He *never* started his 7:00 A.M. show on time. The show before his signed off at 5:00 A.M., so when you tuned in anytime during those two hours, all you heard was white noise; radio lingo for that whooshy static you got when the transmitter has been shut down.

So, during the summer of Attica, I sat in my kitchen, despairing and anxious, well on the way to my final destination, the mental hospital. I always got up before seven to catch the beginning of Larry's show—his first, misanthropic words of the day. Me and tens of thousands of other people, all asking the big question: When was Larry going to show up? When was he going to turn on the station? Maybe, you thought, this would be the morning he'd really do it, not show up at all.

Then you heard it. The static was replaced by total silence, a sudden emptiness that, paradoxically, meant the transmitter had been switched on. You sat up straighter, with an expectant smile, and waited. And then it came, the familiar mixture of grumbling, objects dropping, a chair squeaking, and cursing. Larry was on the air.

He ID'd the station, gave the time and his name, then played his opening music. A march! At 7:30 A.M., surrounded on all sides of the dial by news, weather, traffic reports, easy listening, and rock and roll, Larry played Sousa's "Stars and Stripes Forever," real loud. The music ended, he grumbled his way back on, ordered his bagel, and the show was off and running, straight till nine o'clock.

I remember, hunched over in my chair one morning, intently concentrating on the white noise. My wife came in, looked at me, and said, "What are you doing?" I whipped around, put my finger to my lips, and said, "Shhhh! I'm listening to the radio."

On weekend nights it was Steve Post. Steve, like Bob Fass, had a rich, deep, beautiful voice. Fass was always mellow (possibly with the aid of some special smoke), but Steve was a bubbling cauldron of Jewish angst. He was passionate, whiny, and very funny, with a sense of timing in his monologues as practiced and graceful as a ballet dancer.

Post often had guests on his show—usually friends who were writers, actors, or comedians; people like Marshall Effron, who could impersonate anyone—a mean southern sheriff or a fumbling bureaucrat—with total realism.

Steve had the rare quality of being able to entertain and move you with his own stories, then fall back with equal art and professionalism to play the straight man to his guests. They specialized in mock interviews—the kind you might hear on any straight radio or TV show; and they were so good at parodying "real" interviews that no matter how often you heard them do it, you'd still almost be taken all over again.

One night, my first wife and I were lying in bed. I was listening to WBAI with headphones on (she could become dangerous if deprived of sleep). Post was interviewing a serious-sounding man who claimed to be organizing an event at Madison Square Garden called the Sex Olympics.

Steve asked his guest about the various events he had lined up for the Olympics.... "Mr. Klein, can you tell us a little about the categories of competition?"

"Well, Steve, first let me say I'm proud to be here on your fine radio station. It's a privilege to talk to your wonderful listeners."

"Well, thank you, Mr. Klein."

"Don't mention it."

"I won't."

"Good."

"The, ah, categories, sir."

"Ah, yes. Well, Steve, the first event, and one I think will be a real crowd pleaser, is men's hundred-meter bed-hopping."

"Sounds challenging."

"You bet it is, Steve. Competitors will jump from one mattress to another, having sex with a different partner, never, of course, touching the ground—that would result in immediate disqualification."

"Naturally."

"Or unnaturally, Steve. We don't rule anything out during the event."

And on and on they went. Mr. Klein, whoever he was, went on, with Steve's help, to describe, in detail, the various events, scoring system, and awards at the first Sex Olympics. They talked for about forty-five minutes, then they decided it was time to take calls. This was where the real circus started. Most of the callers were regulars, happy to toss the two guys all the straight lines they could use; and some of the callers, I thought, were pretending to be furious at hearing such blatant vulgarity on the radio.

Inevitably—after all, you were dealing with a possible listening audience of millions of people—there were callers who had tuned in accidentally, had never heard WBAI before. And these people, you could hear it in their voices, were astounded—truly scandalized—to hear anything so vile coming out of their radios. One listener who identified herself as a "churchgoing woman from Queens" was so outraged she could barely talk at first. Then she found her tongue....

"Sir, I don't know who you are, but I don't understand how you get the nerve—the unmitigated gall—to say such disgusting things on the public airwaves!"

"Madam-" Steve attempted to interrupt.

"No—please let me speak. I am absolutely amazed and it makes me sick to my stomach that people such as you are allowed to be broadcasters. I have *never* heard such putrid filth in all my life. You should both be locked up!!"

"Madam, I just want to assure you that I am not one of the organizers of this event, but I do feel that Mr. Klein deserves as much airtime as any other honest businessman."

"Honest?! Honest?!! He is nothing but a smut peddler. He's a filthy degraded smut peddler who should be thrown in jail to rot for the rest of his life!"

Now, Mr. Klein, who has been holding his peace all the this time, speaks up....

"Would you mind telling us your name, madam?"

"I don't mind telling you my name. It is Rosemary Anne Connors."

There's a thoughtful pause....then, from Mr. Klein: "Rosemary Connors. Rosemary—oh, of course. I knew I recognized your name. I'm sorry, Miss Connors, your application for the women's freestyle oral sex event was rejected. You'll be getting an official notice in the mail."

"What?! What did you say?!! I can't belie—"

"Well," said Steve, cutting her off, "why don't we take another call? ...WBAI, you're on the air."

"Hello? Hello? Am I on the air?"

"Yes you are, sir."

"Thank you."

"What is your question, sir."

"I'm a midget."

"I'd just like to say, Steve," interjected Klein, "that I understand that many of your fine listeners are midgets."

"Yes, they are."

"Hello? Hello? Am I still on the air?"

"Yes, you're on the air."

"I want to ask Mr. Klein—"

"Yes, this is Mr. Klein."

"As I was saying, I'm a midget."

"Good for you, sir!"

"And I would like to know if I can send in an application to be in one of your events?"

"Well, I appreciate your request, sir, but frankly, right now we're up to our ass in midgets."

And that's when I started laughing so hard I fell out of bed. I actually slipped off the side of the bed and landed on the floor. My wife sat up, looked down at me lying there, laughing so hard that tears were coming out of my eyes. She shook her head in disgust and said, "Are you listening to that radio station again?"

That radio station.

Carol, like a lot of people in and around New York, saw WBAI as a place for children and misfits on both sides of the microphone. To her, it was just a low-class hangout for unsavory minorities, a haven for fools, perverts, and professional revolutionaries.

Well, whatever it was, it was *my* hangout. The people on the air, the "personalities" on WBAI, were my friends, my comrades in arms in a hostile, crazy world. This was one of the great appeals of WBAI: it was always so personal. Everybody there spoke directly to you. Absent entirely was the insipid prophylaxis of seamless announcer's drivel, of shrill, offensive commercials. What you heard was just pure, unadulterated Human Being.

On WBAI, they played music no one else would, announced every demonstration and poetry reading in the city. They tried experiments on the air that were either strokes of genius or insane, outrageous provocations. Like, for instance, playing "The White Dove" eighteen times in a row.

You could tune in and hear long uninterrupted talks with Henry Miller, Malcolm X, Alan Watts, Timothy Leary, Allen Ginsberg. They recruited famous actors and public personalities to read classic novels like *War and Peace* and *Ulysses* in their entirety, thirty-six hours in a row, uninterrupted.

If Bob Dylan or Joan Baez had a new song, it was played first and often on WBAI. In 1968, Abbie Hoffman and Jerry Rubin called in from a pay phone—directly from the scene of the Chicago Police riot, shouting out the news, choking on the tear gas—straight to WBAI.

The station, naturally, was against the war in Vietnam, and its news reports (and reporters) were always right there for you: at demonstrations, at press conferences, asking questions no one else would ask, revealing secret statistics and government reports that no one else had the nerve to deal with. The news people took great personal, legal, sometimes even physical risks.

The station had one reporter who shuttled back and forth between the United States and North Vietnam. His news reports from the field (while reporters from the major stations and networks were sitting in Saigon, gobbling up Pentagon press feeds) were back-scored by the sounds of American bombs falling around him. When he returned home, his portable tape deck became a station icon: it had received several dents when he dove for cover.

The FBI came to visit, demanding copies of WBAI's tapes (which the station refused to give up). WBAI was denounced by various government bodies, criticized in churches, condemned by "right-thinking" people everywhere.

With all its excesses and its undeniable streak of perversity, WBAI was nothing less than a living switchboard, a transmission station for what would eventually be a permanent shift in American culture.

I had gone into the hospital in the fall of 1971, and it was late 1972 before my sanity returned and I had the presence of mind to notice the world again. Something about it had changed. While I was "away," the peace and love of the sixties had given way to outright anger, even hatred. And, as always, WBAI was right in the middle of it.

As a WBAI listener in the early seventies, I had four strikes against me. I was white, male, straight, and Jewish. I had struck out before I even stepped up to the plate. Of course, all of these divisions and hatreds within what was called "the Left" had been steadily accumulating throughout the late sixties, but I hadn't paid much attention. I had enough troubles in my own life.

The operative words were "revolution" and "liberation." When the time came for the hated oppressors of the world to pay up, WBAI became debt-collection central.

WBAI might have been hard to listen to, but where else could I go to hear what was really going on? I especially hated the anti-Semitism. It was cheap and it was dishonest; a way for a lot of two-bit megalomaniacs to score points with their own communities. It was truly painful for WBAI's Jewish listeners—to put up with such stupid, dangerous bigotry from their own radio station.

Despite the difficulties, listening to these angry voices charging out of the radio, no matter what their grudge or platform, was nothing less than thrilling. They were burning with a kind of fervor that was impossible to tune out. The people on WBAI were, for all their excesses and faults, smart, informed, and courageous. They spoke passionately from their hearts.

It was on WBAI that I first heard Malcolm X. I was in bed at two in the morning, listening to a black broadcaster, and she put on tapes of Malcolm X's speeches. In one speech up in Harlem, he was talking to a crowd about police brutality, giving his formula for dealing with it. He said: "I tell you what, if a snake bites your child, and you go out looking to kill that snake, you don't have to find a snake with blood on its jaws, *any* snake will do!"

Whoo! I sat straight up in bed. The man's fury, his force, shot straight out of the radio like a burning arrow.

Women yelled, and cried, calling in to the station, putting their pain on view for the whole world to see. Gay men and women sat in the studio, telling terrible stories of brutality and shame. Prisoners called in from cell blocks and talked about conditions that made you thankful you had a clean bed and a safe room and some decent food to eat. It was a crashing graduate school course on the eternal dark side of America. You could hardly stand to hear it, but it was hard to tune away.

Naturally—as with all revolutions—there could be as much stupidity and bigotry from the oppressed as there was from the oppressors. This was the world in small, and WBAI had its share of standard-issue morons, but even they were interesting. We, the public, had spent years listening to ignorant, bigoted straight people hosting and calling up on other radio stations. Now, courtesy of WBAI, we could hear ignorant, bigoted gay people. We grew up with a racist educational system, forced to read whole libraries of boring, pretentious white poetry. Now we could hear boring, pretentious black poetry. Maybe you didn't want to hear it, but you couldn't hear it anywhere else. And that in itself was worth something.

I had been listening to WBAI, eating it up, sometimes actually surviving because of it, for twelve years when I heard the call. The program director, Rick Harris, seemed to be speaking to me, like a voice from on high, asking me to apply for the job. After sending in my résumé, I phoned up and he told me that there were many people responding—they would be sifting though the various applications before making their choice. Anxiously, I waited for him to get back to me. He did, a week later. I got the job! I started in two weeks, the beginning of April; coincidentally, just as I was leaving Park Slope and starting my new life with Susan in Manhattan.

Assistant program director was a volunteer job. No pay, just the privilege of helping to program "The People's Radio Station." That was all right with me; I still had my store, I still owned my building. I had plenty of money in my bank account. And Susan was happy that I seemed to be doing something responsible. She didn't really know much about WBAI, but assumed, no matter how left wing it was, that a job down there was like any other job, a straightforward, adult "position" that could lead to better things up the ladder, manager or whatever.

I had been working at the station about three weeks when, on a day that the program director wasn't in, I decided to clean up his files. I came across a folder labeled "Applications for Program Director Assistant." Whoa! Secret info. Now I could see who I beat out for the job. I opened it up and, aside from my résumé and letter, there was only one other letter (sans résumé) in the file. It was handwritten on a smudged piece of paper and the words were very large and slanted upward, sometimes right up to the edge of the page. Sentences tended to end abruptly, cut off in their prime.... *I am writing about the job of program director's ass—Although I am legally blind, I don't think—*"

It turned out that in addition to my "competition" not being able to see very well, he also had a recurring drinking problem.

This was the guy I aced out for assistant program director. It was a bit of a blow to my self-esteem and for a moment, I had a bad feeling about my new job, but I shrugged it off. After all, I was working at my favorite place, meeting all the "stars" I had listened to for years. I was happy enough.

Little by little, I got to know the staff. The people who worked at WBAI, on and off the air, were, for the most part, true members of the counterculture. Some of them were hopelessly mired in the sixties; the clock had stopped somewhere around 1968, and they were stuck in a perpetual state of yippie-Woodstock dreamland. A great many of them had never had a job in the outside world, never even considered living a "straight" life. Though a couple of people were married, no one had any children. There was a lot of pot smoking and pill taking going on around the place. Strange stares, sudden blowups, and meaningless giggling were not uncommon. Friday afternoons the chemical-alcohol party started early and continued late into the evening. Sometimes, on Monday mornings, there were papers strewn about, sticky stains on the desk and the floor.

There were frequent temper tantrums—voices raised in despair or frustration. It was, after all, a lot like show business. There were real prima donnas at WBAI. People who were stars, who had tens of thousands of fans. The place was a huge stew-pot of artists, music experts, dropout intellectuals, doped-up techie-genius dorks, and lefty lawbreakers. Not to mention the fact that everyone at WBAI was, of course, intensely political. A lot of the arguments concerned politics; there were threats, tears of rage, explosive disagreements on the slightest issue. It wasn't your typical office.

They were a tight group and slow to warm up to me. To them I seemed strange, almost unnatural. I didn't smoke pot, didn't drink, I didn't get involved in their arcane drug discussions or go to their parties. They were always worried, and this was not entirely sixties paranoia, that the Feds or the city cops had an undercover officer in their midst. I could very well be a narc.

They all knew I owned a store; a marvelous thing to them. They had no way of knowing, of course, how crazy and erratic I really was, that my store was just a place I had created to talk to people, not a real business at all. That I often threw bills in the trash and had barely made any profit on my "business" the whole time it was in operation. I don't think any of that would have mattered to them, though. They were satisfied that, aside from a tendency to lose my temper, I was a straight member of the vast, mysterious bourgeois sea that surrounded their little island bastion.

To them, I was a businessman. So it made sense, five months into my job, that they would offer me the position of assistant manager. I would be running the operations of the place on a day-to-day basis. I was as qualified to manage the financial and administrative affairs of a radio station as I was to command an aircraft carrier or teach astrophysics at MIT, but I didn't care. I was moving up in the world. I was impressing Susan with my ambition and, truth to tell, I did think that I could clean up some of the chaos that reigned supreme there.

I met with the new manager elect, Steve Post. We settled on a meager salary and he told me I was to start July 1. Steve told me he would be up at Cape Cod on vacation, but since it was summertime there shouldn't be any real problems. He was coming back at the end of the first week of July and would show me the ropes then.

I was thrilled! Assistant manager! I thought how proud my father would be; I was an executive finally, a real man.

My first day on the job, I wore a sport jacket and actually got my shoes shined. I arrived early, organized my desk. I was impressed with myself. Assistant manager. Imagine. Then it all started.

9:01 A.M. The phone rings. A man starts yelling at me before I can say a word. When I got him to calm down, I discovered he was from an electronics supply place, and that over the last three months we'd accumulated twenty-two hundred dollars of unpaid bills. If we didn't pay up pronto, he said, we were going to get our ass sued. I promised him I'd send him the money right away. He hung up on me. The phone rang again immediately. It was the phone company. They told me the service was going to be cut off. The phones cut off?! Absolutely. In ten days if I didn't pay a substantial balance of the bill—three thousand dollars!

9:15 A.M. There had been three more angry calls. I was sweating because the old, cracked air conditioner had choked and died when I turned it on. I was trying to figure out the account books, when I looked up and saw, standing in the dorway of my office, a big fat man in a crumpled gray suit. He was the kind of fat guy whose stomach is itself like a separate person that seemed to enter the room before he did. Behind this man was an even larger man, a missing-link type individual in work clothes, gripping a big handcart. The first man introduced himself: "I'm Marshall Rivkin," he said. I stood up, put my hand out; he slapped a piece of paper into it: "I'm here to repossess your postage meter. Where is it?" he said.

I looked at the paper; it was a legal document. *Whereas, the said amount not being paid*...Then I realized, he isn't just *any* Marshall Rivkin (I had known a couple of Marshalls in Laurelton when I was a kid), he was *Marshal* Rivkin, a New York City Marshal. And he was here to take away our postage meter for nonpayment of the bill. Rivkin was bored, pissed. "So, where is it," he said again, "I don't have all day here."

I was temporarily stymied by this turn of events; I didn't know how to react. Maybe I should call a lawyer. Then I thought, he *is* a city marshal, a duly appointed authority. He had a legal paper. Obviously there was only one thing I could do. "It's in the back," I told him.

We walked back to the mail room. There was our postage meter, a huge machine that stamped all our letters automatically. Marshal Rivkin directed his flunky to load the thing on the handcart. He gave me a signed receipt for the meter and they wheeled it out. I walked slowly back to my office, slumped into my chair, upset by this strange occurrence.

Inside three minutes, what looks like the entire staff crowds into my doorway. They're screaming at me: "What did you do, asshole?" "You let them take the postage meter!?" "You idiot!" I was amazed at all this abuse. What had happened seemed reasonable to me. We didn't pay the bill, the company took its machine back. Isn't that what happens in the real world? *Maybe*, I thought, *they don't know what really happened.* So I explain it to them. "Well, you see, we didn't pay the bill." There was a moment's pause, and looks of shock, utter amazement appeared on their faces. Then, "What the fuck is *wrong* with you? We never pay *any* bills!!"

They were right. WBAI never did pay any bills. Or we paid as little as possible to preserve the minimum amount of services and supplies to keep us on the air. We stiffed anybody and everybody, major corporations and little old ladies in Vermont who made Save the Whales stickers for us. We were equal-opportunity deadbeats. There was really no money to pay the bills, certainly never enough to keep anywhere near current. I found out real quick what everybody else down there already knew: WBAI was perpetually broke.

Ten minutes later, as I pondered the notion that paying bills was considered a crime at WBAI, the building manager came in. I introduced myself as the new assistant manager. He shook his head, a pitying smile on his face, as if to say, "Where do they find these poor suckers?" He reminded me that the rent was due and that he expected me to mail it out immediately. I promised him I would. He frowned: "Yeah, well, I hope you do, because you don't want another mess like last month, the dispossess and all." Dispossess? Jesus!

I sat in my office surrounded by a sea of overdue notices that had arrived in the afternoon mail, trying to make sense of the checkbook, which even to my totally unpracticed eye seemed to be showing an unbelievable deficit.

The phone rang again. At this point, I was afraid to even answer it, but I picked it up anyway. It was Steve, calling from Cape Cod. He sounded sick. "I'm going to need a little extra time up here," he said. "I'll be back on July 15." He was about to say good-bye when I started to tell him about all the overdue bills. "You can handle it," he told me. "But wait—" "Have to go. Bye."

And so it went. Constant abuse. Day after day. At night I'd come home and fall on the couch, completely exhausted.

At the end of the second week, Steve called, still in Cape Cod. He sounded worse than before. "I'm still feeling a little tired, I think I'll be up here till the end of the month. How's it going down there?"

"Terrible," I told him. "We have no postage meter. They may turn off the phone service and we can't pay the rent." "OK," he said, "I'll see you in two weeks." So, the truth dawns on the yokel from Queens. I'd been sent, without any training, directly to the front of the front lines. The rawest of recruits. If I lived through it, I might get a Purple Heart. If I didn't, there would always be another fool to take the job. Still, I thought, I'd only been there two weeks. Surely I could get on top of this mess. I resolved to dig in, but no matter how hard I tried, in the end it was a hopeless endeavor. The overdue notices, the warnings, the threats continued to pour in.

And it wasn't just the attacks from outside that drove me to the brink—I was fighting a determined resistance movement from inside the station as well.

Trying to manage a left-wing nonprofit organization like WBAI was like trying to pilot an airplane where all the parts, the wings, the tail, the body, want to fly in opposite directions. On top of that, this was a radio station. Everybody there was loud and vocal. No one had any trouble telling me just what they wanted, or didn't want, or what their opinion of me was. Worse, more than half the people I dealt with, on-air personalities and off-air workers, were volunteers. There was no way to get them to do what I wanted unless they felt like doing it. And since this was the People's Radio Station, the bastion of political correctness, I always had to be careful what I said to people, lest I crossed some invisible line of bias and bigotry.

The moment I became the boss at WBAI, I became, instantly and forever —*The Man*. I was assailed from all sides: Advocates for the Handicapped, gay men, feminists, lesbians, the *Black Caucus*—everybody was at my throat.

I remember one particular day—it was really the last straw for me—sitting at my desk, engaged in a shouting match over the phone with a man who had done some work on our main station air conditioner. He is insisting on getting paid for the work he had done (quaint notion). While I'm attempting to deal with him, the head of the women's department, a militant lesbian feminist, came in and shoved a paper into my hand. "What's this?" I asked her.

"A requisition for two hundred dollars to tape a woman's music concert in New Hampshire."

I shook my head, "I don't think we have the money for that now." The guy on the phone started threatening me, telling me if I didn't pay, he would come in and shut down the air conditioner. I'm trying to deal with him and the woman is standing right over me.

"What do you mean?" she said, quivering with indignation. "This is a very important concert and we need the money." I covered the phone with my hand. "Look," I told her, "we just don't have the money, alright?" The air-conditioner guy is still talking. "Oh, really," she said, her voice seething with contempt, "why do I know you'd find the money if it was a *men's* music concert?"

"A what? A men's concert?" The guy on the phone is screaming now—he's not only going to shut down the air conditioner, he's going to take the whole thing out till I pay up. "Hold on a second," I tell him. The woman is furious now:

"You're not listening to me!"

"Yes, I am."

"No, you're not listening to me. And you know why?"

"No, why?"

"Because you have your *dick* in your ear! That's why!!" She slammed her fist onto my desk, turned, and walked out of the office.

I tried to reason with the air-conditioner guy—get him to wait another week for a check, when the head of the Black Producer's Caucus came into my office, followed by four members of the Caucus. They recently perceived outright racism on my part because I wasn't able to pay for transportation and housing expenses to a political rally in Washington, D.C. They surrounded my desk, and the chairman shoved *his* paper at me.

"What's this?" I asked him. He couldn't wait to tell me: "*That* is a list of twelve nonnegotiable demands from the Black Producers Caucus. If they aren't met by Friday, we're walking out." I asked them to wait a second because I had to get back to the air-conditioner guy. "I guess you have more *important* business," the chairman says, clearly implying that I would just get off the phone if he were white. The air-conditioner guy had one final word: "Pay the fuckin' bill or you can kiss your air conditioner good-bye"—and he hung up.

I looked at the paper in my hands. "You have three days to meet our demands," said the chairman. "If you don't we're walking out, and we will picket the station—and you."

"Picket? What, me? Wait a minute," I said, but they were already on their way out.

I sat in my office, blown away by all this blistering hatred and denunciation. I was ready to call it quits. I couldn't stand trying to run this halfway house for disturbed delinquents. I was in a state of such constant rage that I thought I was going to explode, and I could never explain to Susan why I was so angry all the time—who could explain WBAI to a normal human? Finally, a year into the job, I couldn't stand the place anymore. It wasn't the station. I still loved WBAI. What I couldn't stand was my job. I couldn't continue to be the boss there anymore: the father everybody loved to hate.

I handed in my resignation in June, almost a year to the day after I started. I told Steve I'd give him two months, till the end of August, to find somebody to replace me, and he could forget about trying to change my mind. I just wasn't cut out to be a manager. On my way home that night I sat in the subway car, brooding. Here it was *again*. Another failure. Another attempt to make something of myself that had resulted in total disaster.

A few weeks earlier, the beginning of May, WBAI had held one of its three yearly fund-raising drives. Regular programming was suspended, and the on-air people pleaded and yelled at the listeners to come through and put their money where their ears were and support the station with financial contributions. Everybody got exhausted and slap happy during these drives. They ran out of things to say, sometimes they literally ran out of breath. One way they had of giving themselves a break was to get the management to come on and tell the listeners the real facts about the wretched state of the finances. I was invited to talk but I always refused to go on the air. It was fine for Steve Post. He was a longtime radio personality and a great fund-raiser, but me?—I couldn't imagine it. Not just because it was scary, though that was part of it, of course, suddenly speaking live to tens of thousands of people. No, it was another kind of feeling that kept me out of the studio.

After working at the station for a year, I had developed a kind of superior, condescending attitude about speaking on the radio. To me, it seemed childish, even a little crazy. This was strange, considering I had always loved to listen to WBAI, and before that, when I was young, I counted on the radio to see me through hundreds of lonely nights; but now, when I was working only fifty feet from master control at a radio station, it seemed to me that talking on the radio was a silly, childish thing to do.

It was incredibly presumptuous, I thought, grandiose almost to the point of mental illness, to assume that thousands of people were even interested in, not to mention fascinated by, anything you had to say. Was there any difference, really, between airing your personal grievances on the radio and ranting and raving on a subway platform or a traffic island on Broadway? The locked wards, as I knew from personal experience, were packed with people who knew they had *very* important things to tell the world.

During the spring fund-raising drive, right around the time I was getting ready to tell Steve I was jumping ship, the program director called me into her office and proposed that I do a regular weekly radio show. Naturally, I didn't take her seriously. First, because she had an ulterior motive. I was her boss and she was always trying to get on my good side, what little there was of it. More to the point, I didn't give her proposal any real thought because a part of me didn't consider being on the radio to be a serious thing for an adult person to do. I told her thanks but no thanks. She needed to look for somebody else, somebody who had a burning desire to flap his mouth to the millions.

A few days after I handed in my resignation, when everybody knew I was a lame duck, the program director repeated her offer that I should take over the recently abandoned Thursday morning show. Well, if nothing else, it was flattering. Now, when she didn't have to waste time being nice to me, she was still asking me to go on the radio. She told me to think it over and get back to her.

During the last two months of my tenure as assistant manager, I kept thinking about the program director's offer. I didn't tell a soul about it; I felt like confessing my desire to go on the air was like saying I wanted to take drugs. And of course, what kind of blowhard hypocrite would I be if I admitted out loud I wanted to have a show of my own? I had always refused to go on the air when asked. I had even shown outright disdain for those special people around the station known as "air junkies," the ones who jumped at the chance for even a few minutes behind a live microphone. And yet, and yet, the more I thought about it, the more the idea appealed to me.

I caught myself peering through the window of master control, looking at the people talking on the air. I found excuses to go into the studio, looking for the chief announcer or asking somebody an innocuous question.

At the beginning of August, I told the program director I thought I might "try it." She gave me a date to start, the first Thursday in September.

CHAPTER TWENTY-ONE

My new show aired Thursday mornings, from 7:15 till 9:00 A.M. For the first "season," September to June, I paddled my way like a baby duck through the unfamiliar waters of live broadcasting.

Unfamiliar is an understatement. The whole endeavor, at first, and even after you've practiced it for years, can seem absurd and unnatural.

Consider it. You're sitting alone in a room behind a console full of meters and dials, speaking into a metal object (a microphone) connected by a wire to some unseen hookup that leads to a whole other bunch of wires that lead to a huge piece of equipment standing near you in the studio. This piece of equipment is connected by other wires and cables which eventually reach another, more complicated machine (a radio transmitter) located at another location several blocks, maybe even miles from the studio. This transmitter beams radio waves, whatever *they* are, through the air—*through the air!*—to another machine, a radio receiver in somebody's house or car. Somehow, by some miracle, these waves are turned back into almost the exact intonations and idiosyncrasies of your own voice so that someone, either around the corner or fifty miles away in another state, hears what you're saying.

It's necessary to have the blind faith or, perhaps, the rank lunacy to assume that people are really listening to everything you say. It's like praying to an unseen god or talking to people who have died.

My first year on the air I was cautious; I did what I figured it was people did on the radio, with, naturally, a WBAI twist to it. Every morning I read articles aloud from the *Times* and commented on the stories. I brought in copies of unusual magazines, like *Soldier of Fortune* and *Funeral Director's Monthly*. Of course, you could never beat the *National Enquirer* or the *Weekly World News*. "Nurse Has Alien's Baby!" "Your Toilet Paper Can Kill You!!" I played a lot of records. Favorites of mine that you'd be hard-pressed to hear on any other station: mixes of march music (like Larry Josephson), Mario Lanza, polka, Dixieland jazz. Sometimes I put on spoken-word recordings of John Donne or Dylan Thomas. I began to get calls off the air, letters came in. I knew I had a few listeners.

Midway through my second year, toward the end of January, the sixth anniversary of my father's death, I thought I might say something about him on the air. The night before the show I had a terrible dream: I was trying to get into the station to do my show but it was surrounded by barbed wire. Right in front of the only entrance was my father, holding a huge butcher knife. He pointed his finger right in my face and told me, "You're not going to talk about *me* on the radio!" I woke up shaking. It was just before dawn, still dark outside. I went down to the station, got on the air, and talked about my dream. Then, in a great gush of words, I talked all about my father. About how he left when I was little, about missing him. His world travels. Living with him after I left the mental hospital. Visiting him in Turkey before he died. How I hated him and loved him. How much I missed him.

I left the station that morning in a state of exhilaration I'd never felt before. It was as if I had coughed up a knot of anguish that had been lying in my stomach for thirty years. When I picked up my mail later in the week, I had a dozen letters from people telling me about their awful-beautiful times with their own fathers, and letters from fathers about how hard it was to make sense of themselves to their children.

That next Thursday I talked about my mother, my life with her, her suicide, all my still-mixed-up feelings. More letters. Calls poured in right after the show; I was talking to listeners for more than an hour after I signed off.

From that point on, I was launched. I told stories about growing up in Laurelton, the cemetery, old girlfriends, shrinks, going crazy, the hospital, my marriages. About jobs, kids, sex—anything personal that I was feeling and thinking. I talked straight ahead, hardly a pause for breath, for at least an hour, sometimes more.

I was amazed, though I suppose I shouldn't have been, by the response. People told me dark secrets. Once when I was talking about giving my baby a bath and worrying that I was going to drop her, a woman called on the air and told me that a few years earlier her husband had left their one-and-a-half-year-old baby in the bathtub for a few seconds to answer the phone and when he got back the baby had drowned. Her voice was weary and empty as she told me that she never again felt any love for her husband. I was speechless after she hung up and put music on for the rest of the show.

My show attracted a sizable listenership of shrinks: psychologists, psychiatrists, social workers. One woman wrote, in what I thought was typical shrink fashion, "Dear Mr. Feder, I am a psychoanalyst, practicing on Central Park West. I find your program fascinating. In the mornings I warm up for my patients by listening to you. You are the perfect narcissist." That struck me as odd. I never thought of what I did on the air as narcissism. It never had that closed-circuit self-referential tightness that I think of when I picture a true narcissist. I was talking about my life as a way of making sense of the world. And if people heard me and found themselves in the same boat, well, so much the better.

Very quickly, after the personal stories and streams of consciousness started, I was as hooked as anybody else, addicted to the risk and freedom of leaping onto the airwaves; I could hardly imagine living without it.

Meanwhile, in my "other" life, my existence *outside* the radio studio, I was still married, still had a child, and still went to my shrink, Dr. Ruth Ziegler, whom I'd been seeing for more than six years. In September of 1982, I went to her office for my first session after her summer vacation. When I walked in, all set to yell at her for abandoning me for the whole month of August, I was stopped dead by what I saw—shocked by the change in her appearance.

Of course, even under normal circumstances I would have expected Ruth to seem "new" to me, after being away for a month. But what I saw when I walked in and dropped down into my regular chair was not just the usual "stranger" but an almost completely new individual.

Ruth was usually perky and confident, always focused, certain of her opinions. In fact, that happy, strong ego of hers was the very thing I counted on as the antidote to my perennial negativity. Now, she was sunk in her chair, eyes dark and downcast, looking ten years older. She gave me a quick, sad smile, barely managing a dim "hello." She was so obviously beaten down and miserable that it was impossible to think of bashing her for "leaving" me in August. And it was equally impossible for me to unload the wagonload of complaints and worries I had saved up for her. The only thing I could decently say was: "What's wrong?" She smiled sadly. Tears filled her eyes. "I can tell *you*, Mike, because we've been friends for a long time."

She tried to deliver her story in as clinical a fashion as possible. "My husband and I were at our country house. He was up on a ladder, painting some shingles on the barn, when he said he felt dizzy and slipped down to the ground. We took him to the local hospital and they told us to take him into New York for some tests. Mike, he has inoperable brain cancer." And then she began to cry in earnest. Not sobbing; she couldn't or wouldn't do that—but steady, heavy tears. She was caught between her professional responsibilities and her abject misery and fear. It was heartrending. I wanted to get up and put my arm around her, let her lean on me and cry as much as she wanted, but I knew she wouldn't have that. So I just sat there and watched her cry. After a couple of minutes, I asked her some questions. *Were they sure about the diagnosis?* They were. *Was he in pain?* He was on pain-killers. *How much time do they think...?* A couple of months. More tears. I was twisting in sympathetic anguish. What could I do for her?

I have to confess, to my shame, that as I sat there aching for her, I was also angry that I had to witness this display of raw agony. Now that I knew what she was suffering, what possible excuse could I ever come up with to tell her about *my* miseries?

The next several weeks with her were an exercise—well-meaning as it was—in playacting. For her, I pretended to talk about my problems. For me, she tried as hard as she could to overcome her misery and pay attention to me. I could never stop thinking about how awful she must have been feeling. I pictured her husband in a hospital bed, hooked up to all kinds of machines, wandering in and out of pain and consciousness. I saw her home alone, in her dark house, crying her eyes out. Even when I wasn't with her, when I was home in my own apartment, I imagined her in her apartment, walking around by herself, sad and lonely.

Just before Christmas, I got a call from her secretary, telling me Ruth would be out for a couple of weeks. I saw her again three weeks later. This time she wasn't crying. She was calm and composed, but any fool could see that the life had gone out of her, that her husband had died.

She was determined to move ahead with the business at hand. Well, she may have been ready to continue, but I wasn't. I couldn't. Our conversation was very stiff. Formal. The next week, figuring that she had steeled herself enough, I told her that I didn't think I could work with her anymore because I could never erase the images I had of her all alone and grieving.

She was irritated with me. "I'm a professional," she said, adamantly, "I can handle your problems." She told me I was making a mistake, but I didn't think so. I told her I was leaving and I hoped she would be alright. And so, after six years with Ruth, my good mother, I was on the road again. Wandering the highways and byways of neurosis, looking for a new parent.

A few weeks later, I found my next shrink, Dr. Klein, an older, distinguished man who was a professor at Columbia. He, like my old pal Mr. Bernstein, was a refugee from Hitler's Europe. He had something of an accent, though I couldn't tell exactly what it was. Dr. Klein was handsome—had that old-world European charm and courteous formality but was more reflective, sadder, and wiser than Bernstein. I liked Klein because he was smart and ironic, and because he seemed to have a detailed road map to the terra incognita of my mind.

So, my life went on. I saw my new shrink. I talked on the radio. I played my part as a husband and a father. I tried to get used to—it seemed hopeless most of the time—the competition with my little daughter for my wife's attention. Talking on the radio to all those thousands of people each week was great, but it could never replace what I had lost in my house—

that precious time alone with my wife at the end of each day, talking and talking.

As if this significant subtraction from my life's meaning wasn't bad enough, real tragedy struck in the winter of 1983—I ran out of money and had to get a job.

For the past several years, ever since my parents had died, I had been living, save for the little cash I made at my bookstore and at WBAI, on income from the money I got from the brownstones I owned in Brooklyn. However, in a virtuoso performance of self-destruction, I managed to get mixed up with a bunch of real-estate thieves—lawyers and brokers out in Brooklyn—and lost my buildings. I became a minority partner in a co-op scheme that was full of illegalities and nastiness. I lived in Manhattan and the brokers were on the spot, so it was easy to convince myself that they knew best. What they knew best was intimidating the tenants into moving out so that they could renovate the apartments and sell them for more money. But my partners proved to be only amateur crooks and ultimately the deal blew up. The tenants organized, took their grievances to court, and the whole business unraveled. The real-estate broker and lawyer lost their licenses to practice and the buildings were sold to the tenants for practically nothing.

I was relieved not to own those buildings anymore, not to have that responsibility. What was even a greater relief was to be done talking on the air about the rich grinding the poor under their heels, *while* I was a landlord—a breathtaking exercise in hypocrisy. But now I was faced with the grim reality of having practically no money. Years of living without working had spoiled me rotten. I hated the very thought of getting a job again. Being trapped someplace, nine to five, reporting to a boss. Horrible!

One Thursday morning I was whining on the air about my dire straits. A listener, a lawyer, called up and offered me a job as a paralegal in his midtown law office. So, with ill-disguised despair, I bought some "real" clothes, found a tie hanging in my closet, and rejoined the rest of the army marching to and from midtown Manhattan every morning and night.

Working in a big regimented office was a squeezing, sickening experience. Doing barren, repetitive tasks in an airless cubbyhole, day after day,

I started to drift away in a daze of boredom. Four months into my job, as spring blossomed outside, I sat in my hole at my little desk, hand-stamping a huge stack of documents.

When giant companies sue other giant companies, which they do on the average of three times a day in this country, they have to produce documents—truckloads of copies of files, financial records, printouts, plans, manuals, handwritten notes, anything that might concern the dispute. Each and every one of these pieces of paper has to have a stamped number so that it can be referred to later in court filings. Someone has to stamp them. Someone like me, a kind of modern-day Bartleby the Scrivener.

There I was with a big, heavy metal stamper in my hand, stamping one document after another. Grab one piece of paper off the stack, put it on the blotter, and *kachunck!* 000001, grab another one, *kachunck!* 000002, grab...stamp, grab, stamp. While my hands stamped, my mind reeled off into a haze of depression and bitterness. Somewhere, no more than thirty blocks from where I was sitting, my little girl was running around a playground, laughing and swinging. My heart ached to be with her. I wanted to magically lift up and over the skyscraper I was toiling away in and instantly transport myself to wherever she was. Susan was in her nicely furnished office, sitting in her big leather chair, being the doctor, making real money. Friends of mine, ex-WBAI broadcasters, were on the radio at other stations, getting paid to talk! And I was here, a grown man, stamping, *kachunck!* millions of foolish pieces of paper. *Who the fuck cares if Worldwide Integrated Systems triumphs over International Metacom Industries!!?*

I worked myself up into a rage, stamping with tremendous force. The desk shuddered; the shock of the stamper hitting the blotter sent waves of pain shooting up my wrist, into my shoulder and my neck. I grabbed another document off the pile. A brochure. The company we represented owned a chain of fancy health spas and gyms. The whole, slick promo was full of happy, healthy smiling faces of thirty-year-old assholes wearing Rolexes, working out in their designer togs on bicycles and weight machines. I hated these fucking people. I began to stamp them all, right in their upwardly mobile crotches. *Kachunck!!* 000089, a muscular handsome young exec on a Stairmaster gets stamped right in his balls! *Kachunck!!*

000090, a gorgeous blonde media consultant gets it right between her legs! Bam. Boom. I was really getting into it now; viciously neutering these morons. *Kachunck!! Kachunck!!* I looked up, and there was my boss, the guy that hired me. He took the brochure off the desk, paged through it, looking at my demented sexual defacements. "Mike," he said, "maybe you should take a break for a while."

I was alone in the cafeteria, sipping coffee and looking out the window at the windows of five thousand other offices full of people doing the same stupid things. *Jesus, how did I ever get into such a spot?* Wasn't there some little part of my life I could make interesting? Sure, I still had the radio show, but there must be something else. Something new to keep the blood from freezing in my veins.

PART FIVE

RICH AND FAMOUS

CHAPTER TWENTY-TWO

That summer I noticed an ad in one of our neighborhood newspapers for people to join a writers and directors workshop for playwrights. A couple of years before, I had written a one-act play about my crazy family in Laurelton; I had vague daydreams of getting it produced somewhere, so I decided to join the workshop.

The Seventy-eighth Street Theater Lab's Writers and Directors Workshop met in a small theater a couple of blocks from my apartment. It was a fairly representative group of lower-level New York theater types, some actors, in and out of work, a few (in our own minds) undiscovered David Mamets and Samuel Becketts. And a couple of directors looking for some material to work with. We were a mix of amateurs and semiprofessionals. Generally, it was an intelligent, decent bunch, but, inevitably, we had our resident jerk—our village idiot. Claude. He wrote modern play versions of heroic stories like the *Iliad*, usually about men and war. Claude was cement-headed and utterly devoid of talent, and, naturally, prolific. His stuff bored us all to death but he had paid his fee like the rest of us, so he got to have his drivel acted out.

One night, during Claude's latest sword-and-sandal extravaganza, I flipped; I couldn't take any more of his shit. I asked him why his main character, who was supposed to be a poet, was spending all his time making ridiculous patriotic war speeches. Claude explained (the man actually spoke this way), "Poets and writers have always heeded the trumpets of war." "What!?" I snorted and rolled my eyes.

I saw a woman a few seats away smiling at me and rolling her eyes too. I'd noticed her once or twice before, but not with much interest. She was a few years older than me, maybe in her mid-forties, and very mousy looking. She had pale, pasty-looking skin, very short hair, almost chopped off. All in all, she was generally blocky and unfeminine looking. She never said much, a silent type, and when she talked she spoke in a subdued, almost monotonous Southern drawl.

She smiled at me, complicit in my disgust with Claude and his silly blathering up on the stage. I moved over and sat down next to her. "What a fool," she said. She really had a thick down-south accent. "Poets and writers, going off to war. What trash! *He* ought to go off to war." I laughed.

Up close, I saw she had a quick, childlike smile. And despite her otherwise flat demeanor and frumpy appearance, if you looked for it, there was real wit and intelligence gleaming in her eyes.

In the next few weeks, Vicky (that was her name) and I became pals. We went out for coffee after the workshops. Little by little—it never came easy, because unlike me, Vicky had no compelling need to recall her past—I learned as much of her story as she was willing to tell.

Vicky was originally from Georgia. Her parents were both history teachers and she had been surrounded by books her whole life. Her mother was, despite all her education and her brains, a typical southern woman of her generation. Which is to say, in all things she subordinated herself to her husband. According to Vicky, her father was a dictator, sarcastic, imperious, and downright mean. She practically flinched every time she mentioned him. As a girl, Vicky had been taken by the theater, but she followed a more familiar path. She majored in English lit, mostly drama, and got her doctorate. She taught for a while at a college out in the Midwest and managed a small regional theater. Due to some disagreement at the theater and, like everybody in that world, knowing she must eventually end up in New York, she quit her job and, like tens of thousands of striving souls before her, made her way to the Big Apple.

That was about a year earlier. She now lived by herself in a crummy studio apartment on the Lower East Side and worked as a stage manager at an off-Broadway theater on the West Side. Vicky had acted a little in her time, but she really wanted to be a director. She was smart, she knew everything there was to know about the theater, and was always going to plays and readings. She had directed a couple of very small productions and readings but was looking all the time for a real project.

The time came for *my* play to be read at the workshop. It was embarrassing, seeing it actually come off the page and out of real people's mouths. I could see all the flaws, but all-in-all it didn't seem so bad. And I was relieved to hear that Vicky thought the play had some virtues. I told her that I was entirely new to this world, that the only experience I had was doing monologues on the radio.

Vicky, realizing my complete ignorance regarding the theater, decided to culturally adopt me. She got free passes to a lot of plays and performance pieces and convinced me to tag along. Some of the stuff was amazing to me, the untutored rube. We saw dazzling mind trips by Richard Foreman or oddball brilliant pieces at La Mama, the experimental theater downtown. We also went to traditional plays—Shakespeare and Molière.

One night we walked up four flights of stairs in a beat-up building in Chelsea to see a dance performance. We sat on rough wooden bleachers in a stuffy, steaming-hot loft space—no more than five of us in the audience. The set was papier-mâché and balsa-wood white rocks on a bare stage. We sat and sweated and waited. Suddenly, a woman, barefoot, dressed in a short white robe, came leaping out from the wings. She ran around the stage, circling the "rocks," leaping onto them and dropping down and hugging them. The circling and running and hugging went on for several minutes in complete silence. Then, from the wings, two other women, dressed the same way, came running out. They leapt and ran and then they all started warbling and screeching at odd intervals. I think the running time of this piece was, roughly, eternity.

When the silly leaping, warbly rock-dance was at long last over, we—all five of us in the audience—applauded. The performers left, then came back out on stage. We applauded even more. They bowed and smiled. You had the feeling that it would be a sin, like being cruel to a child, not to applaud.

Theater, I came to see, was always a risk. The audience had tremendous power: it could doom the performers to total despair or raise them to wild exhilaration. It was a contradiction. There they were up on the stage, sticking their necks out, *projecting*, trying to be stars, and yet they were almost insubstantial, like thin weather vanes, their self-regard at the mercy of every wayward gust of wind. No matter what the quality of the stuff I saw, I was always impressed by the utter courage that theater people showed.

At the end of the spring of 1983, just before the workshop was about to break up for the summer, Vicky invited me to come to a place called the Performing Garage, down in Soho, to see Spalding Gray in *Sex and Death to Age Fourteen*.

In the back row of the theater we sat and waited. A tall, pale, nervous man carrying a notebook appeared from behind a curtain. He sat on a plain chair behind a small wooden table, took a sip of water from a glass, then plunged into a jumpy, brilliant, obsessive, nonstop monologue that lasted about an hour and a half. It was about growing up in a crazy Christian Science family in Rhode Island, complete with a sad, mad mother and a remote father, and teeming with terrifying and hilarious internal and external sensations.

I was amazed by this display; it went further than anything I had seen before on stage. The man's *courage* in sitting there, right in front of people, inviting them to step right inside his guts and take a guided tour, astounded me.

Watching Spalding set me to thinking. I had never in my life imagined going up on a stage. Though I admired actors, I couldn't understand them at all. They struggled and twisted themselves into unfamiliar shapes, walking up and down, trying to delve into their "motivation," doing strange vocal and physical exercises before performances. Trying to get into character. This consuming drive to impersonate someone else was incomprehensible to me. I had enough trouble impersonating *myself*. If I were to pretend to be someone else, I would surely fly off into space. Then I thought, well, Spalding—trained actor though he is—was only telling his own stories. That was something I'd been doing for years. Going on stage didn't seem so far out of the realm of possibility.

A listener of mine, a guy who owned several parking lots in Manhattan, had once let me know that if I ever wanted to give "a speech," as he called it, he would front the expenses. I took him up on it. I scheduled a one-night performance for the beginning of August at an off-Broadway theater in midtown. At the last minute I realized I needed somebody to figure out the microphones, sound system, and lighting. I called my friend Carlos. Actually, Carlos was a fan, a devoted listener of my radio show. In fact, he was what you might call a superfan. He'd recorded every program I ever did, no matter what—stories, silly music, phone calls, fund-raising pitches…everything. He taped the shows off his radio at home and dropped them off at the station during the week when I wasn't around. After a year of this, embarrassed by the one-way flow of things, I sent him money for the blank cassettes. I first met him when he came down to say hello during one of the fund-raising drives.

Carlos was a short, husky man in his early thirties. He had thick, dark, messy hair, a round face, and wore thick, horn-rimmed glasses that he perpetually cleaned on the tail of his shirt. His most defining physical characteristic was carved on his face. Carlos had terrible acne: angry little forests of red on both cheeks and his forehead. And pockmarked scar fields beneath and around the present inflammations where the acne had chewed his face for decades. He was sloppy, wore cheap white shirts outside his pants, and beat-up shoes he hadn't shined or cleaned in years.

For money, Carlos occasionally did small moving jobs. He was really an artist, though: a terrific painter. He had serious notions of showing his work, getting an agent, and finding a gallery, but he never got to the point of actually putting together a set of slides of his work or even bringing them around to a gallery. That was hard enough to do under any circumstances, but Carlos had some special obstacles in his way.

He had had a nasty childhood. His father, a rich businessman, had left him and his mother when he was a little kid. The old man had remarried and lived in New Mexico. He was an autocrat, a remote, stiff bastard who, as far as I could gather, hadn't shown much affection for Carlos in the first place. Carlos's mother made a nothing living as a secretary at a trucking company in Queens. They lived together in a tiny three-room apartment in a middle-class project in the Bronx.

Carlos's mother was always a little drunk. Sometimes she was dead drunk and spent whole days sleeping it off in their apartment. She was a decent woman but had a flighty mind and a weak will. Carlos carried her around on his soul like a five-hundred-pound weight. Carlos drank too, but he was never drunk. Always in control, he never weaved or slurred his words. He was like a lot of people you run into—never without a certain minimum of alcohol in them. Just enough to make life bearable. He carried a quart bottle of scotch with him wherever he went and was always just a little high. When he wasn't working—moving furniture, driving a van—he was more than a little high. He glowed with good humor. Always laughing, sometimes too loudly, about some obscure thing that struck him as funny. And as long as he was a little smashed, something was always striking him funny.

This was the basis of our relationship: to Carlos, I was the self-confident performer, fearlessly retelling the horrifying adventures of my life for all to hear, and Carlos was the eternal listener. He and I had suffered the same way, but he suffered in silence.

There was no rehearsal for my first live show. Carlos arrived at the theater about two hours early, hooked up what we needed in terms of microphones, cables, control boards up in the light and sound booth, things I could never have understood.

The theater was big, maybe three hundred seats. In my ignorance and excitement, and despite having gone with Vicky to dozens of plays and performance pieces, I ignored every rule and ritual of the theater. I was sitting on the stage, with all the house lights all the way up while the audience filed in, greeting people who called out hellos, answering questions. At almost the last minute, it dawned on me that I should probably have waited in the wings, like other "actors."

It would have been almost impossible to find a better audience.

At the end of the story, they stood up and applauded loud and long. It went straight to my head. I felt like I was swelling up to twice my size. *Look at all those people, drinking up every word I utter. And having such a good time, too.* I couldn't imagine why I should ever stop talking.

Later, after the audience had gone, I sat on the stage, struck with wonder. Carlos, who I'd heard laughing way above the audience from the light booth, was putting away the equipment. Vicky was sitting opposite on a folding chair. She had a very serious, critical look in her eye. She told me that if I was considering a serious run at stage performance, I would need to rehearse, learn a few rules of performing—some discipline. She was willing to help me out.

I walked out of the theater—it was about ten o'clock on a Friday night—with Carlos and Vicky on either side of me. She was quiet, as usual. He was laughing, poking fun at me for talking as if I would never stop, and excessively basking in the praise afterward. "Oh, please, please, please, Mike," he said, "can I have your autograph?"

I was euphoric, bloated to the gills with the praise and applause I'd just gotten, and my two pals' behavior seemed suddenly irritating to me. We split up at the corner of Fifty-fourth Street and Eighth Avenue, and I decided, since it was a mild night—to walk home to my apartment on Seventy-ninth Street.

On the way up Broadway my head was buzzing like there was a bee-hive inside it. Visions, images of faces in the audience circulated rapidly in my mind's eye: shining, laughing, flushed. People on their feet, applause, recognition, admiration—for *me*. The elation was ten times anything I'd ever experienced on the radio. I felt great power surging through me—*I could change the natural course of things—heal the sick, raise the dead.*

When I got home, close to midnight, I told Susan all about it—every last little detail. I felt like I had been reborn, that there was a whole new world out there, just waiting to hear me.

The next day, I called Vicky and we agreed on a time the following week to rehearse. Now that I'd found the philosopher's stone, the fountain of youth—performing—I could barely restrain myself. I called the Seventy-eighth Street Theater Lab and met that afternoon with the owner. I scheduled a week of performances—in a month's time.

I had an idea for a series of shows called *The Family Romance*—four nights, each night about a different member of my family: first, my mother, then my father, then my sister, then, last but of course not least, me.

CHAPTER TWENTY-THREE

Rehearsing, something I had never done before, turned out to be an excruciating experience. Vicky and I sat in an empty office, she at one end of a long table, me at the other. There was a sickly bright fluorescent light directly above us. Vicky had her usual deadpan face and a legal pad in front of her as I told my story: blood and guts, jokes, obscenities, flights of ecstasy, moments of crunching sadness, my eyes jumping and my hands waving. She sat there, peering at me with her small sharp black eyes, occasionally smiling or twisting her mouth up or down, frowning acidly. Sometimes she nodded, made a note on her pad. If I stopped, hanging out there all alone, to get some scrap of response from her, she said, "It's not *my* story—just keep going."

I felt like I was roasting slowly on a spit.

When I finished, with an extravagant flourish, Vicky still sat mute, motionless as a lizard on a rock. I glared at her: "So, what? Tell me something!"

"Weelll…" she said in her slow drawl, giving me, finally, a tiny smile, "you got a good story there, old buddy, but you need to stop explaining everything." This pissed me off. She obviously didn't understand me at all. It was what I *did*—explain things. "What do you mean?" I asked.

She got a wary look in her eye, as if I was going to climb onto the table and take a running jump at her. Directors have to be brave, I guess—dealing with raving, egocentric performers. "Well..." she said, "you *tell* us something happened, then you *explain* what it meant."

"So?"

"All you got to do, buddy, is tell your story and let the people figure it out themselves: you have to trust the audience."

A month later, I'm doing my four shows, this time charging five dollars a head because the theater, oddly enough, wanted some rent money. And Vicky thought it would be nice if we could all (me, her, and Carlos) go home with a little spare change at the end of each evening. It was a small house, maybe seventy-five seats. Again I invited my radio audience, and, this time around, my friends, even my wife. I hadn't wanted Susan to see my earlier shot at showbiz because I had no idea if it would be a flop or not. I dreaded the thought of failing in front of her.

The stories went off pretty well. More applause, more adrenaline pumping through my body. I thought I could really get to love performing. It didn't hurt to come home with some spending money, either.

At the end of the week, Vicky and Carlos and I sat in the theater.

She went over my mistakes. I crossed and uncrossed my legs when I was sitting on the high stool I used, swiveling my ass around on the seat like it was a hot plate. I waved my arms around too much and stared at one place in the house too long while I was talking, so parts of the audience felt left out. Vicky was dubious about my frequent, seemingly gratuitous asides—my unplanned, unrehearsed comments and diversions. Once again, she told me I should let the story tell itself and trust the audience.

Carried away by the terrific highs of performing, I booked some more shows at the theater lab in the next couple of months; I even got a few good reviews in the local West Side papers. Slowly and surely I learned a bit of craft up on stage.

I saw some more of Spalding's shows and stole as many acting techniques and stage movements as I could. For instance, Spalding keeps a glass of water on his table when he performs. And, at exactly the right moment, just after a devastating revelation or a particularly ironic observation, he stops, looks at the audience, takes a long slow sip of water, then resumes where he left off. The great art of the pause. Unknown to me theatrically. Unknown to me personally. With me, everything was either full speed ahead or dead stop. Up there, in front of real people, I was moving cautiously into the strange land of *the middle*, of the pause and the considered gesture, the controlled shrug and the half-smile.

I branched out, got a few bookings at some clubs and theaters closer to the heart of things, in mid- and downtown Manhattan. Vicky and I, the odd couple, spent a lot of time together, going to theater and rehearsing.

In the spring of 1986, after I had been performing for almost two years, I started working at the West Bank Theater on Forty-second street, right off Ninth Avenue.

A lot of the places that featured performance work and new theater pieces were attached to restaurants and bars. Usually in the basement. The fare changed every night, stand-up comics, jazz bands, solo performance artists, musicals, six-character plays.

I loved the West Bank Theater. You went through the restaurant, past the bar, down the steps, and there it was, a dark room with black walls, a low ceiling, and about seventy-five seats arranged around tables. It was a cabaret—drinks, coffee, and entertainment. It had that special feeling of condensed, alcohol-soaked bonhomie and edgy artistry; it was a place you could walk into and shut out the workaday world completely. I understood why Vicky loved the theater so much. You get bashed and kicked, humiliated, ignored, rejected, and abused out *there*, but the theater—dark, warm, quiet, lit by colored lights, infused with artifice and dreams—was a kind of paradise.

The stage was a small black-painted wooden platform, no more than eight inches off the floor and about ten feet wide by six deep. You performed in front of a black curtain, behind which were wires and cables, extra lights, gels (colored plastic filters to fit over the lights), some old props, and a couple of chairs. The dressing room was tiny and cramped, like in a lot of small clubs and theaters. It was also the back office of the restaurant. So, while you waited to go on, nervous and pacing, you were kept company by ringing telephones, adding machines, computers, and waiters coming in and out to fetch supplies.

For me, the dressing room was way too remote from the audience. I took to sitting behind the stage curtains or hovering in the wings while the house opened, waiting impatiently to go on. As soon as I was introduced by the emcee, I would push the curtain aside and stride out to sit on my stool, placed smack in the middle of the stage, no more than two feet from the nearest table.

That was how it had to be for me: I discovered I wanted to be as close to the audience as humanly possible. Distance scared me. It made me feel like I was too tall, or too tiny, like Alice in Wonderland. I needed to be right *there*.

In the theater there's a basic concept, the fourth wall: an invisible boundary line between the audience and the performance that's there for everybody's protection—to preserve the art and magic of the performance.

I wasn't sure what made me hate and fear the fourth wall, but I sure as hell had no use for it. I also developed some other performance problems. In dressing rooms before shows, I was always angry. At times, almost enraged. Everybody has their version of stage fright, mine was to get angry. For days, sometimes weeks before a performance, I was like a dog with a bad itch. Everybody, everything—at work and at home—got on my nerves. I had always been psychosomatic, but now, right before I was due to perform, I was getting regular heart attacks, lung collapses, and various forms of cancer.

The night of a show, I paced back and forth in the dressing room, muttering and cursing out loud. One time, I got so mad I punched a hole in someone else's stage prop and picked up a chair and smashed it against the wall. Vicky was pissed off by such unprofessional behavior, such stupid shenanigans. She came into the dressing room to calm me down: "What is this *nonsense*?"

"I don't want to do this!" I told her.

She stared at me, frowning. "Go ahead and look at me like that," I yelled at her. "I don't care!"

"What is your problem, buddy?"

"My problem? I'll tell you what my problem is." I walked up to her, nose to nose. "I just do not want to have to go up there and talk to those people." I paced, I fumed. "What do they *want* from me!?" Somehow, I had conceived the nutcase notion that I had been kidnapped, locked up, and was being forced at gunpoint to tell people a story.

She tried to calm me down. "Mike," she said, her hand resting on my shoulder. "You need to stop this now. Those people out there are your *friends*...they came here because they want to hear a good story. Lighten up, buddy, they're on *your* side." Little by little I calmed down, then, inevitably, I lapsed into a kind of melancholy, sitting there, my head in my hands, almost crying. The best I could do, I learned from Vicky, was to take whatever emotion I was feeling right before the show—irritation or sadness, bring it on stage with me, and start my show with that.

July 1986. I'd been doing a couple of shows at West Bank about my days as a probation officer in Brooklyn Family Court. It was a Friday night, my last show. After the performance, a listener to my radio show came up to the stage to say hello and introduced a friend she'd brought along, Sam Freedman, a fairly well-known arts writer for *The New York Times*. He shook my hand, told me how much he had liked the show, then asked:

"Would you mind if I wrote about you for *The New York Times*?"

I reeled, trying not to fall off my stool. The only reason I could formulate a few responsive sentences was because I had just told a good story and gotten a decent reaction from the audience. I nodded my head maturely. "Sure," I told Sam Freedman, "that would be great." He shook my hand again and told me he would talk to his editors and be in touch with me in a few days.

Vicky and Carlos were sitting with me at a table in the empty club. I was drinking a double scotch, feeling glazed and unreal. Vicky was flushed; Carlos was clapping me on the back.... *The New York Times!*

Vicky, of course, was the first one to come to her senses. "Now look here, buddy, lots of people get articles about them in the *Times*. It doesn't make you Lawrence Olivier. You just stay focused on your work." I looked over at her. *Work? What could the woman mean? I was going to be in* The New York Times. *What did work have to do with anything?* Vicky shook her head and frowned. If she thought she could get away with it, she probably would have slapped me to sober me up. Even Carlos caught on to her concern and managed to get a serious look on his face. Through the rosy haze of incipient stardom, I could detect their anxiety, but their worries seemed far, far away.

When I got home and told Susan about the *Times*, she seemed to wobble a little on her feet and had to sit down on the couch. She looked at me as if I had been magically transformed, abandoned my old self, and walked into our house a different person, a stranger.

"*The New York Times?*"

"That's what I said." Her jaw dropped. She shook her head. Something new had entered our lives....

Three days after the performance, Sam Freedman came to interview me on my lunch hour at work; three weeks before the article was supposed to appear, I gave my two weeks' notice to the law firm. Obviously, since I was on my way to fame and fortune, there was no longer any point in continuing to impersonate Bartleby the Scrivener, hiding in some little corner, wasting away on my stool. They wouldn't be seeing me anymore, that bunch of time-is-money, fussy little barristers. I was headed straight to the top!

Vicky was deeply disturbed when she heard I'd quit my job. In fact, she had warned me not to do it. It was an old truth: *don't quit your day job;* the bleached bones of would-be stars littered the gutters of Manhattan.

September 7, 1986, a Sunday morning. Up at 6:00 A.M. to get the *Times*. I rushed home, threw the extraneous parts of the paper—"Thousands Believed to Have Perished in Monsoon Floods," "Cancer Seen as a National Plague"—onto the living-room floor. And there I was, on the front page of the entertainment section! This was not just the regular entertainment section. This was an extra thick, special version, published only once a year—"What to Look For in the Arts in the Year Ahead." The *front page!* Yes, and I was continued! onto another page, with a picture of me on stage.

All my life seemed to pass quickly before me, my childhood in the attic, my lonely fearful teenage years, my horrible first marriage, insanity, the hospital. All the sad, silly, wasteful things I had done and lived through. I was forty-one years old, and now here I was...famous, described by Samuel Freedman as a "master storyteller."

A little later, with the newspaper on the table...Susan and I sat next to each other, talking in whispers. The article was there between us, a sign from the heavens appearing in our living room, seeming to alter everything between us. And believe me, what had been going on between us for the last couple of years needed altering in the most drastic way....

Since my money had disappeared three years earlier, in 1983, and I had started working as a paralegal, I had fallen badly in Susan's eyes. By the fall of 1986, when the *Times* article hit, it had already been six years since she had gotten her degree and she had developed a good, high-paying practice. Her friends and colleagues were all psychologists and psychiatrists, and they all seemed to be married to other shrinks or doctors or lawyers. They lived in big six-room apartments, made tons of money, had brand-new expensive cars and big houses in the country. More than a few of them were fixing up another bedroom for their second kid. We, on the other hand, lived in a "small" four-room apartment, had a beat-up used Datsun, worn-out furniture, and practically no extra money once the bills were paid. It was understood that this was clearly my fault for having been so self-destructive and passive. I agreed with her. Since my money had vanished, I had lapsed into a wistful, hopeless melancholy.

Susan wanted me to straighten up and do the right thing for the family. Write, get a book or a play published, *make it* as an artist, a radio personality, or a performer. Or, just drop all this talking shit. Get my Ph.D. in English. Go to law school—*be* somebody. Sure, my radio show still counted for something in her eyes. In the beginning, the first couple of years I was on the air, Susan was impressed with my success. Thousands of New Yorkers listened to me; her friends listened to me. Her own *analyst* listened to me. She herself never missed a show.

But after three years or so, the glamour had seriously faded for her. The trouble was, as usual, my fatal lack of ambition. Doing an *unpaid* radio show in the middle of New York City was in Susan's eyes just a stupid waste of time and talent. The fact that she wasn't very interested in my show anymore took some of the joy out of it for me too. After all, part of the reason I tried so hard on the air was because I knew she was at home, drinking it all up. By 1983, with my daughter and our "poverty-stricken" financial state, our relationship was unraveling at the edges. The final nail in the coffin was...another child.

That summer, just after I joined the theater workshop, Susan announced that she wanted to have a second child. It would be perfect. We'd have two kids then, just like all her friends—be a *real* family. She wanted—and was determined to have, this time around—a boy.

She announced her new plan to me in late August. At first I thought, well maybe so. A family. Two kids. Me, the father, that's *normal*, right? It would be the final triumph over my twisted childhood. It took me less than a week to sober up from this sentimental daydream. *Two* kids! No, no, no. Our marriage was already on shaky ground. I had resigned myself over the last three years to sharing my wife's attention with my daughter, but another kid? It was too much.

Susan was resolved to have this new child no matter what. We argued. We fought. The situation escalated into permanent rage on both sides. Things couldn't go on this way without an explosion. One afternoon, we got a baby-sitter and went to the pub across the street. We sat at a small table against the window, ate in silence for a few minutes, then we were into it....

"Well," she said, "are you going to agree? Are you going to do this?"

"No. I can't." She glared at me. "Look," I said, "do I have to tell you my whole story again? I had no father growing up and my mother was crazy. Shit—you *know* all this!" She didn't want to hear it.

"This is probably something you wouldn't know," she said, "but what most people do to repair their damaged childhoods is give their children what they never got themselves."

"Maybe, but I'm doing that right now with Sarah. It's all I can do to try to be a father to one kid. Two would be too much."

"Look, I want to have a *real* family."

"We have a real family already!" I was leaning across the little table, pleading with her to see things the way I did. I counted out the points on my fingers...."Susan, see what I'm trying to say here. You have a good career, you love your work. I have a job, I just wrote a play. I'm on the radio, maybe something will come of that someday."

"Maybe."

"Fuck you, maybe it will! ...you know—I don't want to have the same old argument over and over again. What I'm saying is: we're healthy. We have a smart healthy kid. We go places, we do things, we talk. Why isn't that enough?"

"You wouldn't know about real families."

"Yeah, that may be true, but what's that got to do with what's going on right now?"

"Children without siblings are lonely and self-involved. It's better for children to have a sibling, all the studies prove that."

"I don't want to hear about fucking studies. I'm talking about you and me—about our lives right now." Our voices got louder. We were in that kind of bitter struggle between couples that makes everything around you disappear. Susan was pale with rage. She glared at me. "You're being selfish, as usual." She leaned back, fixed me with her haughtiest look. "I mean this. I want another child. And if you cared for me at all or had any respect for what I want, instead of being selfish like you always are, you would see how much this means to me."

"And what about me? Are you paying attention to what I'm saying?"

Looking at her sitting there, bristling and ready for war like a battleship, I could see that nothing was getting through to her. She had made up her mind—that was it. "Let me tell you something," she said, "I want this boy (it *was* going to be a boy) more than *anything else in the world*. If you can't do it, I want you to leave right now while I'm young enough to find another man who can do it!"

I leaned back in my seat and looked at her. And right there, at that precise moment, I had the feeling, an absolute certainty, that my marriage had just ended.

I should have left right then and there, gone across the street, packed a bag, and found another place to live; somehow explain it all to my daughter. But I didn't have the strength. I couldn't picture being out on my own again in the world. I'd been alone so many times in my life. Now I had a family, no matter how imperfect Susan thought it was, and I couldn't imagine leaving my kid the way my father had left me.

I gave up and gave in, but it was like dying. "If we have a baby," I told her, speaking, it felt, like someone frozen inside a stone, "it's going to be your baby." This didn't faze her a bit. "Well, but you still have to do your share," she said. "You have to do as much as you're doing now."

I nodded silently. She looked at me for a couple of seconds, then got up and left.

From that moment on, Susan was nothing to me but an irritating presence. I went out of my way not to touch her. If I passed her in the kitchen or the hallway, I turned sideways. I spent two nights out of three sleeping on the couch in the living room.

We had sex maybe eight times in the next year, always during the period when she was most likely to conceive. For me it was a duty, part of an odious bargain. She finally got pregnant in July 1984, roughly ten months after our terminal exchange at the pub. From that time on, my irritation escalated into barely suppressed rage. When her stomach started to bloom that fall and winter, I was filled with disgust. When she'd been pregnant with Sarah, I felt awe; there was an unsurpassed beauty to her, carrying our child. Now she seemed like nothing but a fat, bloated cow. I hardly touched her from the moment she told me she was pregnant till a couple of months after she gave birth.

CHAPTER TWENTY-FOUR

M y son, Ben, was born in the spring of 1985. I was, by now, well used to treating Susan like she was a stranger. We went about our business, pretending to do family things for our daughter's sake. We had people over once in a while for dinner, took summer vacations. We still had sex, sudden bangings together, fueled, for me, exclusively by anger. What it was for her I didn't know and I didn't care.

I paid practically no attention to my son. Susan fed him at night. If he cried, she went to see what was wrong. If she brought him into bed in the morning, I turned my back on him, filled with a blind fury. Then I jumped up and walked out of the room and out of the house. When I fed him in his high chair or changed a diaper or took him out in the stroller when his mother or the baby-sitter couldn't do it, I was stone faced. I hardly spoke to him. Once in a while, I would break down and pick him up or play with him a little, but if I could help it, I tried not to see him or hear him. All this filled me with a twisting, bitter guilt. But some powerful, underground river of black intent kept pushing me away from him.

I talked to my shrink, Dr. Klein. I hoped he could give me a magic formula for breaking through the bitterness and anomie. Despite my own instincts to remove myself, I hadn't entirely given up hope. I kept searching to find some crack in the glacial wall between me and Susan, a path back to something resembling harmony, even affection. Nothing changed, though. Susan had what she wanted. What did I have? By July 1985, three months after my son was born, I was having an affair.

A week before my birthday, June 16, I had been, as usual, making sure all the listeners knew that I wanted birthday cards. Even the odd present would not be unappreciated. It was a yearly ritual—this shameful begging for cards, half joke, half serious.

When I came into the station on the Sixteenth and picked up my mail, there were, in fact, a number of cards, some of them heartfelt. Along with the cards was a large, heavy, brown paper–wrapped box.

I brought the box home, sat down on our bed, and opened it. Susan, Sarah, and the baby were out. Inside the box, right on top, there was a card from the sender, wishing me happy birthday and saying: "From a fan to a star." Substituted for the word "fan"—glued onto the paper—was a small pink plastic fan, and in the place of the word "star" was a small, silver star. Corny but touching.

There were several smaller packages in the box, each carefully wrapped and tied with a pink or red ribbon. Each containing a present. As I opened each gift, I was amazed by how perfectly apt they were, how obviously the sender had picked things that meant something to me. Some were things I vaguely remembered mentioning on the air. There was a bottle of good scotch; an old carved wooden cigarette box; and two hand-painted silk ties with funny writing and symbols on them. I was impressed by the careful attention, the sheer personal quality that these gifts represented, from a woman I'd never met, who seemed to have known me all my life.

The woman who sent it all—Rose—said she was an avid listener. What I did on the radio meant a great deal to her, and all these gifts were a token of gratitude for all I had done for her.

I knew instantly that I wanted to meet this woman. I was sick to death of my life at home and here was someone reaching out to me with both hands. I was ready *yesterday* for a lifeline like this, but I waited a couple of weeks before I actually called her. For the first time since I moved to Manhattan to be with Susan seven years earlier, I seriously contemplated having sex with another woman. My moral code, though it wavered a bit from time to time, was essentially out of the Old Testament: the *Lord* was waiting to zap me the minute I transgressed. I knew the instant I spoke to this woman on the phone and arranged to see her, I would be stepping over a line that, once crossed, might never be recrossed.

The first time I saw Rose, she was sitting alone on a bench in Central Park. It was over in the east eighties, not too far from where she worked as a social worker at the New York Foundling Hospital.

We had arranged to meet on a Friday, after she got off work. It was a not-too-hot day for early July, pleasant really, but I was, as they say in the mental health field, agitated. I had walked across the park from the West Side, trying to shake out some of the excess current that was crackling through my bones. Truth was—all rationalizations to the contrary—I was going to meet *another woman*! I might fool myself with little scenarios in my head about "just getting together to talk" or "it's only this one time," but the truth was I had higher (and lower) expectations. I *wanted* something to come of this. I wanted a woman who I could be with, talk to, someone who appreciated what I did and who I was. I longed for something new, someone else to put my hands on.

I rounded a corner on the park walk, and there she was—as she described herself: "long hair, wearing a white blouse, a black skirt, and black shoes." Much, much too prosaic. The minute I set eyes on Rose, she looked to me like the Madonna, just dropped from heaven. A round, curvy, sexy Madonna, with glistening auburn hair and big, beautiful, sympathetic, emerald-green eyes. She stood up as I walked over to her, and—so formal—we shook hands. I remember her hand was cold, mine was hot.

I sat down next to her. There were kids all around, chasing balls, screaming; dogs barking; people walking by; and suddenly, we were alone in the midst of hundreds of other beings. Something seemed to place us on a faraway plane, in some idyllic wonderland. I felt like a shy teenager on his first date with a really good-looking girl, but, and here was reality intruding, also like a doomed character from a myth, caught up in the toils of some fateful story.

Rose was one of those people who shine—who have a natural gentleness and strength you can actually see.

It was lucky for me that she was blushing so much. It gave me time to recover a little decorum and self-confidence. After all, I remembered, I was the "star" and she was the "fan." At least I could work off that.

We talked for a little while and then sort of naturally rose up off the bench and started to walk—no particular direction. And it wouldn't have made any difference if there was a direction; I seemed to be always walking straight into her. I don't mean bumping into her, though there was a little of that—I mean I actually felt that I was walking straight inside her. What part was lust, what part magical connection, I couldn't tell and soon gave up trying. We just walked and talked.

Rose was about ten years younger than me, around thirty. She had been working as a social worker (another therapist!) at the Foundling Hospital for four years, after graduating with an MSW from Brown in her mid-twenties. She worked, not with the orphans at the huge hospital over on Third Avenue, but with the mothers who were giving up their kids and the families who were adopting them.

Every day, she was faced with raw human misery, but from what I could tell by listening to her and watching her as she explained her job, she thrived on helping people in despair. She couldn't imagine being in the world and not helping people.

We talked our way around the park, into the evening, way beyond the time I should have been home for supper—seven, eight, nine o'clock. The sun set, the pastel-colored streetlamps came on in the park, and still we walked. Sometime around nine-thirty I realized, with a guilty lurch, that I should be home. But I didn't want to go home. I wanted to go wherever she was going. Discretion, however, guilt, sadness took hold of me and told me I was going to have to leave—go home to my family. I suddenly remembered the feeling I had when I was little and my long-estranged father, who had come over for one of his rare visits, announced that he was "going home." It was a sad, sharp ache. I didn't want him to leave me then, and I didn't want to leave Rose now. As for her, it seemed like she would have stayed out till dawn, gazing at me and listening to me talk about my life. She was obviously stuck on me. It was almost scary—less intensity might have made me more comfortable—but I wasn't about to turn this gift down. Finally, at the western entrance to the park at Seventy-second Street, about seven blocks from my apartment, I told her I really did have to leave. She put her hand in mine and I felt a kind of velvet warmth go straight through me. It was hard to let her go. I walked away and turned around and she was standing just where I had left her—looking at me. I waved. She nodded. I walked on, turned and waved to her again. Then I was too far down the street to see her, and when I looked around again, she wasn't there.

I walked the next couple of blocks in a state of euphoria. As I neared my apartment and my steps slowed, I could see her there in front of me, beautiful, her rounded, kind face, those great, wonderful green eyes, and that hair. Big breasts rounding out her clean, clean white blouse. Ahhhhh. I thought: this is one of the few times in my life I had looked forward to something and wasn't disappointed.

Two days later, swallowing about ten gallons of guilt, I dialed her number again and we went out for burgers at a restaurant a couple of blocks from her apartment on the West Side. Inside of five minutes, I was holding her hand across the table and looking into her eyes.

I saw her again soon afterward, and again. Within a few weeks we were having sex.

Like all such furtive comings-together, there was an element of danger and guilt to our meetings. Maybe that adds a constant spice to such experiences for some people, but I don't think it did that for me, at least not after the first couple of times. What quickly became essential about my time with Rose was the time itself. Not the sex, not the danger, but the sense of shelter and peace she brought me.

So now I was an adulterer. I had broken the bonds of my marriage vow. When I had married Susan, I had never dreamed I would do such a thing. I intended to live with her, and be faithful to her, till death did us part. In all the years until I met Rose, I never so much as kissed another woman on the cheek. It just wasn't seemly, I thought. Now here I was, with another woman. Spending time, holding hands, kissing, having sex. The true infidelity, though, in the way I saw the world, was in sharing my intimate thoughts and dreams with Rose: *talking* to her.

Some nights I was over at Rose's apartment for hours. I, who never went out with the boys, didn't have any outside interests to speak of, who really never went anywhere, was coming home very late. Sometimes I lied and said I was at a movie. Sometimes I didn't bother to lie and merely said I was out "somewhere." Susan never said a word. She either didn't want to know or, what seemed sadly believable to me, didn't really care, as long as I kept coming home and didn't make a big deal about it.

I spent the year between the summer of 1985 and the summer of 1986 waiting for Susan to come to her "senses" and apologize for all the wrongs she'd done to me—then maybe I wouldn't be "forced" to find love and attention outside our home. Very likely she was waiting for me to do the same—apologize for whatever she conceived to be my great sins. It never happened. Like soldiers in the trenches we fought our nasty little war every day for more than a year, always trying to gain another inch of ground.

Then had come the day of my rebirth as a real person—and maybe our rebirth as a couple—courtesy of the *New York Times* Sunday entertainment section.

There we sat, right across from each other at our dining-room table on a September morning, seven years into our marriage. I could see Susan was really shaken up by the turn of events. Looking at me she said, in a strange, small voice, "I don't know who to be now." I put my hand over hers on the table. This was as close as we'd been in years. But before we could say another word, my son, Ben, got up and commenced to babble.

Our daughter, Sarah, was a big talker, but she was like the sphinx compared with little Ben. He *never* shut his mouth. He babbled and burbled, started to form words as early as was scientifically possible for a baby. He fell asleep talking and woke up talking. Like a puppy, everything was fascinating to him, every day the same things seemed brand-new and exciting. He was popping with enthusiasm and wanted to communicate every last little feeling.

So, on this morning of my resurrection, little Ben woke up and made his way into the living room. It was time to play! That's the way it is—when babies get up, the world gets up with them.

He wobbled over to me. Ordinarily, in my awful way, I would have stiffened up. But today, because of The Article, I was brimming with enough confidence and contentment to be affectionate. I picked up the paper and held it up to him. "Look, Ben, Daddy's picture is in *The New York Times*." He laughed. Sounded good to him, whatever the hell I just said. "See," I said, getting down on the floor with him, "it says right here...'Feder's ability to charm the audience with authentic tales...' Pretty goddamn impressive, eh?" He laughed again, ripped the paper out of my hands, and swatted me in the face with it.

A couple of hours later, about 9:30 A.M., I was on the floor, feeding more sections of the *Times* to Ben so he could rip them to shreds, when the phone rang. I picked it up and a brisk voice asked: "Is this Mike Feder?"

"Yeah."

"This is Universal Pictures in Los Angeles. Would you please hold for Debbie Blumberg?"

"Who?"

"I have a call from Debbie Blumberg, would you please hold?"

Would I hold for Debbie Blumberg? Well, sure, why not? It's what the men in my family did. We have been holding for Debbie Blumberg for generations.

"OK, I'll hold." A couple of seconds go by.

"Mike Feder?"

"Yeah?"

"This is Debbie Blumberg, Universal Pictures. Mike, we read the article in *The New York Times*, and I just wanna say, Mike, we *love* you out here!" They love me out there. I'm wondering what the fuck this woman is talking about and how on earth she got a copy of *The New York Times* at six-thirty in the morning, California time.

Debbie Blumberg, who loves me, tells me she is the vice president for development at Universal Pictures and wants to talk to me about some ideas for screenplays based on some of the stories mentioned in the article.

My agent, Artie, had warned me that the minute the story appeared in the paper, I would get calls like this.

Oh, yes, I had an agent now. As if justifying Vicky's most elemental fears about my uncontrollable ego, I had acquired, in the six short weeks in between meeting Sam Freedman and the appearance of the *Times* article, a lawyer *and* an agent. Jake and Artie.

Jake was a guy I had known for a few years. A show-business lawyer who managed the music career of a friend of mine in Brooklyn Heights. Deciding that I might be in need of his services if my career took any sort of real leap, I signed him up to help me. He told me I had to have an agent to handle any offers that came in when the *Times* article appeared.

Artie was right off the rack in central casting. A short, hyperactive Jewish guy in his early thirties who never stopped moving. He was always pacing, waving his hands, yelling at somebody on the phone, jumping in and out of cabs. He wore his hair a little long, sported expensive leather jackets, and draped himself in gold—a necklace, a watch, a thick ring. He had several clients, mostly actors, including one real-live up-and-coming movie star.

His office was in a huge refinished loft in the West Twenties. I was let in by his assistant, who told me to walk right in. There was Artie, a little churning dynamo of a man, sitting behind a vast ultramodern black-metal desk plumb in the middle of the whole space. He flashed a big grin and gestured for me to sit down. He was on the phone (Artie was always on the phone—sitting or walking, day and night, in a cab or on a plane).

I sat on the other side of his desk and watched him do his thing. And he, never missing an opportunity, was well aware that I was watching him. "No!" he shouted into the phone, cutting the air with his free hand. "You listen to me, babe. We're not talking shit here—we're talking real— so please do me the courtesy—no, Bob, no—you are *really* not getting it. When I say fifty K to sign, I *mean* fifty K!—no—no, Bob—Bob, listen to me for a second. Let me say this one last time, because I don't have all fucking day here." His face was red, he was practically screaming. "We get fifty K on signing or we *walk*! OK!?" He slammed the phone down. Then, instantly, he broke into his big grin again, jumped up, and came around the desk, beaming, thrilled to see me. He grabbed my hand and said: "Hey, the famous Mike Feder. Jake tells me you're a genius."

He took my breath away. I couldn't think of a thing to say. We sat on a huge leather couch. Artie leaned over, put his hand on my arm: "Mike, I, of course, have no way of knowing what you may have heard about me, but let me tell you this—I would never take on just any schmuck just because he thinks he's hot shit. Believe me, I see them all the time. But I trust Jake."

He leaned in closer, put his hand on my arm. "Mike, I can tell you're no dope—not like a kid who never had any experience. Well, let me tell you, babe, I'm no kid either. When I take on a client, I work my ass off for them. And if I say so myself, I am very good at my work." He waved his arm in a circle, taking in the whole loft, which was, in fact, nothing short of breathtaking. Two stories high, more than a hundred feet long, fifty feet wide, big beautiful plants, trees actually, in decorated ceramic pots, a fantastic garden just outside a huge picture window. Large, silk-brocaded chairs, beautiful antique lamps, a state-of-the-art kitchen area against one of the walls.

Upstairs, in a sunlit open space, his assistant was sitting at a polished natural-grain wood desk, whispering into the phone. It didn't take me long to decide—*Fifty K or we walk, babe!*—Artie was obviously one tough customer, just the guy I needed if I was going to play in the big leagues. Quickly comprehending my world-class naïveté, Artie told me that I shouldn't say anything to anyone who called but refer them immediately to him. So, when Debbie Blumberg commenced talking about meetings and options, I told her she had to call Artie. She took the number, told me how wonderful I was again, and hung up.

I got three more calls in the next half hour. Two more from movie companies, and one from a television producer, all from California.

The rest of the day, friends and members of my family called to congratulate me. In the afternoon, I got a call from Artie. He had already fielded six "legitimate" offers from movie and television companies. "Mike," he said, "didn't I tell you you were going to hit it big!? Take it from me, you're gonna be rich, babe."

Jake called and told me he had heard from a friend who had been at a power brunch, that an editor from a big publishing house had been talking about me, saying he hoped he'd have a chance to publish a book of my stories. It was all coming true—my wildest daydreams. After each call came in, I gave Susan the news. She was dazzled, looking at me with awe. I hadn't seen such a look in her eyes since our first days together.

And so it went into the evening. I sat there, like the newly crowned king, in my four-room West Side apartment, receiving congratulations and attention from all sorts of people. Agents, lawyers, production companies, magazines. Aside from calls from complete strangers, I got calls from people I hadn't heard from in decades, barely recognizable acquaintances from as far back as high school.

The only person I didn't get a call from was Vicky, which I chalked up to pure perversity and small-mindedness. I might have worried about her, but I was flying too high to bother. Besides, she and I had a rehearsal scheduled for the next day. Artie had gotten me to book a show that coming Saturday night at the West Bank Theater. So I still had to rehearse. Yes, even I, the anointed one. No doubt Vicky would talk about the article when I showed up at her office.

I was flying pretty high when I arrived at Vicky's office. On the phone with the club that morning I discovered that the show was completely sold out—overbooked! We went into the conference room and she took her regular seat, arranged her pad and pencil, and looked at me. I sat in my seat, waiting for her to say something.

Nothing. She was obviously not going to join in the celebration. But I wasn't going to play her game, I wasn't going to fret and fuss, have a fit. I could afford to be mature...magnanimous. I just went ahead and rehearsed my show. I finished and she made a few suggestions, then she reached down into her bag and produced the *Times* article (which also featured her name as my director).

She said: "Now listen, buddy, don't get carried away with all this. You still have a story to tell this Saturday night."

"OK," I told her, grinning, "nooo problem, babe." Big frown from old Vicky. She was in no way anybody's "babe." She had met Artie for about five minutes the week before when he went down to West Bank to check out the room. He was polite to her; she was barely civil to him. Timid-nostalgic-artistic-southern woman of indiscriminate sexuality meets Mr. Hollywood-Hebrew-macho-glitzman.

She looked at her pad and shook her head. She was trying to be level-headed—something I had very little talent for. Finally, she broke into a big smile, came around the table, and gave me a hug and a kiss. "You just do the right thing this weekend, ace, and we'll all feel good about it."

On the way home from Vicky's, on the M104 bus up Broadway, I sat next to a woman reading Sunday's *Times*. I waited till she got to the enter-

THE TALKING CURE / 239

tainment section, and there I still was...*the man to look for in the coming year*! She didn't seem very excited by the article—that was irritating. She had read it all the way through, following to page eleven, where my picture was. What an exquisite moment. There I was, the actual man in the story, right next to her, and she didn't even *know* it. What great, secret power I had. I was overcome with a tremendous sense of humility. Here, I thought, this woman is sitting next to a legitimate phenomenon, a master of his art, soon to be famous, but does he say anything to her, does he preen like a peacock and try to get her attention? No, he does not. He is humble. He is just like anybody else—he pays his fare, he rides the bus. He is still a man of the people.

The room at West Bank was packed. Peering at the house from behind the stage curtain, I could tell this was not my usual crowd. There was a feeling of power and money in the room—of *weight*.

When I came out there was a lot of applause, too much, really. Most of these people had never seen me before, but based only on what they read in the newspaper, they were giving me practically a standing ovation before I even opened my mouth.

I took a deep breath and started talking....

You know, I was just sitting backstage—a dressing room the size of a postage stamp...made me very claustrophobic.

I absolutely hate being jammed into crowded places. At least I've got a little extra space up here on this stage. I remember one time I was in one of the worst traps of my life—I thought I would actually die.

It was the summer of 1968, the summer of the Chicago Convention, the police running amuck, clubbing people; the assassinations of Martin Luther King, Robert Kennedy...there were riots—rebellions in cities all around the country. All of this and the Vietnam War blazing away.

It was a warm evening late in August. I was sitting looking out the window of my apartment—it was street level—looking at what appeared to be hundreds of happy couples walking by. I was not sharing their happiness.

The phone rang (proving that it worked) and it was my father on the other end. He was down in Louisiana—my father was an engineer—building a fertilizer plant.

My father built steel plants, chemical plants, bridges, dams, tunnels, and, incidentally, did a little work on the side for the U.S. government—something he only hinted at but never really confessed to. We only found out he was spying for a CIA front, the Agency for International Development, years later—after he died.

In any case, by the late sixties, my father had confined his wanderings to the continental USA.

My father, who was, in fact, calling from Baton Rouge, says, "Hey, wanta take a trip?"

I was always glad to hear my father's voice. Here's a guy who had been going away my whole life—for sometimes two, three, six months at a stretch. Mostly all I ever got from him were postcards, maybe a letter once in a while or a very long-distance call. So, naturally, seeing him so rarely, I jumped at the chance of going down to visit him.

You should understand that my father had always been larger than life to me, and the reason for this was simple—I never spent much time with him. If familiarity breeds contempt, unfamiliarity, given the right mix, can breed pure fantasy.

My father wasn't all that approachable even when he lived with me—and when he took off, never to return, he became a kind of mythical figure. And he enriched this myth by looking and acting more than a little like Ernest Hemingway. My father was a big guy, over six feet, maybe 220 pounds, very strong and tough—grew up in the depression, did a lot of heavy work. He could be rough, coarse, even violent sometimes—he had a terrible temper. I'd actually seen him, the few times he was home and took me to a ball game or the zoo—I'd actually seen him hit one guy in the mouth and another time push a man halfway down the stairs in the subway who had banged into my father and not apologized.

I was a timid kid and such behavior was amazing to me. I thought he was something right out of a movie.

Wherever my father went he was the Boss. When he sent me a photograph of himself from some remote corner of the world, he was always the biggest guy in the picture and everybody else looked like they were his employees—they usually were.

So, I drop everything in a second. I call in sick the next day at work and take a cab out to the airport, where there was ticket waiting for me—to New Orleans.

Now, you understand, this is August and it's the deep Deep South. Only people who actually come from Louisiana or someplace on the Gulf of Mexico can understand what it's like down there in the summer. This is a place where you might go if you've been bad in a former life.

When I get off the plane the temperature is around a hundred degrees and the humidity must be ninety-five percent. I think I'm going to melt walking the fifty yards from the plane to the terminal.

Nobody does anything down there in August except ride around in the car to catch a breeze, stay in the house with the air conditioner on (if they have one), or just lie, semi-comatose, in the shade.

My father meets me outside the terminal. And I am not disappointed. You know how it is sometimes; you haven't seen somebody for a long time and you're yearning to see them again—suddenly there they are and somehow it's never quite what you expected? Well, not with my old man. Here he is again, just the way I've always remembered him—a very big guy, joking, energetic, young-looking for his age (he was fifty-one then), with a big, smoldering cigar stuck in his face. To this day I love the smell of cigars because they remind me of him.

His face is red—too much sun, I guess, and also because he has a tendency to eat and drink too much (red meat and beer); his blood pressure always hovers up near the roof, but he doesn't care. Living for tomorrow is not a big thing with my father.

A red face maybe also because he was one of those guys who seemed to shave with an ax or a rusty butcher knife—his face always looked like rough sandpaper. His hair, in those days, was just beginning to turn a little gray. My father, rough and tough, just like old Hemingway.

He takes my suitcase and throws it in the back seat of his top-down convertible—tosses this heavy suitcase with one hand like it was a matchbox. This is the suitcase I thought I was going to have a heart attack dragging across the terminal. I think he used to do these things for effect, as if to say: "You're with a real man now, kid, gimme that suitcase!"

When we got to the motel, I discover that we're staying in the same room. I am not happy to hear this. All my life I have been fortunate enough to have my own room: first, in my small house out in Queens, up in the attic—it was my own little kingdom—a lonely kingdom but a private kingdom nevertheless. After that, I lived in studio apartments, always alone, pathologically alone, like Dostoevsky's underground man. I had developed, over this time, a terrible fear of sharing my space with anybody else. On the rare occasions when I brought someone home with *me, I always made sure that was I sufficiently nervous (no big stretch), or just plain cold enough so that a girl understood she wasn't invited to stay over.*

And there was another reason why I was upset to discover we were in the same room. I was with my father so rarely that I had never seen him with any of his clothes off, not even in so much as a bathing suit. (He didn't go to the beach because his back was bad and he wasn't able to swim.) And, I guess, he was also— no other way to put it—a prude.

So, between his attitude about such things and my own perpetual shyness, I was surprised to discover I was going to be sleeping in the same room as him. Immediately I go into a kind of teeth-chattering state of anxiety. Now, despite his own conservative attitude about things, I knew why only I had a problem— because he grew up in a generation where people were right on top of each other, where you just didn't get that much privacy.

I want to ask him to get me a separate room. But then I think—what's that gonna sound like? Is he gonna think I'm some kind of sissy or what? At the very least, if I ask for another room he'd be insulted. I mean, he has invited me down here to be with him. And after all, it's not as if I was going to sleep right next to him in the same bed—my bed was on the other side of the room.

What I really dreaded, though, was the idea of: (a) him seeing me naked and (b) me seeing him. What is this all about? I don't know—maybe I just didn't want to be so familiar with him—he had established the strangeness between us by leaving me and I wasn't going to do anything to let him off the hook so easily. But that's all retrospective psychoanalysis. Anyway, I grit my teeth and just shut up. He gets a couple of beers out of a small refrigerator in the room and that helps lighten things up a little.

After I unpack, he decides he's gonna take me right out to see his fertilizer plant. Naturally, I expected him to do this, I mean it's natural for a father to show off what he does to his son, but with my father, this stuff had an added dimension to it—one that I know is going to seem sadly familiar to a lot of the men out here tonight: my father always competed with me. He was always having to show me who the tougher guy was. Not that there was much of a contest. I grew up, shy and weird and asthmatic, surrounded by doting and/or hysterical women. My father was not around to demonstrate the manly art of being a man.

But that's the way it always was with him—if we were throwing a ball or pitching horseshoes, he always tried to make it clear who was the better man. One thing he did that always certified this, and it was the easiest way for him, was to show me his plants, his bridges, his constructions. He would always point out to me the tallest building on a site, the largest erection in the place and ask me what I thought of it. Sure enough, it was his, he built it.

Once, when I was a kid, he took me out to Long Island, where he was the foreman in the construction of a huge tower at the Brookhaven National Laboratories—where they did nuclear experiments. We drive up to this gigantic, thick, white tower—a smokestack of some sort that must have been three hundred feet tall—and he says: "There it is, kid—that's my tower!'

So we drive to the fertilizer plant way out in the backwoods, somewhere a few miles outside Baton Rouge—which is no big metropolis to begin with. It's very humid, to say the least, and so hot I can hardly take a breath. Most of the people we see were just sort of lying, like dead bodies, on the side of the road.

The plant is very close to the bayou—the swamp—and a thick, almost yellow-colored mist hung over us just about at the level of a low tree branch.

Everywhere, men are toiling away like ants. There are shirtless guys carrying around big pieces of lumber and steel reinforcing rods. There is the sound of heavy machinery—a slap-thump, you know, the kind you hear at big construction sites: hoomp-bamp! hoomp-bamp!—and hundreds of pipes everywhere, in pieces, joined to other pipes, coming out of huge metal containers and tanks; and steam was hissing and billowing out, joining with the mist drifting in from beyond the trees.

In construction sites up north, there are always a few men you'll notice—usually they're a bit older, guys with flannel shirts or steel hats hanging around telling the other guys what to do—foremen.

Well, when you combine that standard behavior with the southern way of doing things in August in the Louisiana backwoods, you get a lot of hanging around.... A bunch of good ol' boys were drinking coffee and yakking with the "girls"—girls no matter if they were in their forties, you understand—they were the girls. "Sheee...you don't mean that. Why, I was over to Charley McBride's last Tuesday—no, I believe it was last Wednesday..." Dippin' and divin' and bullshittin' all around. But when me and my father come up, all the talking stops temporarily because my father is the big boss from up north.

There's a brief silence and one of the "girls," a woman with a tight yellow dress and a beehive hairdo, says, "That your boy, Phil? He sure is goood-lookin'

—just like his daddy." And she gives my father a little dig in the ribs with her elbow.

Well, I gotta tell you—I am shocked. I can't believe it. What is this? A reference to sex? In front of my father?

My father's face turns even redder than it was. Like I said, my father was a prude—at least I thought he was. Around me, he never referred to anything sexual. No—wait a minute, he did, one time. We were driving home from a Knicks game—I was about twenty—he was taking me back to my mother's house, and we stopped for a red light on Queens Boulevard. You understand, at this point, I had seen him for a total of about twelve hours in the last six months—and he says to me—out of the blue: "Well, um, Mike, what about girls?" I did a triple take and practically jumped out of the car. "Girls!!?" There was a frozen moment, the light changed, and that was the end of my sex education from my father.

But now, here, this woman is saying to my father, "Phil, you gotta bring your boy over to my house. You know how you like my cookin'!" and she bats her eyelashes at him.

Jesus Christ! I am suddenly forced to entertain the thought that my father is messing around down here. But—my father didn't do that! He just worked, he built things. It was very confusing to me—confusing to my leftover little-boy's pure, romantic notion of my dad the adventurer—and maybe, though I couldn't have been conscious of it at the time, still a left-over feeling of my father betraying my mother somehow, though, God knows, they hadn't so much as touched each other in two decades.

Well, anyway, he laughs nervously and hustles me back into another office—the real office, where the boss has his desk. This was more like it. Immediately he is my old father again, explaining things, showing me blueprints of this and that, telling me how he's going to make six different kinds of fertilizer that will turn Louisiana green overnight and make the fields sprout six foot ears of corn.

On and on he went, and of course, it really didn't matter to me what exactly he was saying. I was happy just to be where my father was, smell his cigar smoke—just look at him and hear his voice.

Whenever I visited him in the locations of his grandeur, I was never disappointed. If you've lived even a little, you begin to understand that such idealization could be extremely dangerous, but I was twenty-three and pretty retarded in my development—not once did he seem to have any faults.

So I just sit there, soaking up his "bossism." Being around him like this was like having my identity recharged, or charged—there wasn't a whole hell of a lot of it to begin with. I could run for months on just ten minutes of exposure to my father's self-confidence.

Suddenly, the whole trailer tilts. I think it might be an earthquake. There's a lot of noise and laughing outside, then the door to my father's office bangs open and I see the biggest man I have ever seen outside a basketball game or the circus. This giant looks around for a second or two, grins, and says, "Well, hi there, e'r-body!"

This guy was Bill Green; he was the one who actually ran the plant for my father—day to day. Bill Green came from Texas and he was the goodest of good ol' boys. Now when I say he was huge, I don't mean to say he was fat. I mean this guy had to be at least six-five, maybe more, and had to weigh at least three hundred pounds—but there was nothing fat about him. He was an amazing sight alright, but the strangest thing about him was that he had a tiny little head, or maybe it was just a regular-size head, but it looked small on a body that big. And another weird thing about him—as big as he was—he didn't have a big, booming voice. He had rather a quiet, almost gentle voice. He was so massive that I'm sure he must have known that people's initial reaction to him was fear, or maybe down-right terror. So what he did was to develop a very calm, quiet voice. He never made any sudden moves.

And yet, despite Bill's gentleness, I disliked him. Why? Because he was intruding on my father's legitimate turf, stealing away his command. To take away my father's power was to take mine away too. So, after shaking hands, the polite thing to do, I just glared at him without saying anything.

My father tosses me the car keys—"Take a ride around, " he says, "we'll be done in about an hour." Frowning my best frown, just in case anybody doesn't know I am upset at being cast aside—I snort and leave the office. Some of the girls kid me a little on the way out of the office—but I am too pissed off at my sudden banishment to even talk to them.

I get in the car and drive around Baton Rouge for a while. God, what an alien world! Gun shops, old mossy-looking mansions like in a forties movie—people with worn, torn clothes, cars so old they look like they are from the thirties. And everywhere the simmering, steaming heat. I stop in a general store and get a bottle of Coke out of an ancient refrigerator. I could hardly understand what people were saying, their accents were so thick and they spoke so slowly—too slowly for the buzz-saw New York ear to comprehend.

I drive around for a little while longer, then make it on back to the plant site and pick up my father. He drives us back to the Holiday Inn.

At about five o'clock, my father says: "We better go over to the coffee shop and get something to eat; we gotta go to sleep early because we're getting up at dawn."

"What for?"

"We're going fishing."

Fishing. Well, OK, me and my father have gone fishing before. Besides, whatever he wants to do, you know—it's OK with me.

"Yeah," he says, "we're going fishing in the bayou. It's an overnight trip, a camp-out. It's a little rough but you'll like it."

Oh—an overnight. Now I'm in my second major anxiety attack since I arrived. I am already trying to get used to the idea of being in the same room with my father, now I'm going to have to sleep in the same tent!? And who knows— probably with strangers along, too.

Sure enough, my father says, "Oh, yeah, and Bill— and Bill is coming with us.

Oh, no! I hate this. This is terrible! I'm a city boy, one-hundred percent bookworm, concrete-playground, neurotic city boy, and now I'm going to have to go out God knows where and sleep on the ground?! And let me tell you, this is not the Adirondack State Park we're talking about here. This is the bayou—a swamp—a fucking jungle, for Christ's sake! Hot. Nasty. This is a place where there are diseased malarial mosquitoes, snakes, and alligators—not Bronx Zoo alligators in little glass "environments," but out there—right next to you! This is real. And on top of all this I am going to be crammed in, trapped, sleeping next to people. And yet, and yet, you see, I am excited about this too, because I am finally getting a chance to be right out there with Ernest Hemingway—my father. If I have come down here to soak up my father's essence, to get from him what I thought I needed to get to be a real man, not a puling little momma's boy—well, then, what better test could there be than to go out there in the wild and confront the Big Fish?

Next morning, it's dawn, around 5:00 A.M.—the sun is just coming up—my father shakes me awake. No matter—and again, this may seem familiar to some of the men out there—no matter what time I ever got up, even if it was two in the morning, my father would be up a half hour before me. Get up, cold shower, get those clothes on, and get out for a day's work! You know how it is with these guys from this generation: "Hey, you still asleep?! Jeez! I can't believe you're still lying there. I already been up for five hours, built the Hoover Dam, made breakfast for an entire logging camp—and you're still asleep?!"

Anyway, it was reveille at dawn. By the time my eyes open, he is headed out the door. "Hafta check the car." Right—check the car—air pressure, carburetor, axles, steering ratio.

I take advantage of his absence and jump out of bed, grab my clothes, and run into the bathroom. I get dressed in there so he won't see me. So there we are, both suited up; we grab a cup of coffee at the motel coffee shop and hit the road.

Off the main highway to a one-lane blacktop, then off that road onto a dirt road, into the woods—the scenery getting more tangled and thick as the road gets narrower and bumpier.

We arrive about a half hour later, coasting to a stop on what is now no longer a road but just a dirt track—at Bill Green's trailer. Bill has planted his trailer as far as it was possible to be—away from any human habitation. He lives, literally, right next to the swamp. Right outside the trailer an old World War II army surplus jeep is parked.

We go into the trailer and there's Bill, with his head almost banging into the roof. "Well...good mornin'! How y'all doin' this mornin'?" He hands us two steaming mugs of black coffee that looked like boiling tar. I am already buzzing from the first cup of coffee but I am with the guys now and I don't want to seem freaky so I sip this molten lava. Whoa!

My father and Bill are talking and getting out fishing gear to load into the jeep—so I look around the trailer. It is a total, absolute mess. It seems this guy surely has never been married, never lived with anybody—except, I suppose, with his parents once upon a time. He is the original, wild American boy—just right out there on the frontier, doin' it.

The trailer is full of guns: shotguns, handguns, rifles, ammunition, gun-cleaning oil, gun rags, gun magazines—and there are at least three cats and four dogs, all scratching and meowing and barking and running in and out of the door. Inside and out, the trailer, which was one of those old silver-bullet-looking *things*—*is scratched and dented all over. It looks like a tube of toothpaste some giant has drop-kicked over Niagara Falls.*

The walls are bare except for two framed pictures. One was a fly-specked commendation from the Army: "For bravery in action…" The other picture, hanging over a sinkful of dirty pots and dishes, was of Bill, looking young and uncreased in his uniform in front of what looks like a medieval church. There he was, as huge as ever, wide grin, with his arm around a beautiful blond girl. Bill came back into the trailer to get some more gear, and I asked him, "Who's that in the picture?"

"Aw, that," he says, "that's nothin'—that's not important." And he opens the fridge to get a can of beer. Not important, but all of a sudden there is a small chill in the air, and it's not from the fridge. So, I shut my mouth immediately.

Bill is slurping down the beer—it's still only about 6:00 A.M., right? And this is the third beer I've seen him drink already. In fact, it's only the third of what I would guess had to be at least three dozen cans of beer he drank that day. I have never seen, before or since, anybody drink as much beer as Bill did. In his refrigerator there were three big thermos jugs of coffee he had made for the camping trip, a couple bags full of coffee beans, and maybe three cases of beer…. Nothing else—not milk, not bread, not butter—nothing but beer. And there were several more cases of it—Coors—stacked next to the refrigerator. This guy chain-drank beer. As soon as he finished one can—he sucked it up just like a regular person would drink down a tiny cup of orange juice….shusshupphe!—he would crush the can in his fist like a piece of tissue paper and toss it into an overflowing garbage can full of beer cans.

After loading up and tying down all the provisions and equipment on the back and sides of the jeep, we get in and spin out of his front yard onto a dirt road that runs alongside the river.

Bill drives like a maniac. I knew right then and there that I was driving with a person that might very well kill me. He is going thirty miles an hour around tight bumpy turns that run right over the lip of a hill going straight, fifteen, twenty feet down to the river. And on the straight parts of the road—this bumpy, pitted dirt road—he was doing forty or more, driving with one hand gripping the wheel and the other hand wrapped around a beer can. He threw empty cans over his shoulder into the back—(which I had to dodge or get beaned in the head)— then reached back and snatched another one from the seat next to me. And I'm thinking to myself—yup, this is it—I'm probably gonna die.

Well, I thought, I haven't been a really bad person—I probably won't go to hell. Of course I haven't done most of the things I wanted to do in life—being so scared all the time—and that was a shame, to die so unfulfilled. But still, I've seen a few things, done a few things, and besides, to die in the company of some real guys, true warrior types—well, that was alright—that was the way to go. My father would take care of me in heaven. I looked at my father, who was riding in the front—his hands were gripped onto the roll bar and his cigar was clamped in his teeth. I couldn't see his face so I couldn't tell if he was enjoying this or not. I imagined he was—it was the kind of thing he liked—cruising at the extreme edge of life.

We finally, after about twenty minutes of this carnival ride from hell, slow down and stop. We have arrived at a beat-up, rattling wooden dock, half floating out onto the river. The sun is full up now, but it's pretty shady where we are because the trees are heavy with broad, almost prehistoric-looking leaves and thick vines. The flowers growing on the banks are also huge and alive, more like animals than plants—bright red, blue, yellow—all different colors. They look hungry.

Birds are sitting in the branches and on logs near the bank, staring at us, making what seems to me to be unfriendly-sounding noises—like they were irritated that we had showed up without an appointment. There are strange—to me strange—noises everywhere: grating sounds, cackles, hisses. It is ominous. I look over at my father. He has a wide smile on his face. I can see he is loving this.

We get into a boat tied to the dock by a worn rope, and then we are out on the river—into another world entirely.

The noises die down almost immediately, and we hear almost nothing but the occasional cry of a bird, the mosquito buzz sound of the outboard motor, and the slow whooshing of the water along the sides of the boat. Sometimes there is a quick splash near the bank, maybe an animal jumping into the water.

The bayou snakes around and around. Down in southern Louisiana, the Mississippi breaks up into thousands of little tributaries that run in all directions. The river we are on is a kind of casual, old river, a river that retired from service many eons ago. It hardly seems to move at all.

As we putt-putt slowly on, with the big, strange trees leaning over the banks, time seems to slow down until it almost stops. I feel a warm, mellow glow spread through me, I am almost—it was a completely unfamiliar feeling to me—I am almost relaxed, drifting and drifting....

"Wouldn't do that I was you," said Bill.

"Do what?" I ask him.

"Trail my hand in the water there."

"Why not?"

"Gators," he says, tossing a crunched beer can into the bottom of the boat.

Gators?! Alligators?! Yup. Sure enough, I look over the side of the boat and see, not five feet away, two huge black eyes staring at me. I whip my hand back into the boat. Whoa! I am astounded. I look at my hand to see if it is still all there.

We go on and on and it gets wilder and wilder. We pass overgrown fields, broken-down old shacks in the distance, the odd crumbling dock with a boat tied to it. Not a soul in sight.

After about half an hour more, Bill cuts the motor and we float over to a dock. Bill pulls the boat over, ties it up, and walks up the bank to a dilapidated shack about fifty feet into the woods.

In a minute, he comes out, followed by a kid about fifteen or sixteen years old. He is wearing nothing but a pair of faded red shorts—no shirt, no shoes—carrying a rifle in his right hand and a khaki-colored duffel bag in his left hand.

They get into the boat and the kid sits just opposite me at the front. I look at him—he is like an alien creature. He is medium sized, maybe five-eight or so—thin but very wiry-steely looking, with short, sandy hair and strange, wolf-looking pale blue eyes. His fingers look knobby and bumpy, like they have been broken many times and healed funny, and all over his body he has these tiny, and some not-so-tiny, white and red scars. He is sunburned all over—a dark tan color. The gun is a lever-action Winchester, model 94—thirty-caliber. I knew a little about guns because I had always been fascinated by them and in fact always wanted one. But, of course, out in Queens, at least in the fifties and sixties, there wasn't a whole lot of wild-game hunting going on.

Bill explained to us that the kid is our guide. His name is Joe—Bill pronounced it "Zzho"—and he is a Cajun.

Now, I don't know what a Cajun is—some combination I thought, of Indian, French, and black. But whatever he is, Joe is definitely not something I have ever seen before. Up close, I can see his skin is a reddish-tan color, almost like the dirt and mud on the banks of the river. He kept his mouth shut—didn't so much as smile.

Like I said, for me, it was like seeing somebody from outer space and I'm sure he felt the same way about me. Here I am, with my sneakers and jeans and my "Dump the Hump" (Hubert Humphrey) T-shirt, my imitation street-fighting-man-Jewish-Emilio-Zapata mustache and my curly thick dark hair. He was a little creepy with that cold, flat wolf-glare of his—it made me feel a little like a rabbit or some other form of about-to-be-devoured prey.

Looking at him, I was also thinking, he was our guide? We're already out in God-knows-where, so where could we be going, to what wild, lost place were we headed worse than where we were now—that we needed a guide?

Fear is gathering at the corners of my temporary relaxed state—little rodents of worry and doubt nibbling at me. In fact, the river almost suddenly got more dark and narrow—the trees grew even closer, closed their heads almost directly over the stream now so that the sunlight was only filtering in patches. The grating noise of animals and birds was getting louder, more frequent. I felt hard eyes staring at me from behind the trees and under the water.

Finally, we pulled over again to the bank of the river, or what I at first thought was the bank of the river, pushed aside some thick green foliage, and emerged into an even narrower, darker stream. We pursued this little watery path for about ten minutes and then, parting some more thick plants and vines that hung down from the trees, emerged into a little wide-open lake. Jutting into the lake was a small promontory—just bare, red-brown dirt with one huge oak presiding over it—this was to be our campsite for the night. We coasted the boat over, tied it up to a stump, and got out.

We climbed up the bank, put all the fishing gear and other stuff down, and started to put up the tent. And...my worst fears came true. It was a small tent, and I mean small, like Boy Scout–sized, an army surplus tent. I'm thinking... we're all gonna sleep in this canvas closet? Oh, shit. Trapped. Claustrophobia squared. I gritted my teeth—calm down, calm down, be a man. I resigned myself to one long night—I knew I wouldn't get one minute of sleep.

Everything had been progressing in a dreamlike state all day. It was getting to be late afternoon, almost early evening. We figured we'd better go out on the water and get some fishing done before dusk.

This was a whole different experience from being on a northern lake. In the north, there's a cool, crisp, clean feeling to the water and the woods. On a lake in, let's say, upstate New York, if the moon is out, everything is bright and sharp, all toned up and fitted correctly. But down on the bayou it's something completely different—there's a flat, fuzzy, soft feeling to everything; muddy, misty, steamy, lazy....But still, the silence out on the water—that reverential beautiful peace is mostly the same.

We threw our lines in and waited....

The air was fairly still and all you heard was the sound of the sinker hitting the water—plop—and the sound of the slight breeze rustling the leaves in the trees on the banks. Far away, there was the tiny buzz of a small prop plane, maybe a crop duster. In the east, the sky was deep violet and in the west it was turning orange-crimson-red.

Then, a shift—things got completely still and even more humid. In an instant the sun slipped away and the sky turned blue, then black, and filled with stars. This few minutes we had, of suspended beauty, of the turning of things, was ended by the sudden attack of every mosquito in the state of Louisiana, each one the size of a B-52, descending on us like crazed kamikaze pilots. We pulled in our lines and made back to the shore as fast as we could—rubbing insect repellent all over ourselves.

We jumped out of the boat and rubbed more of the stuff on our bodies—onto every space available—under our clothes, on our eyelids, everywhere. The only one who didn't bother with this at all was Joe—he was beyond such city-slicker silliness. He didn't care about the mosquitoes and the mosquitoes didn't care about him, either.

I don't know what it was—either his blood was too acidy for them or he was so scarred up they couldn't get through to his veins. In any case, the guy was immune.

Sufficiently coated with antibug glop, we went and gathered up some wood and soon had a good fire going. We sat around eating big, thick slices of fried beef that we speared out of a black frying pan and slurped up big delicious spoonfuls of baked beans from a pot at the edge of the fire. Delicious! Bill was taking a break from beer and was passing around a quart bottle of bourbon—the stuff must have been a hundred proof.

The mosquitoes and the bugs were amazing. They had no fear whatsoever, no sense of danger—as if no man had ever tried to squash one of them before. I felt something on my shoulder and reached to swat it off. I felt something big crawl right into my palm. I whipped my hand around and looked at this thing—it looked like a prehistoric animal, armored and horned. I was disgusted and tossed it onto the fire, where it popped like a small firecracker. I shivered—"Jesus, what was that?"—my father thought this was pretty funny: "Whatsa matter, never saw a locust before?" A locust? Shit, that was something from the Old Testament! Where was I?

There was a sudden, crashing noise twenty feet away in the bushes. I jumped. "Hey, calm down," Bill said, "It's not even their feeding time yet." Ha-ha. They're dying laughing.

Supper went on, more beef and beans and bourbon—we were getting pretty mellow, pretty loose. I realized that Bill and Joe were talking about guns. Not to be left out, I volunteered: "Hey, I saw plenty of guns at the Chicago convention." (On TV I saw them, but I didn't tell them that).

"Yup," I say, the old-time cowboy now—"plenty o' guns."

Joe looked at me—totally blank. "Whuzat?" It turned out—and this was incredible to me—that he had no idea what the Chicago convention was. In fact, he didn't know what a convention was at all. He just knew that there was a president and he lived in Washington, which was somewhere up north. How the president got to be the president, Joe had no idea, nor did he care in the slightest. Astounding! This guy's background and culture were completely foreign to me— he could have been from someplace in the Amazon jungle.

I instantly develop a very unfortunate attitude toward this kid—extremely condescending. How, I think, how on earth can anybody be so stupid and ignorant? Jesus, America is truly doomed. How can this guy live and function in the same country as me and my friends?

I didn't say anything like this, of course, but that's exactly what I was thinking. I look over at my father, a political aficionado, an old City College communist from the thirties, and wonder what was he's thinking. He didn't seem to care much about it; he was just slugging down the bourbon. I look back at Joe, who, as usual, is regarding me with those dead-blue eyes of his.... And I'm thinking... my life, all my glorious days on picket lines and demonstrations—all my political science courses, all the candidates and the war protests and the riots in the streets and blacks and whites and assassinations—this strange, wild guy doesn't know or care one bit about any of it; his idea of life is fishing, shooting, and going to the tavern and maybe getting in a good knife fight on Saturday night. He is a caveman.

By now, we are all half drunk—except Joe, whose calm demeanor never flick-ered. The air is thick, warm, and very humid. It is determined by the great white hunters, Bill and my father, that it is time to turn in because we are going to get up at dawn to get in a good day's fishing.

Joe, carrying his rifle, goes to lie down on a blanket spread out under the oak tree while I have to get into this miniature tent. Bill is over on one side of the tent, my father in the middle, then me. Thank God, I thought, at least I didn't have to sleep between these two guys—who knows but they might both roll over at the same time and crush me like a bug.

But let me tell you, even if I weren't lying between them, this was small com-fort, friends—things were bad enough as they were. I was lying, sweating, hot, covered with sticky mosquito gloop, on top of a humid-damp sleeping bag, right next to my father—two inches away from him. I hadn't been so close to him in— well, ever, that I could remember.

After all, he took off when I was four.... When I was a baby, I guess, he must have held me. And I dimly remembered that sometimes when he came home from work when I was a very little kid, he would lift me up in his arms—but for twen-ty years now, we had hardly even so much as shaken hands with each other. It was a terribly unsettling feeling to be so close to him.

My father was practically asleep already. He was one of those guys that has either no conscience or a very clear one, anyway—because he could fall asleep the second his head hit a pillow or a rock in the middle of swamp, as the case may be. You know these people? How do they do that? How do they get away with such blissful freedom? I, of course, am just the opposite—I could toss down an entire bottle of sleeping pills, smash myself in the head with a sledgehammer, and still lie there stark awake, turning every little detail in my life over in my brain.

Anyway, sleep was totally out of the question. After all, here I am in a pup tent, right next my father, snoring, and right next to him snoring even louder, like some giant warthog, was Bill. All this and the night was so astoundingly humid you could wring the pillow in your hands and probably get a full cup of water. The tent itself was so damp from humidity, when I touched it it felt like it was raining outside. I was sweating like I'd never sweated before.

I lay there, thinking about Joe, lying outside, asleep with his rifle in his arms. And suddenly, I was ashamed of myself—all the nasty, condescending thoughts I had about him before, his "ignorance," his "primitive" nature. What was I with all my knowledge, anyway?—such as it was at the age of twenty-three? Oh, yeah, I could march and yell and carry signs, I could make ironic jokes and read Henry James, and so what? Next to him, in his world, I was like a two-month-old baby. I would starve to death if I wasn't near a supermarket—the slightest movement in the woods earlier had sent me into the shivers. And never could I imagine sleeping outside, under the stars, on top of the dirt, on a thin blanket surround-ed by bugs and snakes and wild animals. Live and learn....

Despite all my nerves, I must have drifted off for at least a little bit, then I was awake again, aware of a certain...urge.

I had been essentially so worried all day long, everything was so strange and overwhelming, and I had been drinking beer and coffee and bourbon—I realized that I had not once pissed all day long.

So now, here I am, in the middle of the jungle, nine o'clock at night, dead, pitch-black outside except for the starlight, and I have to take a piss. I'm about two feet from the tent-flap opening, but my father is between me and it and he's asleep. But I'm worried—if I get up, move around, make a noise, what will hap-pen? Maybe these two guys will think it's an animal and thump me with an ax, and then—if I even did make it outside the tent—maybe Joe would put a bullet through my head with his trusty Winchester. I wanted so much just to get out of there and get to the bushes, but to do that I would have to bump into or at least touch my father—and that, for some reason, caused me unbearable anxiety.

So I lay there, completely rigid, hot, covered with sweat, the snoring in the tent getting louder and louder till it was rumbling around in my head like a hun-dred bowling balls. I am tense as a wire and my bladder is expanding and expand-ing. I feel now that any sudden movement might cause it to blow up. I have graphic, awful visions of my bladder exploding and flooding my body, poisoning me.

Finally it gets so bad, and I am so absolutely convinced that I will explode and die, that I make a very small, careful motion to get up and get out of the tent. And as I move, ever so slightly, the snoring stops as if both of them have just been waiting for me to move—and Bill chuckles. There's a pause. I say, "I gotta go, I gotta go." And Bill says, "You go out there this time of night, son—and some-thin's gonna eat you."

Oh man, I couldn't believe it. I said, "Are you kidding me?—cause I really have to take a piss."

My father starts to laugh. Big joke, right? These creeps, they think it's hilarious. What do they do with it? Do they absorb it into their bones? How can they sleep all night after drinking all that stuff?

I make a move to get up, and Bill says, "I'm serious, kid—you better not. You get out in them bushes, there's bobcats, there's snakes."

Jesus! Of course, that's it for me. As bad as I need to go, and it is as bad as I have ever needed to go, I am not going out there in that antediluvian swamp to have my tender Queens College genitals ripped off by some ravaging beast.

So, I don't move again—I stay right where I am. I know I am going to die. I picture what heaven might be like—will I even go to heaven? The back of my body starts to go numb from my head, right down my spine, down through my legs and feet. The beginning of death, perhaps—but no, I'm not off the hook yet—I can feel a rash breaking out all over the front of my body, itching and burning everywhere. My nose starts itching and then running and my eyes twitch and jump and the muscles all over my face begin to quiver.

Just at the very moment when I am saying my conscious good-byes to the world as I've known it in my brief twenty-three years, I open my eyes...and yes, the small spot of tent right over my face is lighter—the sun has begun to rise. In my terror and hysteria, I have lost track of time entirely and now it is actually dawn.

Instantly, as if they had set an alarm clock, my tentmates, these two bears, stop snoring, get up, and immediately go outside. I can hear them walking around outside, then I hear some sticks breaking and can smell the fire.

It is safe for me to move now. I get up off my sweat-soaked sleeping bag and slowly, like a man who had been in a coma for years, feel my way blindly outside the tent. Like a zombie, I walk over, stiff-legged, to the bushes and piss. A never-ending stream gushes out of me—relief! But, not relief, because unfortunately, I have been through so much, have wound myself up so badly, that I am over the top now and I have become one huge, twitching nerve—a veritable carnival sideshow of psychosomatic explosions. I start to sneeze and can't stop, my nose runs like a river, over my mustache, down the back of my throat, I feel like mice are running through my body, my teeth ache, my head is throbbing, sharp pains stab my muscles, my bones feel as though they are actually cracking. I see colored lights moving. I am about to fall over.

I stumble over to the fire. They are both sitting around, drinking black coffee and eating bacon. I realize they are staring at me—I'm sure I was a sight to see—

but now I can only perceive them through a swimming haze. I feel, suddenly, a great, towering red hatred for them, these son-of-a-bitch, John Wayne, he-man fuckers.

I look at my father. How could he take me—his own son, a sensitive youth— into the middle of this godforsaken jungle and subject me to this torment!? I think of Abraham, ready to murder his own son, the knife poised over his heart. They stare at me—I stare at them—and I feel that I am not of their species. I hate men—all men—I want to kill them, with their greasy, bacon fingers and their stupid grins. So what am I, then? Am I a man? Am I a woman? A visitor from another planet? Some kind of undiscovered freak of nature? Well, whatever a man is, it's not me. A man goes out in the jungle, he puts his head down, and goes right to sleep, in the middle of wildcats, mosquitoes, snakes, hundred-degree temperatures—and then wakes up, yawns, and says, "Whoooie! I feel good this morning! What's for breakfast?"

For a couple of minutes they tried to kid me out of it—tell me to sit down and have some coffee, c'mon, it's no big deal.... But it's no use—I am over the edge. I think they realize then that they have a certified hospital case on their hands— that the fishing trip is over.

Joe is looking at me with intense fascination. He has never seen a human being act like this and probably will never see anything like it again. He is storing it up for telling his friends at the tavern—"Shee, I saw a city boy th'other day, you would not believe..."

I am in a sort of dream—I watch, detached, as they packed up the tent and all the gear and load it (and me) back into the boat. I keep my eyes half closed, I don't want to see them looking at me—I feel so sick and ashamed. I can feel the heat of the sun coming through my clothes and hear the low sound of their voices floating, it seemed from far off.

I am afraid to move or speak.

Eventually, we get back to Bill's trailer—I hardly remember the jeep ride back. And there, like a miracle, manna from heaven, it turns out that Bill has an air conditioner in the little bedroom in his trailer, and—more miraculous—he has a Contac, my favorite allergy pill. He gives it to me with a tall glass of ice water— ahhh! That pill seems so beautiful to me, red and white, like a religious object— salvation—the holy grail. I knew I was going to be saved. I lay back on the bed, and in the cool breeze of the air conditioner, I fall asleep.

I wake up a few hours later, it's slightly dark in the room—must have been around dusk. I look around, realize what had happened, and instantly burn with shame.

I get up, put my clothes on, and stumble into the kitchen. My father is sitting at a small, Formica-topped table, drinking coffee, and Bill is outside, messing around under the hood of the jeep.

My father hands me a cup of black coffee and says, "How are you, kid?" Ahhh...He has forgiven me! I can feel it. I sip my coffee, thinking of what on earth to say. There are so many important things to tell him, so many years of fear and yearning, so much—so much to tell him. But my father must sense I am about to unburden myself of twenty years of confessions and, possibly, accusations—and he wants no part of it. Instantly, the look of concern on his face disappears and he gets that familiar hard look on his face, distant, unapproachable. He pushes back his chair and says, "Well, looks like you're gonna live. We better be heading to the motel." I want to grab him—"Wait!"—but it's too late, he is out the door. I get up and follow him. We say good-bye to Bill, who I somehow know I will never see again. He shakes my hand and I can tell he pities me. God, what a depressing situation.

It is about nine o'clock. I lay on my bed in the motel room, staring across at my father, lying on his bed, reading the New Orleans paper. A tremendous silence lies between us, and the distance between his bed and mine seems immense. I have ruined everything and I just don't know what to say.

After about a half hour of this, he suddenly throws down the paper, lights up a cigar, and says, "Whaddya say we go into New Orleans, get some French food, and hear some Dixieland?" Thank God, I think. A reprieve. This was just like my father—he couldn't bear silence and he couldn't bear doing nothing—it drove him crazy. The way he solved problems was by doing something—taking action. Well, that was fine with me.

We jump into the convertible, put the top down—it was a mellow night, not too hot now—and we burn rubber out of the parking lot, onto the highway to New Orleans.

We park the car down near the waterfront and walk to the French Quarter. There are a lot of lights and noise but it isn't overwhelming like Times Square— its scale is more human. We pass by some sleazy sex-show honky-tonks and then we are in the actual French Quarter—a place that seems out of sync with the modern world. Old wooden buildings, pastel-colored and trimmed—decorated like cakes—iron grillwork, latticed windows, balconies.

You're surrounded by soft, colored lights, and every twenty yards you emerge into some small, beautiful plaza with a bubbling fountain full of goldfish. People are walking slow and friendly, they smile at each other—flowers perfume the air.

And everywhere—music—pours out of nightclubs and houses; bright trumpets and lilting, sliding clarinets, twangy banjos, pianos pounding, and drums thumping. It's as if the very air is singing and dancing.

We enter a courtyard, find a French restaurant, and have a delicious shrimp dish and a few glasses of white wine. Then out again into those soft, pulsing, beautiful streets. The night is shimmering and alive in a way I had never felt it before—my father walking right along next to me. I was happy.

We wind up at Preservation Hall, an old-time wooden, plank-floored music hall, kept just like it was sixty years before. Some of the original guys still played there, old-timers in their seventies and eighties. For a dollar they'd take requests—play anything you wanted. They looked frail, these wrinkled old men, with their faces marked by things I could never have understood—but man, they could still play. That music was still alive—pumping and throbbing.

Dixieland. It's the most triumphant, eternal kind of music. In fact, I don't think there is any kind of music more personal or more human. It wails, it blasts, it throbs—it sweeps you away. Dixieland says: this is life, and that's all there is, but we're gonna go on, because in spite of everything, it's so beautiful. And if it isn't beautiful...well, the only thing left to do is go on anyway....

We sit there, clapping and swaying and pounding our feet on the floor while those eternal old men keep wailing away.

Eventually, though, it had to end. My father looks at his watch—it's one in the morning. And I have to catch a plane at 10 A.M. We walk out of the Quarter, out of fairyland, and back to the car.

On the highway, I sit next to my father with my eyes closed. I don't want this night to end. I feel closer to him than I ever have. I am buzzing and floating with wine and that beautiful music still winging in my head.

Slowly but surely, the magic of the night ebbed away. The wine wore off, the music drifted off. Outside, I could hear cars speeding by on the highway. Here it

260 / MIKE FEDER

was again—another of the endless good-byes that seemed to make up my life. The moon is shining through the window. I look over at my father's bed and I feel so far away from him—as if I am floating out to sea.

The next morning. Business as usual. "Morning. How ya doin', kid? Let's get the show on the road." I throw my stuff in the suitcase, and we grab a cup of coffee for the trip to the airport.

We shake hands at the departure gate and I turn and walk out to the plane, feeling heavy as lead. I get on and find a window seat facing the terminal.

The engines rev up and I look over to the terminal and see my father standing on the observation deck, not thirty feet away from me. The plane is in the shadow of the control tower, and I don't think he sees me.

My father...I never really knew him. I hardly even thought of him as my father most of the time—just some fabulous stranger, traveling all over the world, like a character in a myth or an adventure novel.

And as I saw him standing there, I was overcome with the revelation—he was just like everybody else! His face was heavy and full of lines; his eyes were sad and searching. And at that moment I felt even closer to him than I had the night before—really, truly connected to him by blood and spirit more than ever before. The very fact that we were saying good-bye, that we were separating from each other, meant that we had been together—no matter for how brief a time. And I felt a kind of love for my father that I had never felt before. My father wasn't God. He hurt like everybody else, like me.

As the plane taxis out to the runway, I twist around to see him one last time. I recall the magic of the night before. The plane hits the runway, gathers speed, and lifts off and I hear that music again—feel my father swaying next to me on the bench, chomping on his cigar, clapping his rough, red hands. Me and Father —didn't we ramble!

The show went pretty well but I was a bit manic. My composure and timing were off because of all the hype and the pressure.

After the show, Jake and Artie called me over to their table. Sitting there were a couple of obvious high-power types. I was introduced to Nancy Josephson, one of the top agents and a vice president of International Creative Management (ICM, talent agency to the stars, babe!). She was thrilled, she said, by my moving story.

Nancy Josephson asked me if I wouldn't mind coming down that week to ICM—Artie would make the arrangements—to talk and meet with her and some other people at the agency. I must have hesitated for a split second because Artie smacked me hard on the back and said, "Are you kidding? Mind? Don't worry. He'll be there."

People crowded around me and shook my hand, congratulating me. I was in a spin, dizzy, like I was going to fall over. I looked in the back for Vicky and Carlos, but I couldn't see them over the heads of the mob around my table. When the room cleared a little, I could see them near the sound-board and light board, talking to each other. I thought of waving for them to come over—to share in my success—but I didn't do it.

Vicky, with her doughy, frumpy frown. Carlos, with his messed-up face, his sloppy clothes, and his alcohol laugh. They were both so disheveled and unhip. My friends, yes, of course, but I didn't want to mix them with this elite crew. They just didn't project the right image. I turned back to the crowd at the table. A few minutes later, feeling guilty, I looked back again. Vicky was gone. Carlos stood at the door, holding his old, worn backpack.

The next day, Artie called me and told me that we had a meeting on Wednesday with ICM, and Sam Cohn *himself* was going to be there!

I digress for the pitifully uninformed among you. You may not know who Sam Cohn is. In fact, if you're not in show business, I'm sure you have no idea who he is. Sam Cohn was at the time *the most powerful agent in show business*. I'm not talking juggling acts or stand-up comedians: This was not *Broadway Danny Rose*. Sam Cohn was the sole representative of a couple dozen or so of the most famous movie stars, stage actors, directors, and playwrights in the world. Aside from his personal clients, he was *the Man* at ICM. The big boss. Sam Cohn made careers. If he favored you, you could become a household name. If he ignored you, you had to go look in the mirror to remind yourself who you were. There were probably performers and writers who had committed felonies to land a meeting with Sam Cohn. And I was being invited to see him.

On Wednesday, I was seated at a huge oval conference table in ICM's offices, Jake on one side of me, Artie on the other. There were more than a dozen people at the table, all heads of departments at ICM, their assistants whispering and handing them papers to sign. The literary department, the movie department, the television department, voice-overs (commercials), magazine rights. They were all there, assembled to view the new phenomenon.

We made small talk, waiting for Sam Cohn to arrive and take his seat at the head of the table. He was already more than ten minutes behind schedule, and the waiting was beginning to get on my nerves. I hated it when people were late.

I felt like getting up and leaving. Artie clamped his hand down on my wrist, "Mike, for Christ's sake, calm the fuck down."

I looked around the room. There were people sitting at that table that routinely spent time with some of the most famous, talented people in the world, and no one dared utter a peep about this rudeness. So, Sam was late, no problem. Maybe he was talking to God about a three-picture deal.

I was just on the brink of telling Artie I was going to leave when, finally, Sam Cohn hurried in and took his seat at the head of the table. I sat at the other end, directly opposite him. It's all me and him now, as if an electric current were flowing between us. Everybody else around the table begins swiveling their heads back and forth between me and the boss. "Sorry," he says, "I had an important call." *And what am I, chopped liver?* I can feel Artie next to me, humming with anxiety. I nod. "That's alright," I assure Sam Cohn magnanimously. He folds his hands together on the table. "So," he says, with a sly grin, "what do you want us to do for you?" That catches me off guard. I'm expecting him to launch into a detailed plan to position me as the next Mount Everest. It had never occurred to me that I would be asked what I wanted.

I sense a game going on here; I'm being tested. I grin back at him and say, "I was hoping you were just gonna hand me a check for a million dollars." I can feel Artie having a heart attack. There are some pale faces around the table. Cohn laughs: "I had it with me; I must have dropped it in the hallway."

"No problem," I say. "I'll wait while somebody goes to pick it up." Sam Cohn and I sit there duking it out verbally for a couple of minutes, then he leans back and lets the department heads present themselves to me.

The plan unfolds. Provided I sign with them, a fait accompli as far as everybody in the room is concerned, ICM, being a "total" agency, is going to finance an expensive showcase performance of my fishing-trip story and use their clout to invite producers and studio heads, theater owners, and editors from various publishing houses to come see me. They'll field the offers and craft a stellar career for me. Cohn also thinks it would be a good idea to set up a run for me in some regional theater so that I can polish up my act. Then, when it's ready, bring it into New York.

After the meeting, Jake, Artie, and I walk out on to Fifty-seventh Street. It is a sharp, bright early-fall day. Artie is high as a kite, and Jake, normally very sober, is more than a bit manic himself. They have a couple of decades of show business experience between them, but they have never, they assure me, seen such a big deal made out of a "new" talent.

We go into the New York Deli on Fifty-seventh Street to celebrate. A deli of delis this place is. A *power* deli. There are giant salamis hanging in the windows, six-foot jars of bright-red cherry peppers, revolving glass cases filled with huge slices of cake. With all the stress and attention pouring in, I am suddenly ravenous.

We thread our way through the tables to the back of the room, the only place—according to Artie, the master of appearances—for really important people to sit. The place is vast, and though it is only about eleven in the morning, every table is occupied. Big, heavy carnivores in fancy suits are at work. Heads are bent over plates of salami and eggs. Corned-beef sandwiches, squealing in terror, are torn apart by huge powerful jaws. Phones are urgently being talked into, fingers are waving, eyes flashing. Deals are being made and broken and remade at lightning speed. As we walk past the tables, Artie is slapping hands, patting backs. "Hey, babe, just get in?!" "Joey, what's happenin', dude?!" This little guy is amazing. He really does know everybody.

We sit at a "prime" table where everybody can see us. Ordering immediately, we launch into our impressions of the meeting. Artie is in his chair no more than two minutes when he jumps up and says he has to talk to some people. I watch him head down to the floor to work the house. When he gets back, about ten minutes later, he points to a tall, cold-looking man in a pearl-gray suit. "OK, babe," he says to me, "I just got you a deal."

"What?"

"That guy over there is Jonathan Hirsch—he's head of a production company creating a new sitcom. You're gonna fly out to Hollywood sometime in the next few weeks and write the pilot for them." I'm flabbergasted. "Artie, man, what're you talking about!? I don't know anything about writing TV shows." He is completely unfazed—takes a big bite of his pastrami on rye and says, "You do now, babe."

The fee for my services is to be five thousand to "consult" on the pilot of the show—about a midnight radio talk-show host—and a certain percentage of the royalties each week if the show is picked up by a network.

I am suddenly overwhelmed, reeling from all of this rich stuff. ICM, TV, Hollywood, salami and eggs. I feel the return of an old, unwelcome visitor, disassociation; I'm disconnecting from my surroundings. I watch Artie and Jake talking, I hear myself talking back to them, but it is starting to become unreal. Such a symptom scares me, considering my history. I tell them I have to go home. We split up outside the deli and I head uptown to tell Susan about my newest "triumphs."

Three weeks later, in mid-October, Artie, Jake, Vicky, and I are standing in the Westbeth Theater Complex downtown in the West Village. Vicky had asked them to show us their smaller theater—a nice little hundred-seat space, with the seats rising up, amphitheater-style, from the stage. I like it on sight. Vicky and I look at each other: yes, this is definitely the place. Artie is troubled, though. "Mike" (he rarely addressed himself directly to Vicky), "I don't know about this…it's too small. What you wanta do now is make an impression."

"What impression?" I ask, "this space is perfect for what I do." Artie frowns and waves his hand in dismissal. "No man, you gotta think bigger." He looks around the little theater. "You know what this place says to me? This place says small. '*I'm* small, what I *do* is small, what I will *always* do is small.'" Jake nods his head as Artie talks. Vicky is frowning. She *hates* this pushy little guy. She looks at me to see if I'm buying this shit from him. Am I? Enough, I guess, to follow him and the theater owner into the big room for a look.

The large space at Westbeth Complex is *really* large. It's where Broadway plays and musicals put on tryouts for backers. "Now," says Artie with evident satisfaction, "*this* is what we want." He takes me by the arm and we walk around the room. Vicky stands near the doorway with her arms crossed, silent and furious. As we walk, Artie explains that important people are coming, half of them flying in from the coast (the Coast!). They aren't used to artsy little New York theaters. To them that means limitation—penny-ante, small-time bohemian shit. They see things in the big picture. "Is this guy capable of filling a thousand-seat venue?" Am I, Mike Feder, big enough for them to invest their time and money in? I have to give the movers and shakers a sense that I'm big talent—capable of expanding into whatever-size project they might imagine. I cast a glance over at Vicky, who is having an intense conversation with Jake, shaking her head and pointing her finger at us.

"C'mon, Mike," says Artie, ICM is paying for anything we want. Let's do it up right, OK?" I sigh. He turns me around to face him. He seems pissed. "Let me ask you something, Mike Feder," he says, peering directly into my eyes. "Are you really serious here, or what? Tell me right now, am I wasting my time with you?"

The showcase is planned for three weeks later, the first week in October, in the large room. Vicky and I rehearse my story, but there is a coldness between us. I keep hoping she will understand. I feel lost in all this heavy stuff constantly rolling over me. I want her to help me out, but she's really angry with me for walking down what she sees as a completely wrong path.

I go down to the theater with Carlos. We stand there in the airplane hangar–sized space and look around. Since he is not going to be doing any of the light or sound for the show, he seems to be at a loss for words. We finally talk some about my story, and about what new stuff is happening in my career, but it is uncomfortable. It is clear that since he has no part to play anymore, no way to help me, he doesn't know what to say or do. I can't think of much to say to him, either. We stay only for a few minutes.

On a Saturday night, three weeks later, the night of the showcase at the theater, we watch the crew—there is an entire *crew*—of carpenters, lighting

266 / MIKE FEDER

technicians, and painters, putting finishing touches on the set. This is a long way from my few dusty square feet down on the floor at the West Bank Theater.

They have built a huge stepped wooden platform, about eight feet off the ground, painted black, in the center of the room and hung a gigantic black curtain behind it. My old high bar-stool, which I insist on using, though Artie wants me in a big swivel chair, is set up on top of the platform. It looks very small and lonely up there.

Blinding spotlights are hung from the dark, high ceiling, focused right onto the stage, rendering the rest of the house almost totally dark. I try the stage out, do the sound and light checks. It is very high up there. I feel like I'm looking at people down on the floor from the top of a skyscraper. I climb down and walk over to the far wall of the room, where Vicky and Jake are talking. I look at her and she shakes her head. "Jake here," she says—openly disgusted—"thinks you look great all the way up there on top of that mountain. What do you think, buddy?"

High up on that black stage, in front of that huge black curtain, I'm telling my story. I try to search out human beings down there in the audience, but all I can see through the glare is the occasional pair of eyes shining in the darkness, like wolves' eyes in the forest out beyond the campfire. I'm used to the cozy, chummy nearness of the audience in the small clubs I've worked in. Up there on that altar, I can't feel the people, I can't hear a chuckle or a sigh, or an intake of breath. I'm out of touch. I have a brief image of King Kong, trapped on top of the Empire State Building, ten thousand miles from his home, lit up by spotlights, battered by bullets and confusion—dying.

The feel of this audience is different from anything else I have ever encountered. Preshow, as always, I watch them coming in from behind the curtain. They looked like *Vanity Fair* and *GQ* come to life. All of them have a kind of critical, bored look on their faces. Artie calls it an "industry crowd." He warns me that they won't react as much as a regular audience. They have seen everything, he says, and are very hard to impress.

After my performance there is some polite applause, which I can hardly hear all the way up on my mountain, then the lights come on and people file out, pretty fast, it seems to me.

I stand in the backstage area. Jake and Artie come back. "Great show, babe! Beautiful!" I know that is bullshit. I have given one of the poorer performances of my short career. I'm disgusted with myself. More people show up. Nancy Josephson, some of the other agents from ICM. And Sam Cohn, of course. He comes over, shakes my hand briefly. He smiles, a remote, thin smile, "Good story." I just nod to him. He turns and walks off with the rest of the agents.

I go out front to say good-bye to a few people. I'm introduced to several editors, representing a few publishing houses. Artie sets up some appointments for the coming weeks. Artie and Jake are talking about various appointments and deals, who showed up and who didn't. I sit on the lower step of the stage just out of the circle of light. The theater is empty and black all around me. Vicky and Carlos are nowhere in sight.

CHAPTER TWENTY-FIVE

Another meeting, this time at Crown Publishers. Another conference table surrounded by what seems like a small army of eager-to-please faces. All this corporate converging makes me nervous. I'm just one person, why does it take so many of them to negotiate with me? There are a couple of editors, two marketing people, and three or four executives whose function I never determined.

Crown is having a big hit with Tama Janowitz's *Slaves of New York*, and they want to follow it up with my book. The marketing people even have a title ready: *New York Son*.

The meeting goes a lot more smoothly than my show-business baptism of fire at ICM. I'm more experienced now and, anyway, books are more my line. I'm not being told to become an actor or write a TV pilot. I'm just being asked to write down stories I have already told over the radio and on stage. And I have another reason for cooperating and making sure the meeting goes well. Crown is offering a twenty-thousand-dollar advance, and at this moment, despite my great expectations, I'm well on my way to being totally broke.

When I quit my paralegal job that previous August, I thought I wouldn't need much money, so I only borrowed about three months' living expenses from a friend. This was all I figured I'd need, because after talking to Jake and Artie, I had constant visions of sugar plums boogying in my head. I thought I'd be swamped in big bucks almost instantly, but now, two months into the world of big promises, I realize I only have about six weeks' worth of money left. Susan's income is the main one in the family, but my paralegal job was still absolutely necessary to pay the bills. And Susan and I had *very* separate checking accounts. Our money and our responsibilities were carefully laid out. Even though I'm famous now and about to be rich, babe— if I don't come up with my share of the expenses, there'll be trouble.

Later that week I get another offer, from Harper & Row. Jake and I are shown into a small office where I meet the man who would be my editor. It's a cozy place, cluttered with manuscripts, sun pouring in the window. I hit it off immediately with the guy. He has taken the trouble to listen to the tapes of my stories that Jake had sent to all the publishers. We talk for a long time and I get the sense that he has a very intelligent, thoughtful approach to the book he sees me writing.

I like this editor. I like the feeling of the place, but, alas, he is only offering ten thousand, a paltry sum for a rising star like me, especially a rising star that is about three weeks from bankruptcy. I take Crown's offer.

By the last week in October, I have tentative agreements to develop two of my stories into screenplays. I have a couple of television writing jobs pending. My tapes are circulating at various network radio stations in the hopes that I'll be offered a syndication deal. I have a book contract with a major publisher. I should be happy or, at the very least, content with the progress being made, but I'm not. I'm feeling jumpy, unsettled.

Susan has gone, almost overnight, from shocked disorientation to absolute certainty. My golden future is her gilt-edged guarantee. Each day, she asks me about the latest deals, the newest offers. She is unusually sweet and cooperative. Anything I want to do, she goes along. If something bothers me, a chore, a responsibility, no problem, she sees that it gets done. She is developing some alarming spending habits. Immediately after I meet with ICM and I'm offered the Hollywood TV writing job, and even before I get my book contract, she has magically acquired new credit cards: gold cards, platinum cards, titanium alloy cards. Each day I come home to find we own something new. An expensive coffee table, an art deco lamp, new clothes from fancy department stores for the kids. She gets herself some expensive new shoes, and she buys a Bergdorf Goodman sweater for me. We take to eating out a lot.

All this worries me; she seems so sure of my ultimate and imminent success that I wonder what would happen if by some slim, improbable chance things don't work out. What if I don't become rich and famous?

Around a week before Thanksgiving, my anxiety ratchets up several notches. I am watching the money running out of my bank account like the steady downward flow of sand in an hourglass. I haven't heard anything from ICM about the regional theater run they promised. I call Artie and Jake every day, but though they reassure me—these things take time—they don't have any solid news for me. I try calling Sam Cohn myself, but he is always away or in a meeting. I still have my writing job in Hollywood and some meetings with movie studios planned when I get out there, but that is for later in December. I haven't started to write my book yet but it isn't due till mid-spring. I figure I have plenty of time. Besides, that project seems pretty dull compared to all the other glamorous stuff in the works.

The weather gets colder, the days shorter. That doesn't help. Fall always makes me think of death. My father left in the fall. My mother killed herself in the fall, and my father's plane dropped into the black sea in the middle of the winter. The leaden sky, the shrinking daylight. Fall-winter creeps up into my bones like the chilly sights and sounds of the cemetery: gravestones, stillness, paralysis.

I do practically nothing all day long except wait for a phone call from someone "important." I stop talking to my friends almost entirely. They seem far away and inconsequential to me. How can they solve my problems? They have no money, no contracts to offer or promises to make. I run and rerun grandiose scenarios in my head while I sit in my apartment or take walks around the neighborhood. My life is on hold. I have stopped creating anything. I'm doing nothing but waiting for the golden gifts to arrive, everything that is rightfully mine, so long overdue.

One overcast afternoon, I'm looking out the living-room window, vacantly staring at people emerging from the funeral chapel across the street. The bereaved, the tearful, the bored, the same old parade I have seen a thousand times as a kid. One older man, dressed in a heavy dark

272 / MIKE FEDER

coat, has his arm around a woman dressed all in black, probably the widow. Suddenly he looks straight up toward where I am sitting. I can see his eyes focus on my face. I feel like I'm going to fall right out of the window, though it is shut tight.

I'm over at Rose's apartment at least one night a week. Five minutes through the door and we are in bed, having urgent, dizzying sex. For the first hour I'm there I am almost completely drunk, having emptied half a pint of scotch in about fifteen minutes. When the heat and the liquor start to wear off, we talk. To be accurate, *we* don't talk, *I* talk. I lay there next to her, tension drained out of me temporarily (till the inevitable wave of guilt hits me later)—safe in my hidden shelter. It is a moment of bliss, oblivion. Nobody's husband, nobody's father, nobody's client, nobody's star attraction or vicarious life-support system. Just me and her. Untroubled, quiet.

I've always had a hard time distinguishing between genuine despair and maudlin self-pity. Maybe that's a common problem for drunks and the hopelessly self-involved. Certainly I'm drunk a lot of the time when I am over at Rose's, but really it is after the booze has worn off at a later hour, when I'm clear and calm, that the fear and anguish inside me pour out.

I'm sick to my stomach of all the glitz, the glamour, and the talk of money and fame. The flushed greedy faces, the waves of phony applause from strangers, the meetings, the "big" phone calls. The lust after money and mass adulation are burning me up like a fever. I'm over my head and drowning in all this delusional bullshit. And I'm terrified of failing, failing everyone who depends on me.

Rose hears everything. Insults received, misunderstandings, fears, terrors. Blow-by-blow accounts of my current torments, week after week. "Don't do it," she says, "just drop all this stuff." I sit up in bed, "What do you mean, don't do it?! Are you nuts? I have to do it!"

She shakes her head, frowns, "Don't you see how bad it's making you feel?" I dismiss her entirely. "You know, you just plain don't understand what's going on here. You've never been in my position, so how could you know what you're talking about?" She just looks at me, smiling. Jesus! How could this woman have any idea what I'm really up against?

Ten days before Christmas, there is still no action from ICM about this plan to send me to a regional theater to polish up my performances. Still no solid offers, with money attached, from movie or TV companies, to option one of my stories or write a screenplay. However, there is still my Hollywood trip. Off to the coast to *do* something, finally, even if I have no idea what the fuck it is I'm supposed to do. Contacts, meetings, money... get the motor revved up again. Get the show on the road instead of sitting around, brooding in my apartment, running to Rose all the time to cry and whine. "Should I, shouldn't I?"

I see Rose one last time before I fly to California. I have concluded, in the fudge pot of my conscience, that this trip to Los Angeles will set me on the "right" path again. I will have recognition, money, solid offers, deals that would have me back on the path to the Emerald City. Therefore, I resolve to stop seeing Rose. Why? Because it seems like the *right thing to do*. I have to get back to the correct, legal world of marriage and family.

I tell her my decision. She's hurt. She cries. I try to comfort her in vain. But I do comfort myself with the thought that this kind of thing, this compulsive sadomasochism, is exactly what I'm going to prevent from now on. No causing her any more pain. No causing anyone—even my theoretically unsuspecting wife, and by extension, my children, my *family*— any more pain.

CHAPTER TWENTY-SIX

The production company for which I am supposed to perform my writing wizardry sends a huge white stretch limo to the door of my apartment building. It looks like the Taj Mahal on wheels. It is embarrassing, getting into that glitz-mobile in front of my neighbors and the doorman.

The driver stows my suitcase and holds the door for me. I sink down into the deep, wide leather seat. The car is as long as a bus and done up inside like a *Playboy* reader's fantasy of heaven. The doors are lined with walnut paneling. There is a color television, a private phone, a bar stocked with several crystal decanter bottles of scotch, whiskey, and vodka, and a tray of tiny deli sandwiches—covered in plastic. There is a goddamn red rose in a vase! And to cap it all off, a bottle of Moët champagne rising up out of a silver ice bucket. The driver is so far away from where I am sunk into the back seat, I have to yell in order to get him to hear me. He motions for me to use the intercom. "What's all this stuff back here?" I ask him. "Compliments of Jo-Mar productions, Sir." He clicks off.

I notice an envelope next to me on the seat. It is a note from Artie. "Mikey—I'm out here doing some meetings. Staying at the Beverly Wilshire. I'll see you after you get in. It's all happening, babe!"

We are rolling along the Belt Parkway, heading for Kennedy Airport. The windows are smoked glass. Everything outside, the leafless trees, the frozen ground whizzing by, the other cars, look unreal and far away. I feel like I'm suffocating in here. I press the button to get the window down. The wind on my face is biting cold but it sobers me up a little. I stare at the other cars. Naturally, everybody is staring at the limo, at me. Why wouldn't they? I would. Who *is* that in the limo? Is he famous? Is he a movie star? A rock and roller? Maybe Donald Trump on his way to his private jet. As I return the stares of my fellow highway travelers, I realize they aren't looking at me and my ride with awe. They are irritated, even disgusted. What asshole is this, taking up half the parkway? After a few minutes of such blatant hostility, I get angry back. I bring the window up again. Jerks. They don't like the limo, eh? Well, fuck 'em. Let them drive their puny, stinking Oldsmobiles and Chevys—their pathetic wretched little *used* cars. While they're cranking home to a worn-out wife and screaming kids, a mortgaged, falling-down old house, I'm on my way to Hollywood. I guess that's why they have smoked windows in these things. It separates *them* from you. And you from you, too.

I decide, what the hell, I'll try to enjoy myself at least a little. I switch on the TV. A movie is playing. *The Charge of The Light Brigade!* Errol Flynn. At the head of his brave and daring troops, red uniforms and gold braids glistening in the sun, cantering proud and noble, ready to exact revenge on the evil Khan and his minions. As Captain Errol raises his gleaming sword to signal the charge, I take heart. No more fear. Be a man. I reach over and pour a whiskey for myself. Take a big swallow. Damned fine stuff, that! Steel yourself, old boy. The enemy awaits. This is no time for hesitation and doubt. Onward, onward ride the five hundred! Agents to the left of them, producers to the right, angry wives in front of them! Onward they ride, onward to glory! Yes!!

But wait, wait…didn't they all get massacred?

Another whiskey, perhaps.

On the plane, first-class compartment, of course, I'm given complimentary champagne and offered my choice of steak or lobster. I'm more than halfway drunk. I sit back in the big seat and close my eyes. What a strange way to live. Is this what people do all the time—the rich and the famous? I try to imagine getting used to it. Why not? I think. It's better than dried-out chicken bits and a cramped seat back in economy. I stretch out my legs and try to get into it, but there is just too much Laurelton, Queens, in me. *Mr. Fancy-Pants Hollywood writer. Since when did you get to be such a big shot?* So much for transcending class. My real problem is psychic. I'm so deeply lost in a storm of contradictions and colliding feelings that I can't calm down. And always, always, that little poisonous snake of doubt and fear is still there, flickering its nasty tongue, ready to strike. "Fly away, Mike," it hisses, "drink your fancy whiskey and eat your lobster, make your deals and sign your contracts, I'll still be here, waiting for you." I'm seized with a desperate urge to be off this plane, back down on the ground in New York, walking the streets, anonymous, unknown. By the time we land in L.A., I have a blinding migraine headache.

I'm picked up by another stretch limo and driven to my hotel, the Mondrian. A real power hotel. The whole place—outside, the lobby, the rooms—is decorated in long bright stripes and squares of color, à la Mondrian. My room is a suite, a bedroom and huge living-room office. Kitchen against one wall, a big, fully stocked bar, refrigerator stuffed with cheese, crudités, little bottles of wine, foil-wrapped chocolates.

Out the huge picture window, there is a panoramic view of Hollywood, buildings, glittering lights, brown-purple hills off in the distance.

Walking across the soft, thick carpeting very carefully, as if to avoid stepping into quicksand, I go into the bedroom. I neatly put my two small suitcases side by side right in the middle of the king-sized bed. Sitting on the edge of the bed, in the dark of the bedroom, I look back through the door into the brightly lit living room. My little girl's face pops up in my head. Sarah, with her brainy, quick mischievous smile. I miss her terribly. I miss my baby Ben—the innocent cause of so much of my anger and misery. If he were here now, I'd pick him up and he'd throw one of his teddy-bear hugs around my neck. I even miss Susan. I think of Rose, alone, crying in her apartment. I feel utterly lost, like a little kid who's been separated from his parents in a gigantic department store. At that moment, there is a loud knock on my door. It's Artie, leather jacket, gold necklace, and all. God, I'm glad to see him! A real New Yorker! He grips my hand, "Dude!"

"Artie," I say, "what am I doing here?"

278 / MIKE FEDER

He tosses himself onto the B-52–sized couch. "Get a grip, babe. What are you doin' here? You're here to consult on a TV pilot. You're here to rack up five thousand guzungas! That's what you're doing here. OK? I'll take you over tomorrow, introduce you to Jon Hirsch." He clapped his hands together. "And we got two big meetings—tomorrow, and Thursday." He sticks around for a while, trying to inject a little iron into my spine, then rushes off to a dinner meeting.

The next morning, I meet the producer, Jon Hirsch. He gives me a brief outline, nothing more than a few ideas, really, of the show he has in mind, a couple of characters to work with, some plot suggestions, then hustles me into an office with a word processor and shuts the door. I look around. Potted Palms, framed, signed photographs from movie and TV stars, a big desk, two phones. I sit in the chair and look at the computer. I practically black out and have to overcome an urge to grab the phone, order a cab to the hotel, and get a plane home, but the tiny image of Artie is there whispering in my ear, and I can see Susan's face, all admiration and anger mixed together. I have to dig in.

I write a two-page outline of a story, walk down to Hirsch's office, and show it to him. "Needs more," he says. "Tighten the main character up, give me a little suspense right here"—he stabs a place on the page with his gold fountain pen—"and here." I go back to my office.

Tighten the main character? A little suspense? I'm in a fog, starting to despair in earnest. I'm attempting to write a teleplay about something I don't understand, don't care about, and have no idea technically how to construct. I don't write fiction. The only stories I can tell with any passion or humor, or sense of reality, are my own stories. I sit up straight. *Stop it, you fucking asshole! You need this money.* I have to do this or die in the attempt. Onward. Onward.

Two more visits to Jon Hirsch's office, more instructions and corrections. He is getting just a little irritated with me, wondering, perhaps, who this alleged "genius" is that Artie has palmed off on him.

Hirsch and I keep at it. Back and forth, from my office to his. Around four o'clock, he tells me we can wrap it up for the day. He stands behind his desk, his cold eyes fixed on me, holding my little treatment in his hand. I get the feeling he's going to chuck it in the garbage the minute I leave.

Back at the Mondrian, I sit in the bedroom with the lights out. It is dusk. Man, I hate to see that evenin' sun go down. Anytime. Anyplace. Right here, right now, it feels like it is going down for good—darkness forevermore. I call Susan in New York. She is solicitous, tells me the kids miss me. I tell her everything is going fine and ask her to put Sarah on the phone. I'm so glad to hear that little girl's voice. "Come home soon, Daddy." she says. "OK," I tell her, "I will, I will." I get off the phone. The bedroom is completely dark. I slump down in the bed, staring out the window at the moonscape of Hollywood.

I wake up early. Splash some water on my face, order up some coffee, and shake myself together. Another day, another Hollywood dollar. I pick up the rental car the production company has gotten for me and drive out to Jon Hirsch's office. It is almost Christmas and decorations are up all over town. It is about seventy degrees outside, bright and sunny. Jolly old Santa, his sled, and all his reindeer are strung across the road, hanging from palm trees. On the main boulevard, I drive past a sidewalk Santa, dressed up in his suit and beard. Ho, ho, ho. Ringing his bell. Rich-looking women in flower-print dresses and sunglasses walk slowly behind him. Christmas trees, elves, tinsel, and lights are set up in store windows; and just outside the stores, smooth, suntanned men in convertible Mercedes and Bentleys talk quietly into their car phones.

Back at the salt mines, Jon Hirsch didn't seem so pleased to see me. I guess I am not a phenomenon anymore. A fast drop in less than twenty-four hours, from talent of the year to amateur writer. Well, it isn't his fault. I *am* an amateur writer. Jon tosses my treatment to me. "You need to fix this up—just check my notes." In my office across the hall, I see that almost every original idea, every new character I have come up with has been crossed out or so altered that it is as if I hadn't written anything at all. I spend another whole day writing inside a vacuum, trying desperately to understand what he wants me to do. I am so pitifully out of my element. What I think makes sense doesn't make sense. What I think is foolish and meaningless he pounces on. "Yes. Very good. That's perfect!" Driven by the fear of falling completely on my face and embarrassing everybody, I learn quickly how to give him what he wants. By the end of the day, he is excited, really pleased with "our" writing. We finish after six, a hard day's labor in the creative mills of TV. According to Jon, we have ourselves one hell of a treatment for the network, with plenty of "hard, realistic characters" and some "dynamite real-life dialogue." I stagger out of the office and drive back to the hotel.

Artie and I have dinner that night out near the pool. He is very pleased with me. Apparently Jon Hirsch called him and told him what a genius I am. Man, things happen fast out here in Oz. Artie is, as usual, talking a blue streak, free-associating about deals, contracts, percentages, beautiful cats, back-stabbing assholes: the entertainment business. He points out well-known agents and actors sitting at other tables. I'm already slurping up my second giant coconut rum–punch piña colada–margarita, or whatever the hell it was the waiter was putting in front of me. Artie leans over and whispers. "See that guy? Looks like a bummed-out asshole in his beat-up old sneakers? That guy has a *three-picture* deal, Mike. Do you have any conception?" I look at him blankly. My head is about to roll off my shoulders from alcohol and creeping loss of identity. Artie can see I'm in trouble.

"I'm not feeling right about all this stuff, Artie," I say.

"Hey, Mike, don't you think I know it? You think *I* like this fast-lane shit?" He sure *looks* like he likes it, all sunburned and smiling.

"You don't?"

"No, man, gimme a little credit here. Hey, babe, I'm a New York guy, like you."

So starved am I for sympathy and understanding, I almost break into tears. The little guy *understood*! I'm overcome with gratitude. "Kid," he says, "only two more days and you'll be back in the city."

"That's good."

"But look, babe, we got our most important meeting tomorrow. With the ABC guys. You got to be cool and you got to be sharp. Right?" Right. Cool and sharp.

The next morning, Artie picks me up at my hotel, and we drive over in his bright-red Mercedes convertible to the Beverly Hills Hotel for our big power breakfast. Artie has snagged none other than the heads of special projects and prime-time development for ABC television. A couple of weeks earlier he had me send them a treatment about my years in the probation department, complete with various stories and a huge cast of characters. This is to be the main topic of the meeting—the possibility of creating a pilot, developing a brand new prime-time drama about a probation officer and his gritty adventures in the gritty city. Artie is really juiced. "This is the big one, Mike, this is what we're here for."

We pull up in front of the hotel. A massive doorman, wearing what looks like an admiral's dress uniform, complete with gold buttons and a gold-braided hat, opens the door for us. Artie tosses his keys to a valet. We step onto a thick red carpet and enter the hotel. Out of California into Europe as envisioned by California. Crystal chandeliers, ten-foot gold-framed mirrors on the walls, silk-brocade wall covering. The restaurant has more brocade, more crystal lights on the walls. Huge palms are placed in the corners and at intervals along the walls. On the tables, in big cut-glass vases, are bursts of bright flowers. Smack in the middle of the vast room is an actual fountain—Spanish colonial style, bubbling and splashing, the spray sparkling like diamonds in sunlight, pouring into the room from the green glass roof. Quiet, efficient waiters, sharp and polished as flamenco dancers, move smoothly between tables. And the diners, elegant, perfect, all of them wrapped in the cool, confident aura of the supremely rich and powerful. If gold ingots and diamonds could sit up and talk, they would look like these people.

We are shown our table. The two executives are not there. They'll be late. Of course. It is all part of the game, something I have already come to understand. In any case, Artie and I have time to go over my performance. Because it is to be a performance. I have to be what they think I should be, sound how they want me to sound, if I am going to hit the mother lode. Artie tells me he thinks the guys are excited, possibly *very* excited, by the treatment they have read, but they want to see if I'm the "real deal."

I need his coaching. Not only because I am beginning to slip in and out of functional reality, but because I can't get the feeling of what the "real deal" might be here. What I have seen of Los Angeles, admittedly a small and exclusive part, seems to be gauzy and ephemeral to me, like a Maxfield Parish painting come to life. People I meet, or overhear in offices and in the dining room at the Mondrian, don't seem to think as I understand thinking in New York terms. Rather than brood or cogitate, or explode in bursts of ideas, these people flit, like butterflies, from concept to concept, never seeming to alight on any one solid thought for more than a second at a time. An invisible sense of preoccupation pervades every conversation, every gesture and glance.

Our guests are only ten minutes late. Sandy Edelman and Jeff Bieberman. We stand up to shake hands all around. I touch a couple of cool golden palms and resume my seat. Sandy and Jeff almost look like twins if you don't trouble to examine them closely. Both are suntanned, in their early thirties, graceful, cool, seamless. They are dressed alike. Lightweight, expensive suits, with open-collared pastel shirts, expensive, perfectly shined loafers, no socks. On each wrist there gleams a gold Rolex watch. People at other tables—ours is in the very center of the room—are glancing in our direction. In such exclusive circles, everyone knows, apparently, who everybody else is. And these two guys are unmistakably royalty. Even Artie, the sultan of schmooze, seems nervous—his usual ingratiating smile is outrageously wide.

I can't muster much enthusiasm. Even before these two guys sit down I conceive an intense dislike for them. I don't like their looks or their manner. They have expressionless, almost dead eyes, like sharks. Boredom and condescension drip from them like acid rain. I rouse myself for one last shot, one more go for the gold. At the very least I don't want to shame Artie, who has worked so hard for this meeting.

We ordered. Sandy wishes for a slice of cantaloupe and an Evian. Jeff is more adventurous, ordering one poached egg and orange juice. I'm starved. I could gobble up five scrambled eggs, a pile of home fries, and ten sausages, but this is not the time for vulgar gorging. This is a time to be sharp and cool.

Small talk is made. Artie and the boys—talking deals, rumors, trends. Then Sandy, who in some subtle way seems to be the senior of the two, speaks directly to me. "Mike," he says, in a smooth, superior voice, "We've read your probation officer treatment." He pauses. Artie's smile is frozen to his face. I wait. Sandy looks at Jeff, then back to me. "Powerful," he says, "I was moved." I can feel Artie relaxing next to me. Now Jeff speaks. He is being sincere. I can tell because there is a slight ripple in his previously passionless affect. "Mike, we are definitely *excited*." Bango! The E-word. Artie is suddenly beaming, gratitude popping from every pore. He pats me on the back. Sandy and Jeff look at me across the table. I get the feeling I'm supposed to throw myself on the floor and kiss their feet. I purse my lips, nod, "Thanks." If I'm broadcasting any irritation, these two snots are too far above me to feel it.

We sit for a moment, nodding and smiling, sipping our coffee. They are talking about my treatment, discussing all the hard cases, sad cases, tragedies, and comedies I have known and lived through in the years I spent in the neighborhoods, courts, and jails of Brooklyn and Manhattan. Suddenly, there is a shift, a definite upping of the invisible stakes at the table. Sandy and Jeff look at each other, then lean forward, fixing me with what I suppose for them passes for intensity. Sandy peers into my eyes, he takes a breath: "Mike," he says, "tell us about the streets." *What? The streets? They want to know about the streets?* They probably never even *walked* on a goddamn street. They go from one meeting to another, from one mansion to the next, without even so much as setting one loafered foot on the streets. If they could get away with it, they would have native bearers carrying them everywhere they went. The *streets*!

I can feel my face twisting in a nasty frown and the steam rising out of the top of my head. "Oh, you want to know about the streets?" I'm about to enlighten them in *serious* detail when I feel a tremendous pain in my left leg. Artie has stabbed me, actually reached under the table with his butter knife and jabbed it into my left thigh. I wince and shut my mouth.

Sandy and Jeff wait for me to speak. Slowly, carefully, regaining my equilibrium, recalling why I'm here, I tell them what it's like on the streets. I tell them about the eight-year-old boy raped by his uncle; the wife beaten to death by her insane boxer husband; the old man practically dead from an attack on him by ten viscious kids, all for a quarter. I tell them about crazy corrupt judges and cops, sadistic correction guards, pathological murderers, arrogant, megalomaniac drug dealers. With every word I speak, I feel like I'm betraying these people by telling the stories of their lives to these manicured zombies. It is obscene.

I guess my presentation is strong enough. The meeting breaks up soon after I am through talking. We touch hands. The princes take their leave, and Artie and I sit alone. I am checking my leg. There is a slight tear in my pants where Artie poked me with the knife, a red spot underneath. I can see he is really angry. He turns all the way around in his chair to face me. "Mike, I don't know what your fucking problem is. I go to more trouble than you will ever know, I put my ass on the line for you to get these guys down here. And what do you do? You think you can talk any way you like to any-body!" He is standing up now, shaking his head. I feel terrible, ashamed of myself. We walk out of the restaurant and drive back to the hotel.

Artie has regained most of his composure by the time we arrive. He turns to me. "I'll see you in New York. And look, Mike, when I talk to you next week, I don't know what's gonna come down with ABC here, espe-cially after this meeting. But that doesn't matter right now. When I talk to you again, I want you to be thinking seriously about what you plan to do. Either you want to make it or you don't...OK?"

I go up to my room, feeling like pure shit. I need to talk to somebody who might throw a little forgiveness my way. I sure am not going to for-give myself, not after my performance. I dial up Rose, let the phone ring twenty times, praying for her to pick up. She doesn't. I'm on my own.

Two hours later, another limousine, not a stretch this time, drives me to the airport and I'm on the plane back to New York. This time flying coach. My ticket has been downgraded. I wonder if this is a sign that the big wel-come mat is shrinking. Well, that's fine with me; coach is where I should be, anyway. And besides, I feel like such a fool and a failure, the downgrade seemed like fair punishment. This trip, all my bright, rich prospects.

The plane lifts off from the L.A. airport and suddenly we are out over the ocean. I expected to see land. Maybe I'm on the wrong plane? Maybe we're headed for Alaska or the Far East. Even better, I think. Time to get lost. If I can't have amnesia to get away from myself, I can at least disap-pear into the mists of some faraway place.

According to Salman Rushdie, disorientation means "failure to find the east." I was disoriented, all right. I had no idea where I was or which direction I was headed in. The East, what a great thought. Ten years, hidden in the mountains of Japan, sweeping leaves in a monastery courtyard. No one knows who I am or where I am. Ah, sweet surcease from sorrow. Off we go, jet, take me away.... But no such luck. The plane evens out and we head—over dry land—back to New York. When I arrive at Kennedy, there is another car waiting for me, just a regular old town car, and I know my star has definitely fallen.

CHAPTER TWENTY-SEVEN

Mid-January. Bleak, cold, dead.

After I get back to the city from my trip to Hollywood, I have become, suddenly, a virtual nonentity. The telephone hardly rings. I rarely hear from my agent or my lawyer. Artie is always in a meeting or traveling back and forth to the coast. I call ICM, but all I get are secretaries or assistants to the assistant of whomever I'm trying to reach.

Even my shrink has grown cooler. When I tell him how odd and bleak my world has become, he seems to be unsympathetic. I have the feeling he wants no more of my usual stories, my reports of fresh show-business treasure chests waiting to be opened. And speaking of treasure chests, he wants to know—where is his money? I owe him almost two thousand dollars in back fees, and I can't pay it. I tell him I'm going to get five thousand from the TV company and then start to make things up—promises of future deals that don't exist. He doesn't buy this for a minute.

January, February. Colder, emptier. My situation is getting desperate. The times I'm able to break out of my numbed haze, I'm shaking with fear and paranoia. Inevitably, things in my house are deteriorating badly—heading straight back to the awful days before my burst of potential greatness. Susan is growing impatient. Flashes of her pre–*Times* article disgust and nastiness reappear. She has run up huge debts on her credit cards, thanks to her four-month spending spree, and she is getting warning letters, threats. Why don't I hear from ICM, she wants to know. Where are the movie companies? Where are my fucking agents and lawyers? She demands that I stop lying around, get on the phone, and get some action from somebody.

The only steady beam of light in my life is Rose. Coming back from California, I immediately break my "vow" and resume seeing her. Rose doesn't seem the least bit surprised. Or maybe she is, but she is just happy to see me again. Though I don't know why she would be; all I do is lay in her bed, slugging back straight scotch, and complain about the variety of ways my life is turning to shit.

One gray afternoon, in my shrink's office, I slump, exhausted and defeated, in my chair. "You know," I tell him, "Rose says all she wants is me—fame doesn't matter, money doesn't matter, my troubles don't matter. As long as I'm with her, she says she would be happy." He looks at me with his wise, sad eyes. I appeal to him for some direction, some concrete help. "She says she just wants to dedicate her life to making me happy. Shit. She's probably crazy herself, right?" He seems to wander for a moment, as if he is lost in some personal musing of his own, then he looks at me and says, "There are such people, you know."

Through it all, of course, I still have my radio show. It has always been a consolation, a way to keep my sanity—talking to the listeners about what is going on inside and outside my head. But lately I 'm hard-pressed to tell them anything that isn't dreary and self-pitying. After amusing the listeners with my adventures in Hollywood—leaving out as much of the terror and fear as I could—I don't have much left to say that is interesting or uplifting. I am completely boxed in, full of plots, characters, and horror stories (my daily life)—none of which can be told. I fall back on playing tapes of old stories and take a lot of phone calls.

By mid-February, I am almost out of money. All the fuss and fury (meetings, promises, deals) of the past few months has blown over completely, leaving me stranded on a desert island—wondering where it all went.

The only thing left is my book. I finally sit down at the word processor in my bedroom and try to write, but the atmosphere in my house is too uncomfortable—too crazy. By now Susan has come full circle in her attitude. She is right back in full contempt-and-disgust mode. She is sick of me and my rationalizations about my lost prospects, my busted career.

One gray afternoon, the last week in February, I walk out of the building with Susan, who is nagging me mercilessly about my manifold inadequacies and crimes. I'm headed—actually, I don't know where I'm headed. I just want out of the house, away from her and the kids and my whole life.

She keeps pace, walking beside me to Amsterdam Avenue, talking and talking. I stop in the street. "Look," I say, "don't you have some chores to do, some business to take care of?" She sneers at me: "Well, whatever I have to do, I'm sure it's more than you're doing." I start walking again. She keeps up with me. "In fact," she continues, "it *has* to be more than you're doing, because you never do *anything*." I put my hands up.

"Hey, just give it a fucking break, will ya."

"Ahhh, poor little Mikey wants a break. Life is sooo hard for you...." I stop again. I am seeing red mists in front of my eyes. My hands feel huge and hot. I think I am going to explode. If she says one more word to me, I know I will break her neck. She backs up, right against the window of a liquor store. I follow her, standing inches away. After a long moment, I let out a breath and point my finger an inch away from her eyes. "Fuck you! I'm through with you and your whole fucking life!" I stand there for a second, then walk off, straight to the subway entrance on Seventy-ninth Street, down the steps, through the turnstile, onto the platform, headed uptown.

CHAPTER TWENTY-EIGHT

Midnight. I sit alone in my studio, six floors up, watching, over the tops of the swaying trees in Riverside Park, the lights of the houses and apartment buildings on the Jersey side of the Hudson. The only sound is the wind through the leaves…ssshhhhh…it's early April, about five weeks after I blew up on the street and considered strangling my wife. I have left practically everything behind me: my aforesaid wife (as they say in legal papers), my children, most of my books, all my records, record player, TV, my desk, my papers, my computer—the whole heap of worldly goods and responsibilities were sitting there on Seventy-ninth Street, only thirty blocks away.

Here I have a single bed, a couple of chairs, a table, my electric typewriter, some kitchen things, a few books, and a radio.

The studio apartment, about ten by fourteen with the stove and a refrigerator built into a tiny foyer, is in the Master Arts Apartments, a huge, tall, ominous-looking building that towers over the Hudson on Riverside Drive. Once an architectural landmark, it was originally built at the beginning of the Depression as a residence and showplace for artists. Sixty years later, it has become somewhat seedy, with very little trace of its former panache. There are still some of the original artist tenants, though not many. Quaint old souls, dressed like old-fashioned Village bohemians, still painting or composing and singing in their small rooms.

In the upper stories, there are two- and three-room apartments with couples, even some children, but the predominant species at the Master still seems to be the Single. People who choose that life or have been left behind, either by an oversight or on purpose. A lot of the people I see in the Master seem like fugitives, hiding from some nameless crime. The building is filled with people like me—recluses and cranks.

A listener of mine owns the building. He has let me use this studio rent-free for the last several months, after I went on the air asking if anyone had a nice quiet place for me where I could get some writing done. Well, not a page of writing has gotten done, and, in fact, I hardly set foot in the place all winter. Now, however, after all my troubles, I am thanking God that I have this little hideout; I have been so blasted by what has happened during the last several months that I think without a place to sleep I might be wandering the streets, camping out in the park with my fellow bums and lunatics.

The established fiction, especially for the benefit of my daughter, who can't be expected to understand why her father is suddenly gone, is that I needed the space and time to write my book. But, as usual, I am doing no writing. The typewriter sits on the floor in the corner of the room, covered up with a cloth. I don't want to see it, and I don't want it seeing me either. In fact, when I first escaped here, I didn't want to see much of anything or anybody. Even Rose, whose apartment is only three blocks away. Especially Rose, who has as much of an emotional pull on me as my family. I tell her I need to think, to be left alone. I rarely pick up the phone.

Every morning around dawn, I get up, put on a T-shirt, sweatpants, and sneakers and walk in the park, without a thought or a destination—for a mile, two miles. When I feel like stopping, I sit on a stone bench overlooking the river, my mind as blank and untroubled as the blue sky, and let the day rise and fall around me.

Around three weeks after landing in my refuge, I hear from Vicky. I invite her up and we walk along Riverside Drive. I describe all of Artie and Jake's manipulations and their valiant, doomed attempts to launch me. I ridicule all the Hollywood and show-business types, throwing my grandiose self into the mix.

Vicky and I talk theater. She fills me in on what's going on downtown at La Mama and other places. She invites me to go to some plays but I tell her I'm happy in my hidden fortress.

Back at the studio, drinking coffee, Vicky suggests I think about doing a new story, a performance about everything that has happened to me since last fall. No way, I tell her—no more performing seal for me. She picks up my copy of *The Way of Zen* and looks at me. "You do what you like, buddy, but you know, that stuff you were just telling me, agents, lawyers, hollywood, all that—now that's a pretty good story...." "Right," I smile. "A good story..." The Way of the Theater—Vicky's path to enlightenment.

Carlos comes over. He's tentative with me, unusually sober. We sit at my card table and play chess. Carlos loves chess. He's a rated player in New York. I, on the other hand, play chess like a cuckoo on LSD. The first couple of games, Carlos is puzzled by my ridiculous moves. He is used to tactics, strategy. He ponders the board carefully, trying to figure out my grand plan. Of course, there is none. I have never had a plan in my life, grand or otherwise.

After a few games it dawns on him that I am incapable of thinking more than two moves ahead. He is vastly amused by my clownish chess playing. I guess that's part of my motivation. It brings me tremendous relief to be able to make him laugh again. It takes some of the sting out of my guilt for having left him in the dirt.

As summer approaches, my confidence starts coming back. I'm on the phone a little more often, reestablishing communication with the outside world. When I'm with Rose, sex and scotch are no longer the minimum daily requirements for me to relax. I find myself sitting quietly for hours on her couch, just talking with her.

I go to see my kids more often. In the beginning, after I left, it was all I could do to get on the phone for a couple of minutes with my daughter. Now I'm dropping over to the house to play for a couple of hours, taking the kids out for walks in the park.

I get up the courage to venture beyond my safe little neighborhood and go out to the theater with Vicky. The first piece we see is a monologue, a terrific solo performance by a man from the Midwest, a collection of autobiographical sketches linked together to form a life story. He plays all the characters. The performer is so passionate, so mesmerizing, that I don't notice, till he comes out to take a bow afterward, that one of his arms is deformed, shriveled up against his body.

Back at my studio later that night, I pace back and forth. The experience of witnessing that monologue has energized me. I can feel the juice stirring in me again, the need to tell a story about my terrible six-month merry-go-round.

A couple of days later I get a call from a fellow broadcaster at WBAI, David Rothenberg. He's a publicist and earns his money handling new shows, cabarets, restaurants, and the like. David tells me he has been hired by a man named Marvin Greenberg, who owns a couple of restaurants in Manhattan. This same Mr. Greenberg has just opened up a back room cabaret at a place called Hamburger Harry's—just off Times Square—and is booking entertainment. David, who knows all about my recent misadventures, asks me if I want to work there, tell a story. I put him off, telling him I have an idea for a story, but I'm feeling a little wobbly: I need to lay back for a little while.

"What laying back?" he asks.

"David," I tell him, "I just crawled out of a train wreck. I need to fix myself." He doesn't see a problem. "So, fix yourself! Tell a story." David is sometimes flip and cynical but he is a little like Vicky; if he has any religion at all, it's the theater. "C'mon, Mr. Suffering Jew. Do something for yourself! You'll make a little money, have some fun."

"I don't know. I'm reading about Zen Buddhism now."

"Is it funny? Can you fit it into the act?"

"David."

"When you find the true path, give me a call."

Chapter Twenty-nine

Hollywood and Bust, I call it. I'm on stage again, at Hamburger Harry's Cabaret on West Forty-fifth Street, just one short block off Broadway.

Hamburger Harry's is a jolly, if noisy, place to work. You get to the cabaret through a black-curtained doorway, in the back of the main restaurant jammed with tourists and loud preshow crowds.

At Hamburger's, my powers of concentration have to be pretty good to focus on the show. While I wait to go onstage, I sit in a beat-up orange plastic chair, two feet from the dishwashers and the cooks. The cabaret concept is new here and it has never really made much of an impression on the kitchen staff, who constantly smash pots and pans together, drop plates, and trade stories in loud machine gun–speed Spanish.

The show starts at around eight o'clock, or whenever the last diner finishes his triple root beer–ice cream sundae. David Rothenberg is doing a good publicity job, making calls, placing listings in the papers and such, so the houses are pretty good. Half, sometimes two thirds of the room is always filled. The audiences are cheerful. And the money is great. I keep the whole door price, ten bucks a shot, so even thirty people means three hundred in cash at the end of the night. I give Vicky, with whom I'm working again, twenty percent of the take and keep the rest.

I look at the clock. Five minutes after eight. Long enough. I want to be out there. I peek around the side of the curtain. The houselights are just going down, the people have finished their milkshakes and burgers deluxe, I get up, push the curtain aside, walk onstage, sit down on my stool, look around the whole place slowly, sigh...

You know, I was sitting backstage blowing my nose. It's allergy season and I'm wondering, when will I ever get over all these tics and ailments and complaints I carry around with me? Well, what's new—I say. I was always allergic to something, or coming down with something, some dread illness.

I'm sure this had a lot to do with my mother. To compete with her. My mother was always sick on a grand scale, mentally and physically. In the end, though, competing with her was hopeless—you always lose when you try to beat your parents at something.

Actually, a lot of Jewish boys I've known had this condition—the allergies were a bond of undying love between a boy and his mom.

I went to an allergist who lived far away in Manhattan. I only lived in Queens, an hour and a half away. But to me, at that time, that meant crossing the great divide.

These days, of course, any normal person has a right to be scared on the subway—there's so much violence—you have to watch out all the time. But back in 1960 there wasn't all that much violence. You didn't have teenagers wandering around eating people and throwing them on the tracks. No, what bothered me, what truly terrified me, was that there were so many powerful machines down there, and that it was so dark and so far underground. I was always afraid the station would fall in on me, that the train would smash into a wall or a steel girder and kill us all in a mangled, bloody heap. I was riven with the worst premonitions of disaster. Also, I had read a lot of mythology when I was a kid, and I had a vague sense that the underworld, you understand—THE underworld, might be right beneath my feet, just waiting to grab me.

I should have brought a book to read, I would have been better off....

The train pulls in, lumbering and screeching on the rails, and I get in the front car. Now this is important...I always got on the front car of the train, and even to this day, I often find myself drawn to the front car of any train.

I think it has something do with (and maybe this is just a masculine thing because I don't always see women doing this) some sort of identification with the surge of power that you feel being in the front of the train.

When you're a teenager in the city, one of the most powerful things you have any personal connection with, since there are no bulls or horses or tractors around, is a subway train. When that big steel train comes rumbling and roaring into the station, it just fills your blood with a kind of crazy excitement.

Course, now that I'm an old guy, it just seems like a lot of noise and trouble. The other day, I saw a kid with spiked purple hair wearing a T-shirt that said: "If It's Too Loud, You're Too Old!" Probably true. But anyway, back when I was a kid, I was excited by all that noise and power. So, I always got on the front car. Also, without realizing it, I always sat somewhere near the front window of the car, the one that had all that crisscrossed wire embedded in it—reinforced glass, I guess you call it.

I looked over at the window. I wanted terribly to get closer to it, but I never had the actual nerve, though it tugged at me constantly to just get up, walk over, and look out of it. And why? ...I felt it would be very embarrassing, extremely uncool, to stand up there like some dork, some pinhead, and just be staring out the window of the train. I mean, after all, I was fifteen, for Christ's sake!

Because I wanted so much to look out that window and because I never would, a terrible tug-of-war took place in my mind. The best I could do in my half-assed way was to sit as close as possible to the window and look at it out of the corner of my eye. Oh, man....

So the train keeps rumbling along, stops to let people on and off, and then roars up again into the tunnel, headed for the next station. And I'm sitting there, sniffing, scratching, picking at my fingers and thinking about my mother at home and how she was sick and how her sickness made me sick, and how I never wanted to ever go home again, and all I had to look forward to was being stuck in the arm by some fool in a white coat....

At the third or fourth stop, the doors opened and closed, but just before they closed completely, a big fat hand thrust itself into the gap. The doors opened again, because this hand wouldn't move, and into the car came what we used to call in those days, with our total teenage lack of sensitivity, a retard.... This guy, who could have been anywhere between fifteen and thirty-five, rolls right into the car with a lopsided, nutty smile on his face....

Now on this car—it's the middle of the day, you understand, not rush hour— were about ten other passengers. A couple of working guys carrying tools, a couple of businessmen with their suits and shined shoes, and a few housewives—

ladies going into Manhattan to go shopping. And like most people on the train, they are reading something—bibles or newspapers or paperback novels.

I, of course, had nothing to read. I was too busy playing my long-running starring role, as the Jewish Hamlet from Queens, starkly worried—to be or not to be—on the F train....

Anyway, this guy, the retard, walks right into the center of the car and says—without the slightest preamble or hesitation—"Here's Herbie! Herbie is here!" in a very loud voice, looking around with a big wide stupid grin on his face.

He was kind of slump-shouldered, with thick arms and legs; small, dim eyes; a big, thick jaw; a large nose; and wide, hairy ears. He wore a zipped-up but very loose jacket that ballooned out in front as if he were pregnant. On his feet he had big black shiny shoes. He stood there for a half a minute after his announcement, looked around, then, again to nobody in particular, he said, "Here's Herbie! Herbie is here!"...

And I'm thinking to myself...oh, God, please. I've got enough troubles in the world already—please don't let this retard sit down next to me and drive me nuts the whole way into the city. I want—I think I deserve—a little privacy in the vastness of my misery.

Of course, typical for any subway ride in New York City, people just kept reading their newspapers and books. And what were they supposed to do, after all. If people looked up every time a nut or a lunatic or deranged person came into a subway car in this city, they'd dislocate their necks. So you keep reading. But I did notice a little smile on a couple of faces, little twitches at the corners of mouths of condescension and amusement.

And I, without a book to hide behind—I couldn't help watching this guy Herbie with that terrible sick knowledge that people who are a little bit freakish or lonely, or who live in a very strange family the way I did, have something in common with other people who have problems. Residents, so to speak, of the same warped, leaky boat...I watched him with a feeling of disgust and awful, unwanted identity.

He kept yelling, "Here's Herbie! Herbie is here!" looked all around the car, finally perceived that no one was paying any attention to him, and, without further ado, unzips his jacket and pulls out, of all things, a plastic steering wheel.

I don't know if they still have this toy, but we had 'em when we were kids: a plastic steering wheel with a suction cup you stuck on a dashboard—so you could pretend you were driving, just like Mommy and Daddy.

Herbie goes over to the train's front window—the very window that I had been looking at and never going near—he just walks right up to the window, as if he owned it, and, after moistening the suction cup with a generous amount of spit, sticks the steering wheel right on to the window.

So, in effect, this retard, Herbie, is now driving the train.

And I mean to say, friends, this guy had absolutely no doubts. This was a guy who knew just what he wanted to do. He was not plagued with ambivalence, he did not need an aptitude test or a personal counselor. No, no, he was like Albert Schweitzer or Jonas Salk, or some great adventurer—from the day he was born he knew. He knew he was going to conquer the Zambesi or be the greatest brain surgeon that ever lived, or the most heroic train driver in the New York City subways. Whereas I, of course, had no idea what I wanted to be, or even if I wanted to be.

The train pulls into Continental Avenue, about halfway through Queens now—stops, passengers get on and off, and pulls out again, lumbering and rolling over the tracks, clackety clackety clack. And Herbie was steering the train—and making plenty of noise in case anybody wasn't sure what he was doing—Rumnnnn, mumnnnn!

We go into a hard curve and Herbie just sort of leans into it. The train hits a straightaway and he grips the wheel for more control. Another curve, another burst of speed—wheeooo! This guy was having the time of his life. And since he was so intent on his job, he wasn't looking around at all—now all the people in the car were looking at him with these amused, pitying looks on their faces.

But I wasn't amused—I wasn't pitying him—I was fascinated. Jesus Christ, here's this guy, a moron, a half-wit, and here I am, so smart—me and my high IQ—a handsome devil (at least my mother thought so, and a couple of girls here and there); I can run faster than practically anybody in my neighborhood, throw a ball faster and further, I'm the marbles and baseball-card champ of 130th Avenue...and there's this guy! He looks like a pile of hay, a freak of nature—comes on the train and does the one thing I had always wanted to do—he just goes right up to the window and he's driving the train.

We hit a real heavy turn, which Herbie negotiates beautifully. And at that moment, the door to the engineer's booth swings open and right next to Herbie, who do I see but the engineer, the actual driver of the train.

He's got this little railroad cap on, like in one of my old children's books; a little black guy with gray hair, hunched over the control lever of the train, and he has a totally bored look on his face—like he's in a trance or half asleep. As far as this guy is concerned, he might as well have been at home, watching TV. And right next to him, about a foot away, although the engineer couldn't see him because the door was in the way, was Herbie, standing straight up, legs braced, every muscle straining—driving for his life! Driving what could easily have been the Starship Enterprise *on its five-year voyage through space.*

We were getting to the last stop in Queens, right before the tunnel into Manhattan, really roaring along, with more and more people getting on the train at each stop—and they all saw Herbie, immediately looked away, then sneaked around to look at him again. Though it was getting crowded, there was a space around him; people kept back a little. You know how it is in New York, you have to create a vacuum, a little no-man's-land between yourself and whoever happens to be the nut du jour. But Herbie noticed not a bit. "Here's Herbie! Herbie is Here!" he screamed at the top of his lungs, hands gripping the wheel, driving that old train wherever it had to go....

Well, all strange things come to an end. We get to the stop in midtown where I had to get off. As I left, Herbie was waiting at the window, hunkered down, kind of drumming his right foot on the floor, impatient to drive on.

I went upstairs, and here I was in Manhattan, which I detested. I mean, Queens was hard enough for a case like me, with the occasional person I ran into on the street, but with my kind of shyness and my practically symphonic breadth and depth of neuroses, Manhattan was like a terrible carnival that somebody dropped me into without warning or protection.

I walked the streets—got to the allergist's office, and here was this jerk waiting for me. He was, like most doctors I saw when I was a kid, a Depression and World War II guy—big, tall, bluff, and hearty, about forty-five or so, with a tough, rugged face, a man who made his living sticking long, sharp needles into helpless young people.

Now to be fair a little—I do try once in a while to be fair—this guy, though he was an allergist and an ex-marine, had some dim understanding of psychology, of psychosomatic problems. In fact, he would have had to be deaf, dumb, and blind not to see what a twitchy mess I was. So he shakes my hand, which disappeared inside his, and he says, in a firm, manly tone, "How's Mother?" Of course—naturally—he wouldn't say, "How's your mother?" but, "How's Mother?" thereby immediately making her a principle of existence, a basic fact of life rather than just any mother, or just my mother, an ordinary human being—who I was having trouble enough understanding to begin with.

And what could I say? "Oh, she's OK, she's alright." Just a small problem, Doc, she wishes she never had children, and sometimes I wish I could hit her over the head with a heavy shovel and put us both out of our misery. "Yeah, she's good—she's good."

The doctor sticks a dartboard-ful of needles in my right arm and I get out of there fast. In the outer office, his nurse says good-bye to me—I thought she was going to ask, "How's Mother?" too. As far as I was concerned, all grown women were directly connected by telepathy, if not actual phone line, to my mother....

I walk my itchy, sore, sorry way back to the subway station to get the train back to Queens. It was about two-thirty in the afternoon now, and I could hardly be more depressed. Seeing Herbie driving the train and me not being able to do it really got to me—how did he manage to achieve that? Would I ever do anything I ever really wanted to do?

I knew when I got home finally, my mother would, like always, be in her room, and she was going to be moaning or crying, upset, hysterical—and the rabbi or the doctor or both of them were going to be there. Somebody was going to be there, kowtowing to her, ministering to her—and I'd walk in and have to be quiet so she didn't get more "upset." Shit—my old half-life again; back hiding in my room upstairs, staring out the window at the cemetery in back of my house. What a fucking miserable way to live! The injections hurt like hell, visions of doom rolled around in my head, and I kept seeing Herbie at his post in front of the window.

I get back on the train, headed uptown and out to Queens. As usual, without paying attention, I had gotten on the front car again. I sat there for a couple of stops, leaning forward with my elbows on my knees, my head in my hands, staring at the floor. Then, something came over me—a light lit up somewhere in my brain. I sat up and looked over sideways at the front window, and I suddenly thought: "What the hell!" My life was nothing but a bottomless cesspool anyhow. I didn't want to go home to this woman, but I was going to whether I liked it or not—life was just passing me by, there were a million things I wanted to do and never did a goddamn one of them. That's it! I said to myself, I'm just gonna do it!

I stood up and walked right over to the window—even though the car was full of people (any one of whom could have been, at that very moment, in direct communication with my mother). I stood in front of the window and just put my face right up against the glass—and looked out. The train began to pick up some speed—it was an express train, skipping stations, moving fast.

God, what a view! What an astounding, beautiful world I was looking into! In that moment, I completely forgot that anybody might be looking at me, forgot that I might be making a fool of myself entirely. So what?! Here I was in the front part of this great train that had no thought for anybody else in the world as it surged through the tunnel. And I was at the very head of it. It was the feeling the first sperm must have when that starter's pistol goes off—bang!—and those millions and billions of sperms get out there and start that great race for the egg. The fastest, the biggest, toughest sperm, racing like the wind, knocking everybody else aside, races for that egg. He knows exactly where he's going. Whammo! Well, that's just what this train was doing. It was charging through that tunnel, passing people, waiting in the local stations, passing them like they were nothing but ants....

Oh, I tell you: have you ever had enough guts or child in you to get up there— it doesn't matter how old you are—and look out the front of a train? It's one of the great sights you'll ever see. You have this long, beautiful, dark tunnel, and the train is hurtling through it with the walls only two feet away. It seems like you're going a hundred miles an hour! At the far end, off in the distance, you can see the lights of another station, but in between, where it's really dark, you can see all kinds of red and green, yellow and blue lights—traffic signals. You have no idea what they mean, or you don't care, they look like nothing else but beautiful jewels sparkling all around.

Suddenly, everything in my regular dreary world had disappeared, and it was just me and this train. I was this train, zooming along through this tunnel, going a million miles an hour, and the stops were coming, whizzing by. I could feel my fingers twitching and I wished I had the same kind of steering wheel that Herbie had, because right now I was in charge of this train.

Once we were in Queens, we passed by one of those spots where you can see trains coming in the other direction—there was no wall in between, just iron girders. The train slowed down a little bit, but it was still going at a pretty good speed, and I saw coming in the distance another train. I held my hand up over my eyes and peered into the front window of the other train. And as it got closer, who did I see but Herbie, driving the train, headed right toward me! I couldn't believe it. There he was, getting closer and closer, and then I knew he saw me, driving my train, and it was a moment of identification I can hardly describe to you—a moment that very few people have in common. We were both driving these huge powerful machines, responsible for so many people, lives dependent on us, the destiny, perhaps, of thousands of people in our hands.

We were coming closer and closer. Herbie lifted his hand and smiled and waved at me. I forgot everything. I forgot my self-consciousness, I forgot he was a retard. I forgot I wasn't a retard. I forgot I was a quivering wimp.

I raised my hand and we just gave each other a salute—a kind of grim, professional understanding passed between us at that moment—two great men, responsible for the destiny of the universe, were at the helm.

Herbie's train zoomed past and I kept driving.... I drove all the way into Queens, to the last stop. And finally, as the train rolled into that last station, reality—horrible, sad old reality, returned. I had this sinking feeling in my guts because I knew I was coming to the end of my trip and I was headed back home. I got off the train and climbed onto the bus and I could feel my shoulders start to droop. I started picking at my fingernails, biting my lip, scratching at my allergy shots.

I got off the bus in Laurelton and walked the few blocks to my house and— sure enough—there was the rabbi's car and the doctor's car parked at the curb. And I was thinking to myself, oh, God, I hope her bedroom door is closed and she doesn't hear me come in, doesn't call me, or bother me at all.... I felt such exhilaration.

I sneaked in the house. Fortunately, her door was closed. She was being ministered to in there—being given pills and consolation.... I walked quietly upstairs to my room so that she wouldn't know I was there. I closed the door to my room and I looked out the window. And then the vision came back to me! The charging subway train, driving down the dark, beautiful tunnel a hundred miles an hour, the power of the universe in my capable hands.

It's a tremendous relief for me to be up on that stage, telling stories again, redemption after all my sad, awful failures the past several months. Magically gone are all the demons I used to be plagued by when I was performing. I don't feel angry. I don't feel crazily ecstatic. I'm just happy to be sitting here, entertaining people. So, it is more than a little sad for me when after three weeks fly by I'm performing the last show of my run. I've done well, brought in good crowds, but still, there are other acts Mr.

304 / M I K E F E D E R

Hamburger is considering. I finish the show, thank the audience for listening, and walk off.

After the room empties out, I come back out and sit onstage. Vicky comes up with the cash from the door and we split it up. She's acting a little strange—flushed, like she's had a drink, something she never did. "What's with you?" I ask her. She gives me one of her show-business hugs. "Stephen Holden from the *Times* was here tonight, and he's doing a review of your show in the paper tomorrow." The *Times*! Oh, no! I feel like grabbing a crucifix to hold up. Back, you fiend!

Sure enough, there is an extremely good review in the paper the next day and yet another article the next day in the weekend section about my story and Vicky's directing work. Calls pour in, hundreds of people wanting to see my show. David calls and tells me Mr. Hamburger wants to book me for an unlimited run.

At the end of a show, I have a big roll of tens and twenties in my pocket and a couple of mellow double whiskeys (on the house) resting comfortably in my stomach. I ride home in a cab, watching the lights and the people out the window, a private show staged for my personal viewing. I get back to my studio about ten-thirty, take a shower, undress, and sit at the window, letting the fresh river breeze flow over me. Such a life. What more could a guy ask for? Well, one thing: he could ask for all his problems to disappear. No matter how much I might wish to be, I am not a prince in a fairy tale. I have a complicated real life. Decisions still have to be made about people and my future. Still, sitting there, pleasantly drunk and bathing in the cool breezes, recalling the happy faces of the crowd back at the show, it's pretty easy to dismiss the worrisome parts of my life. There is one worry, though, that I can't quite banish from my immediate consciousness. Something that keeps buzzing around the edges of my contentment like a pesky fly. My shrink is on the verge of firing me.

I'm down to one session a week now, but the money problem remains. I still owe him a sizable back bill of almost a thousand dollars. In fact, it was up to fifteen hundred until a couple weeks ago, when I gave him a bagful of cash from my show. That was all I could afford to give him, so the relentless discussion of my overdue bill continues, session after session.

I denounce Dr. Klein for what I see as his uncaring attitude. He tells me this is just another evasion, a dodge. Increasingly, I begin to see him as abrasive and ineffectual. His little habits, always bothersome, now seem positively obnoxious. For instance, he's always either smoking or trying to stop smoking. And when he's trying to stop smoking, he sucks or chews on something, a toothpick, a pencil, a pen.

One day, I'm in there having the same old tiresome debate about money and hostility with him and the fountain pen he's sucking on falls out of his mouth. I notice, for the first time during the session, that his lips and his tongue are dyed purple. Here he is, the big psychotherapist, professionally interpreting my failure to act responsibly and my hostility, and all I can see is this big purple tongue flapping over purple lips. I hold up my hand to get him to stop talking. "Wait," I say, "let's wait till you pick up your pen." He stares at me, a bit insulted, "I don't need to pick up my pen."

"Yes you do, you need to suck on it."

"Oh, do you think I *need* to suck on that pen?"

"Don't give me that shrink bullshit. Of *course* you need to suck on that pen. You know it and I know it. You're always sucking on something. If you don't suck on that pen, you won't be able to concentrate and if you can't concentrate you won't understand what I'm talking about. So why don't you just pick it up and we'll get on with things."

After a long pause, he says, "Mr. Feder, I do *not* need to suck on that pen. Why don't we continue."

"Look, I don't care if you suck on it. It's OK with me. God knows I got enough tics of my own. You think I'm gonna judge you?" I fold my arms and stare at him. It is a therapeutic standoff. Finally, after another long pause, during which he is getting visibly nervous, he says, "All right, Mr. Feder, if it makes *you* feel able to continue the session..." He swoops down, grabs the pen and sticks it back in his mouth.

The next week, no sooner am I in my chair than he informs me that he is going to "terminate" me if I don't pay up. Three weeks, then I'm out. Terminate me?! What a word to use..."terminate." The only people who would ever use that word besides therapists are the CIA and the KGB.

A week later, my last session. The last few minutes of my last hour with Dr. Klein. I'm sad, and not a little scared to be going out on my own. And a little angry too, because now at the last hour, I detect in him definite relief that this is our final session. It isn't just the money after all. I am really a burden, a difficult, stubborn, sometimes scary patient. Who needs the aggravation?

Just before I leave I ask him, "Can you give me any final words, something I can take with me?" He looks at me with compassion and says, "Well, you have a very cruel conscience." That's it. We shake hands and I leave, closing his office door behind me.

As if having to separate from Klein were a sign, the first warning of trouble ahead, everything starts to unwind. The demand for tickets at Hamburger's has been slowing in the last week until it's down to a trickle. I'm informed that I have three nights left and then my run is over. No more stories, no more happy faces, no more free whiskey.

I sit up in my studio on June 16, my birthday, looking out at the river. There are three boats headed downstream, out to the ocean. For the first time, I don't see them as friendly visitors just passing by my happy little spot on land but as vessels of possibility and rescue ignoring me, abandoning me to longing and despair. The magic spell I have been under for the last couple of months has broken for sure. All my doubts and worries, all my conflicting and heavy responsibilities crowd into the room with me.

Here I am, a forty-two-year-old man, living (as a guest) in a small single room, a quart of orange juice and a half-eaten bagel in the refrigerator. No job, no plans, practically no money. A family waiting for me to make up my mind whether I'm going to come back to them and be a real husband and father. A woman who really seems to love me, patiently waiting to see if I'll leave everything behind me and build a new life with her.

The summer crawls on. I am, as Artie might have put it, "history, babe." I have no prospects, no money, and a blank future. I'm lonely and exhausted by the emotional tug-of-war going on between my wife and Rose. My wife pulls from her side, citing my responsibilities to the kids. They miss me, my absence was unnatural and cruel. I'm making them neurotic. Rose, in her style, pulls from her end. No manipulation, hysterics, or threats. She knows her legal and moral claim on me (*the big prize*) runs a poor second to Susan and the kids. Her only claim is love. In the weeks before I move back, we lay side by side in her bed, listening to her favorite music, country, and looking silently out the window.

The only thing I have left that seems to be free of doubt and guilt is my radio show. Even there, however, in my private sanctuary, the radio studio, I'm tapped out. I have always used my show as a way to explore my moral and emotional dilemmas—stream-of-consciousness style. No subject is taboo, but I am so embarrassed by my failures of the past year that my shows take on a tentative and almost, at times, listless quality. I can't talk about my affair, of course, and I haven't told the listeners that I have moved out of my house. I'm sure they wouldn't forgive me for leaving my kids. So I become furtive and evasive on the air—not very entertaining.

With my show-business career stalled, I cast around for other ways to make money and stay in the flow of things artistic. Vicky tells me she's still pursuing off off Broadway theaters for me but hasn't come up with anything yet. Jake and Artie, the showbiz twins, are not in the picture. They operate at higher elevations and I have slipped beneath their radar. Hamburger Harry's is booked for the next couple of months—singers and bands, mostly.

I call ICM to see if there is a warm ember left from the fire of their earlier enthusiasm. I have yet to write my book, so there is nothing to be gotten from the literary department. My stock has plummeted to zero in the movie and television department. Even Sam Cohn's *secretary* isn't taking my calls, so the whole idea of a regional theater run is dead. There are still two possibilities: the speaker's bureau, where they book speakers for conventions and meetings, and the commercial department. The speaker's bureau usually handles celebrities like retired pro quarterbacks and famous unindicted politicians. My chances there are slim, though the guy in charge says he'll try to line up a few conventions for me. The only thing left is commercials. ICM, along with several other established talent agencies, sends out a steady stream of professional announcers and actors to audition for radio and TV commercials. Landing a good commercial can be a small gold mine.

Naturally, I hate the idea of doing commercials; they're all disgusting, and then there's the hypocrisy of me being a shill for some company and simultaneously holding forth on left-wing WBAI—the people's radio station. At this point, though, such considerations are minor; I need money—something to prove to Susan that I'm bringing home the bacon, no matter how thin and burned a piece it might be.

I register with the people at ICM and within a couple of days they have three auditions scheduled.

I show up at an ad agency's offices in midtown, check in with a receptionist, and am handed the copy—for Iron City Beer, a local Pittsburgh product they want to market in New York. It is for a radio commercial, no more than ten lines or so, wrapped around the sound of bottle tops being snapped open and the bracing, manly sound of Iron City beer splashing into a tall glass.

Looking around the reception room, I see ten other auditioners, distinguished, prosperous-looking men, most in their fifties and sixties, all making notes on the copy, some pacing back and forth, reciting the lines out loud. I actually recognize a couple of them. One is a lead actor on a soap opera I've seen at Rose's house—another a famous Broadway musical star.

My nerves carry me into the men's room. There are more auditioners in there. Silver-haired, brown-loafered, manicured men in expensive slacks and sweaters; actors, radio announcers, all with smooth, deep, masculine voices—real professional; all practicing their lines. *Ahh...that's good! ...Iron City Beer. I drink it, why don't you!* It is like a chorus, a round (with musical accompaniment from the occasional flushing toilet). One guy starts from the beginning of the copy, then another starts after the first, then another and another. *Ahh...Iron City...Why don't* [flush]. *Ahh, Iron...I drink* [flush]...*Why don't...Ahh...I drink* [flush]. *That's Good. Iron... Drink it!* [flush]

I take out my copy, reading and pacing in front of the urinals and sinks along with the others, my rough, not very professional voice submerged in the larger chorus. *Ahh, Iron City!* I find out later on that voice-over people routinely rehearse in bathrooms. The tiles make for great acoustics.

I come back outside and wait my turn in the reception area. They call me into the studio and ask me to "slate"(say) my name and read the copy. *Ahh, that's good...I drink it, why don't you?!* A voice comes over the studio speakers. "Good, but a little more manly please...." *Right, more manly.* "...I DRINK IT, WHY DON'T YOU?!"

"Thank you." That means I'm done, dismissed. I never hear from them again.

I go on a dozen auditions, two for television. It is always a nerve-wracking experience; not just the disgusting idea of prostituting myself, but the unreality of it, being "manly" or passionate or ecstatic about some product I never heard of and wouldn't touch with a twenty-foot pole. And the competition. A dozen, maybe two dozen guys, all superb, polished speakers. Successful, even wealthy men with beautiful voices. Most of them are on a first-name basis with one another. It is kind of a congenial club, one in which I am most definitely not a member.

By mid-fall, I am going on one audition after another, with no response: I'm getting poorer and poorer. I'm grateful for what ICM is doing for me but depressed by my failure and fed up with the whole experience. I call up the commercial agent there—a friendly, middle-aged woman named Irene Black. "I'm sorry, Irene, I can't do this anymore."

"C'mon Mike, they really liked you for Iron City—you almost got a callback."

"Irene, this is such garbage."

"Mike, garbage can pay very, very well."

I sigh.

"Look," she says, "do one more, then I'll stop sending you out."

"You got one more?"

"Yeah, it's a voice-over. They sent out the copy in advance, so you can come over here and pick it up."

I take the train down to ICM on Fifty-seventh Street and pick up the copy. It is a TV commercial for a new frozen-fruit dessert. The script describes a bunch of giant talking fruits, strawberries, bananas, blueberries, walking around and talking to each other about becoming a frozen dessert, then jumping, or being pulled, into a freezer. Irene tells me she's sending a lot of her clients over to the auditions. She has already sent over a strawberry, two blueberries, and a couple of oranges. I am her first banana.

I ride uptown, rehearsing my three lines on the #1 train. The scene reads like this: the fruits are shivering and jostling each other, waiting to see who'll be the first to jump into the freezer and become dessert. The strawberry has just insulted me, the banana, "You think you're so *biiig*, banana, but you look pretty yellow to me!" I get angry, "Oh, yeah, straw-berry, well I happen to know kids like *me* better!..." I practice the banana's lines over and over—trying to get the right sense of bravado, feeling the banana's character. I look up for a second to check which station we've just pulled into, and there are two teenage girls right across from me, star-ing at me and giggling. I must have been reading out loud. Jesus! This is what it has come to. *What to look for in the arts in the coming year. A talking banana.*

The commercial is scheduled for the next morning. All night I practice my lines, walking up and down in my studio, imagining the banana, feel-ing the banana, *being* the banana. The next morning I'm on the train, still practicing. I arrive at the ad agency at 9:00 A.M. for the audition. I'm in the bathroom, surrounded by all the other giant talking, pacing, preening fruits.

In the studio, I state my name and start to read. "Oh, yeah, strawber-ry, well I happen to know—" A voice sounds over the studio speaker from the control room, interrupting me. "What are you reading?" I try to look into the control room, but all I can see is my own reflection in the glass. I look up at the speaker. "The banana," I say.

"You're not the banana, you're the strawberry."

"No, excuse me, I'm the banana. I got the copy yesterday from Irene Black."

"Well, she made a mistake, then; you're the strawberry." *Alright, enough.* I snap.

"I am not the *goddamn* strawberry. I am the banana. I was the banana all day yesterday and all night last night. I was the banana on the train down here this morning." I jump up, practically shouting: "I *am* the banana!" There is a short pause, then, "You're the strawberry. Can you read it?"

"No!" I shout, throwing the copy down and walking out. So much for my commercial career. I move back into my house two days later.

PART SIX
ONE MORE TIME

CHAPTER THIRTY

I return home as a penitent.

Susan never says it out loud, but the understanding is clear. I have acted like a child, abandoned my family, and now I'm expected to do what husbands and fathers are supposed to do.

The week before I move back, I tell Rose. We sit in my studio, holding hands across the table. There is no way I can console her. I never explicitly say I am not going to see her anymore, but it is clear she is being relegated to her old position, waiting for me to come to her. I want her to tell me to go fuck myself—it would be so much simpler that way. But she doesn't, and I'm left with my own hurtful words hanging in the air. As she leaves the studio, she kisses me. Watching her walk down the hall to the elevator is no relief. That I will no longer be pulled in two directions just leaves me feeling bleak and alone.

The first couple of months back, the fall of 1987, I try to stick to the simple plan I have in my head: be as decent to my wife as possible and try to be a real father. And, write my book. There is nothing else I have to do but these three things. Surely, I can accomplish this.

At first things go pretty well. I have chosen a path and am following it. The kids are overjoyed to have me back, and I find some new, previously undiscovered well of energy to draw from. I give myself to them as I never managed to do before, especially Ben. I never really knew him at all—now I play with him for hours, take him out to shop and to see what's doing in the big wide world. At night I lay down next to him, tuck him in and read him stories till he closes his eyes. I smooth his golden hair with my hand and kiss his forehead.

I go up to the studio every day—we have a baby-sitter—and work on my book. I work at the typewriter for hours on end, making rapid progress. The book is past due and the people at Crown are not happy that I've been dragging my feet. Now I'm sailing along nicely and my editor is back in my camp: talking with me on the phone, meeting with me in his office, going over each story as I take it through various drafts. I feel like I have a purpose, a direction. I love seeing the blank white paper waiting in the typewriter for me to fill it with words. It is like taking a clean dive into a sparkling pool.

Things are going well, but as Thanksgiving approaches, I experience a few old symptoms, tiny warning signals: wisps of disgust, muted flares of irritation. Small, quick jets of fear spring up in my stomach and my chest. All of this I try to banish from my mind—*begone, neurosis! I renounce you and all your ways!*

Thanksgiving is hard, but I survive it with only a few gushes of hysteria; I somehow get it into my head that the turkey I had gotten from the butcher is spoiled and that I'm going to poison the entire family. However, the bird is edible and the day turns out to be, if not perfect, at least a reasonable facsimile of a real family event. Yet—no matter what willpower I bring to bear to fight it off—I feel something elemental turn in me that day. A flare goes up in my psyche, lighting up again the familiar flat horrors of my internal no-man's-land. I awake the very next day in a sweat, my hands and feet jiggling, my mind racing with disturbing images. I take a long walk by myself around the reservoir in Central Park. The dead metal grayness is back in the sky and I can't shake the creeping frozen feeling that is rising up in my stomach.

CHAPTER THIRTY-ONE

E arly December. Things get worse. Depressed, I go to bed earlier each night, waking up at three in the morning, stark-staring awake, thoughts zooming through my skull, fear rippling through me.

At dawn I jump out of bed, throw on my clothes, and hit the streets. My hands twitch, my eyes blink.

Susan and the kids get on my nerves again, and this part of my sudden regression is more upsetting than anything else. I'd finally established a real connection between us—and I don't want to drift completely away again into that old, cold rigidity.

I'm appalled by my sudden relapse. Where is my resolve—where has my simple plan gone? Was my pledge of rectitude, taken only three months before, nothing but a self-delusion? I wrack my brain to try to figure out what is getting at me, what force is gnawing at my guts, but it is almost impossible to perceive anything through the wall of fear and anxiety that increasingly surrounds me.

In my studio, instead of writing I pace, fidgeting and mumbling to myself, or I am overcome by a drugged-like torpor, so I can hardly keep my eyes open. It is almost impossible to concentrate on my book. I just can't fail everyone *again*. I have to get a hold of myself. No matter what, this book *will* be finished. I squeeze out the pages, one at a time.

Sometimes it takes hours—between nerve spasms, running to the bathroom, gulps of water right from the faucet—just to produce a couple of hundred words.

Two weeks before Christmas. On a Saturday afternoon, wet and shivering from walking for hours in a freezing drizzle, I step into a tiny coffee shop in Spanish Harlem, way up on the East Side near Lexington Avenue. The minute I enter and sit at the counter I feel better. It's like a foreign country. Every sign is in Spanish, with a couple of tiny English translations in parentheses below them; everybody is speaking Spanish. There is an altar—a wooden shelf, up on the wall over the cash register, with different-colored candles in glass, Jesus, saints, necklaces, flowers, coins. I could imagine I'm in San Juan and not a mere thirty blocks from my own apartment.

The place is small—no more than four tables, and six stools at the counter. Steam rises everywhere, from food cooking in the kitchen, from the big steel coffee machine; from coffee cups, cigarettes, ashtrays. The windows are completely fogged up—not a face or person or car is visible on the other side. I look at the window and try to spell out the name of the place, written in big gold letters. It is La Esperanza (Hope) Coffee Shop.

Hunching over the counter, sipping a burning *café con leche*, I look up at the altar and see, toward the back, a plaster statue of the Virgin Mary: she is wearing a golden crown and is dressed in a light-blue robe. Her delicate hand is raised in an attitude of blessing, and on her white face is a slight smile. She radiates forgiveness.

Inhaling coffee steam, lost in my hazy half-dreams, I notice, out of the corner of my eye, in the back of the shop, one of those old-fashioned wooden telephone booths with the closing doors. It is suddenly very clear to me what I want to do. I go over to the booth, take a quarter out of my pocket, and dial Rose's number. She picks up on the first ring.

"Hi."

"Hi, it's me. Can I come over?"

"When?"

"Would now be OK?"

"Yes. Come over."

"OK. I'll be right there."

I go outside and start walking, through sheets of rain, the twenty blocks to Rose's building. I get there, soaking wet, go upstairs, and knock on her door. She opens it and we are instantly holding on to each other for dear life—we barely have the presence of mind to close the door behind us—it seems like years since I've seen her. In five minutes we are in bed. After practically eating each other alive, we lay next to each other for a long time, in blissful silence.

Christmas comes and goes. I throw myself into the holiday spirit, buying a tree, decorating it with the kids' help, wrapping presents, taking pictures the next morning as the wrapping paper goes flying and the kids get overwhelmed. I am truly happy doing these simple, traditional things, but the great irony is that I am only able to do them because I have Rose in my life. I am filling my tank with love and sympathy at her place, then motoring back home and running on that very same fuel in my own house.

By mid-January, I have finally finished the first complete draft of my book and hand it in to my editor. There will be a lot of correcting, editing, and rewriting to do, but it is finally off my back. Oddly enough, though I should have predicted it, handing in my book doesn't bring me any relief. It just highlights the profound blankness of my life. Now I have no project, nothing to divert me from the onslaught of my self-torment.

I go up to my studio during the long, freezing winter days and sit there, with the window wide open, wrapped in my shirt, sweater, and winter coat, drinking scotch straight from the bottle. The leafless trees in the park creak in the icy wind—the blue-gray Hudson looks like cold liquid lead. I feel like the river is calling me to come and take a swim—I can tuck myself in under the water and finally get some sleep.

I hardly sleep at all now and eat virtually nothing. I shake from weakness and cold and fear. The kids are worried about me, but when I try to reassure them, it only makes them worry more. I got some bootleg Valium from a guy at WBAI. I take ten, then twenty milligrams a day—sitting in a back room at the station, watching the steam heat spurt from a leaky valve on a radiator—practically nodding out with my head on a desk, looking at the open window a few feet away from me, twenty floors up.

CHAPTER THIRTY-TWO

"You're not really gonna kill yourself, are you?" The little guy sitting across from me—Sanford Brodsky, my new shrink— is taking a real chance, I think, provoking me like that. I'm leaning forward in my chair, disheveled, wild-eyed, daring him to prove that he can keep me from doing myself in.

We exchange stares. He's a small, shrewd-looking, sharp-eyed man in his early sixties. Finally, he says, "Go ahead: say nothing for the whole hour if you want—it's no skin off my nose." I believe him, and somehow this loosens me up a touch. I tell him I'm betraying my wife, using my girlfriend like she was a bottle of scotch, that I'm hurting my children, and in general am a worthless, useless piece of shit—better off out of this world. I give him as much of my history as I can stand to hear myself repeat. He listens intently, his little black hawk-eyes never leaving my face. Finally, I grind to a halt, paralyzed by the recitation of the long string of my horrors.

He leans forward, closing the gap between us. This is the first time I have ever seen a shrink do that: "Do you really want to die?" he asks.

I look at him for a few seconds, then, for the first time in about forty minutes, I soften up. I unzip my coat halfway and lean back a little in my chair. Deep down inside, I can feel a click—like a tiny switch has been thrown, a short small jolt of juice has shot off somewhere, penetrating the iceberg lodged in my chest.

Brodsky smiles—a small, ironic twist of the lips, a little gleam in his eye. "You don't really want to kill yourself, Mike, do you?" A couple of seconds go by and my eyes fill up with tears. "No, I don't. I don't really want to do it."

"That's what I thought."

Brodsky and I work out a plan, some simple steps to keep my sanity and patch my life back together. First, "Mike, you got to stop taking those fucking tranquilizers. I won't work with anybody who takes pills." Check! No more pills.

"And you have to get a job, any job. Nobody can do nothing all day without going nuts. Having a job would be like a vacation for you right now." Get a job. Check.

"And you have to get yourself another creative project now that your book is done...you're an artist, you have to do something artistic." Check. Be an artist. Whatever he says. It hasn't taken me more than one and a half sessions—seventy-five minutes—with him for me to consider myself adopted.

"And you have to simplify your life," he continues, pointing his finger at me. "You have to stop seeing your girlfriend." Check, stop seeing my girlfriend. *Hold it...wait—not see Rose anymore? Just be with Susan alone?* This is taking things a little too far. I hold up my hand for him to stop. "Hold it a second."

"What?"

"I don't know if I can do that, stop seeing my girlfriend. It wouldn't be right, just to stop like that. She'd fall apart."

"I thought we agreed—you were going to listen to what I told you."

"Yeah, but—" I hang my head down. He goes on, "I'm not telling you to give up the girlfriend for good—that's something you have to figure out later when you calm down." That is a little relief, but I was worried about right now. "I don't know what will happen if—" He flushes, thumps the arm of his chair.

"Oh, bullshit, don't tell me she's gonna fall apart! Nobody dies from a broken heart!" He stares at me for a couple of seconds. "Besides," he says, "who are you really concerned about here—her or you?"

I sigh. Life without Rose. "OK," I tell him, "I'll call her and tell her."

Leaving his building, I walk to the corner, Seventy-fifth and Third. It is freezing out. I walk across the street to a phone booth, put my last quarter in the slot, and call Rose at work, hoping she isn't in. She picks up after two rings.

"It's me," I say. I want to believe she knows what I'm going to say. "Look," I tell her, "I can't see you anymore." Silence. "It's too much. I'm falling apart." Silence. "And it's no good for you, the way I keep going back and forth, is it?" I can see her in her little office. I know she's crying.

"Are you there?"

"Yes."

"I have to go now—I'm at a booth." Now I can hear her crying. "This is something I have to do."

"Good-bye."

"Good-bye."

I hang up and stand there holding the receiver, my fingers numb from the cold. *OK, OK, nobody dies from a broken heart—she'll get over it. I have to do this. It's for everybody's good.* I start walking up Third Avenue to the crosstown bus on Seventy-ninth Street. It is the day before Valentine's Day. Just yesterday, I'd gone up to my studio to work on the final draft of my book, and I found an envelope from Rose slipped under my door. On the return address section there was a large, hand-drawn red and pink heart with a question mark written over it.

I had gone over to my desk and ripped open the envelope. A Valentine's Day card. "You make my life." At the bottom, more hearts and her signature, in silver ink: *All my love, Rose.*

Walking to the bus, I pass a card store, Valentine's Day decorations, cards, hearts, cupids. A bakery, huge pink candy hearts with sprinkles, piles of chocolate, heart-shaped cupcakes, a gigantic cake with white and pink icing with "Love" spelled out in the middle. What a stupid holiday! Another excuse for store owners to get rich off suckers and fools. I get to the bus stop, stand there trying to rationalize—to convince myself everything was said for the best, that the situation isn't fatal.

It's all very simple, pure existentialism; you say yes to this, you say no

322 / MIKE FEDER

to that. I want to be a father and a husband, I have no girlfriend. The price to pay. I make a phone call, I go home and I live my life. Nobody dies of a broken heart.

Following faithfully the advice of my guru, Brodsky, by April I am back in the land of the living. For two months now I have been working as a recording engineer at the American Foundation for the Blind on Sixteenth Street. I sit on the other side of the glass for a change, while somebody in the recording studio reads a book to be transferred to tape—to be sent out to the blind. It felt odd to be on the "wrong" side of the glass, but right, too—a kind of penitence for the drivel I'd been dishing up to my listeners all winter.

Back on my radio show, I finally lighten up. I can talk to my listeners now without sounding like Edgar Allan Poe. Subjects *outside* my own head suddenly appeal to me again.

The last revisions to the book are done. My picture is taken for the cover, the copy editing complete. Jake, still my lawyer, calls me into his office and presents me with the check from Crown, the second half of my advance, minus his commission—nine thousand dollars!

I reconnect with my kids. I'm able to give them things again—specifically, myself—without feeling like I'm being burglarized. Sarah is eight—given to philosophical musings and complex expressions of her inner feelings. She and I get into the habit of sitting in the warm spring evenings on the stoop of a brownstone down the block from our apartment building. We converse on every possible subject and microanalyze all the passersby.

Little Ben and I are back on track. I carry him on my shoulders, play endless games with him on the living-room rug—take him to the playground, read him stories.

I quit the recording job at the American Foundation. The juice is flowing in me again. ICM has lined up a couple of "lectures" for me at conventions for three thousand a pop. I have an idea for a screenplay about my managerial days at WBAI and begin making notes on the word processor Susan bought me for Christmas.

CHAPTER THIRTY-THREE

L ate September, I'm sitting in my living room on a Friday afternoon, going over the draft of my WBAI screenplay, when Ben bursts into the apartment with his baby-sitter, Ellie. "Did you write a book?" she asks me. "Yeah, I did."

She has a big smile on her face. "Well, Mr. Famous Author," she says in her Irish brogue, "didn't I just now see it in the bookstore window?" Ben comes over, falls onto my lap, and looks up at my face. He's excited too, "Dad, you're in the window!"

He looks a little confused and alarmed, as if it were the *real* me in the window (I have the same problem of course—not that I'd let him know). I reassure him that the actual me is right here. I'm stunned by the reality of it. *My book is out! In a bookstore—no, in a lot of bookstores—all over. Damn!* Crown sent me a copy a couple of weeks earlier, but until this moment the book was still an abstraction, as if that one copy were all they were going to print.

I grab my keys and half-run the three blocks from my building over to Broadway and the nearest bookstore, Shakespeare and Company. There is a copy of my book—*in the window*—right next to other new books by real writers! I walk into the store, over to the new releases section, and there it is again—on the shelf, a copy facing out, and behind that twenty more. Yessir, there I am, *New York Son*. My picture on the cover, right beneath the title.

324 / MIKE FEDER

I don't know how long I stand staring at myself on the shelf, but I snap out of it when somebody taps me on the shoulder. It's the store manager, a woman I've seen before once or twice, Felice. She is a few years older than me, very outgoing but famously blunt, known up and down Broadway for telling people, writers and customers alike, what she thinks of their books, their manners, them. I turn myself reluctantly away from my book to look at her. "Mike," she says, "don't stand around here staring at your book—go home and write another one." Hearing her use my first name is embarrassing; she is probably a listener of mine. There is a strong concentration of my listeners living on the Upper West Side, the center of psychotherapy in New York City. Similar worldviews, I guess.

I am blushing like a kindergarten kid caught doing something extra dumb. "You're right," I admit. Then, stealing another look at my book, I walk out of the store, justly chastised.

Of course, the first thing I do is run to the curb and grab a cab to Coliseum Books on Fifty-seventh Street to see if *they* have my book. Yes!! They do! I hit two more stores, one in midtown, another on the East Side, before I come back down to earth and go home. I am in awe of what I have accomplished. A book, something real, something with shape and weight, has been produced—after forty years of feverish talking, performing, and telling stories.

Later that night, after everybody is in bed—and after I have received all my congratulations—I realize, from past experience, that I have to get a hold of myself, put a leash on my natural manic tendencies. Felice was right—standing around looking at my book is a dead end. Well, I do have one real-life problem to grapple with, something I can fix on: I learn that my book had been born with a birth defect, and it wasn't a small one.

Back in July I had gotten a call from my editor. *Publishers Weekly* had given my book a poor review: in fact, a *very* poor review—my book and I had been ripped up, trashed, and pulped. This was definitely bad news. A decent review in *Publishers Weekly* was one of the two or three essential ingredients necessary for selling a book. The magazine carried short, two- to three-paragraph reviews (unsigned) of most of the new books issued every year. These reviews were small but they were powerful, like drops of nitroglycerine. Every library and, more importantly, every book buyer in local stores and big chain bookstores, like Barnes and Noble, read *Publishers Weekly* as a guide to see what new books they should order, what they were going to sell to the public.

I was devastated by my editor's phone call. How could anyone not like my book!? I knew I was no great writer, but I wasn't that bad, either. All I did was tell stories, just like I'd been doing on my radio show for years, just like I'd been doing my whole life. Thousands of people loved my stories, or said they did. How could anybody take such a disliking to me?

I went to the library and found a copy of the magazine. The review really was a killer. From the intensely personal nature of it, I was convinced the anonymous author listened to my radio show and hated me. I was outraged. I wanted to track down the person who wrote the review and beat him to death with a blunt instrument.

My editor, David, was as upbeat as possible under the circumstances. He told me I did get a great review in the other trade journal, *Kirkus Reviews*, but it was obvious from his tone that my book had had both legs shot out from under it before it was even up and running. He told me that my only real chance now was a good review in *The New York Times*.

Once again, *The New York Times* held my fate in its hands—my future by the balls. Actually, I had to pray that they had a grip on my balls: the worst thing would be if they ignored my testicles altogether. These days there's the Internet, TV, radio. The power of the *Times* is a bit diluted, but in the fall of 1988, there was no Oprah's Book Club, no Amazon.com, no big cable TV book shows. An author still absolutely lived and died by what the *Times* did or didn't say about them.

I waited for the phone to ring, for my editor to tell me that a review was going to appear in the Sunday book review section. And as each week passed without the review appearing, I felt increasing alarm, and a familiar barrenness spreading inside me. Having a book published had given my moribund stock a good boost with Susan. I lived in fear of it plunging back down again.

The weeks dragged on with the book hanging in midair. I did one last speaking gig, at a college just outside Dallas. There was nothing else lined up for a couple of months, the gray winter stretching out in front of me. The light was diminishing, the temperature dropping; I knew my mental state would soon be alternating between shooting bursts of anxiety and sludgy puddles of depression. For the first time in more than half a year I felt a great, almost uncontrollable desire to jump on the bus and run up to see Rose.

Since I had cut her off last February, I try to keep her out of my mind, but whenever I slow down just a little and stop—if I am walking through the park, or on a street corner someplace in Manhattan—I think of her, see her eyes, her beautiful long hands, picture her body.

At one point, I'm sitting in the Half-Moon Diner in SoHo, taking one of my semi-amnesiac breaks from my daily life. I look out the window and think I see Rose about a hundred yards away. I'm sure it is her—the same neat white blouse and black skirt, the same curvy, solid-soft body, that beautiful thick auburn braid hanging down her back. Her head seems bowed a little, as if she might be sad. I jump up from the table and run out the door. She is standing, waiting for the light to change. Just as I am about to call her name, I stop. What if it is her? What then? Try to drag her back into my life—make her my personal nurse and my faithful hand-maiden again? Split my life, and hers too, right down the middle?

Rose, if it was Rose, kept walking and disappeared behind a building.

CHAPTER THIRTY-FOUR

Christmas of 1988. My book has been out for more than three months now and it is languishing seriously, sitting right on the edge of oblivion. It hasn't been reviewed in the *Times* and it is obvious it never will be. I am increasingly angry at Crown. The few ads they placed in the papers talked about how funny my book was—a laugh riot! They instructed their distributors to put the book in the *humor* section of every store. This drove me nuts. I thought it was absurd to put a book of stories about psychotic breakdowns, separations, divorces, and fatal accidents (no matter how full of black humor it was) next to cartoon books and the collected columns of Erma Bombeck. I called and complained but to no avail. By this time, the publisher had developed an allergic reaction to me and my book. Though it had gotten some good reviews from out-of-town papers and a couple of nice blurbs from Spalding Gray and Quentin Crisp, from a business standpoint the book had become a poor investment. I understood that, at least intellectually. Business is business. The last publicity appearance they arranged for me was a book signing at a downtown bookstore, the last stop on my whirlwind, one-city tour.

I take the subway to Rizzoli's at the World Trade Center. When I arrive, a clerk conducts me to a table on which, in the extreme corner, they have deposited a modest stack of my books. Next to my little anthill, taking up the rest of the table, is a huge mountain, copies of the newest book on manners by Letitia Baldridge. There must be three hundred of them. Letitia herself, a grand old dame gussied up like the queen of England, stands in front of the table, greeting her subjects. I sit behind her, like a toad on a stump, watching her shake hands and sign books—for almost three hours. During that time, my signing hand remains uncramped: only three people pick up my book.

By the time Letitia sits down next to me to take a break, the entire original stack of her books has been reduced to a couple of copies. I am grumpy, in no mood for small talk. I ignore the woman entirely. Letitia fans herself a little, sips some ice water, then turns to me with a gracious smile. She extends her white-gloved hand, "Well, Mr. Feder, I just wanted you to know how very pleased I am to be here signing books alongside a fellow author."

Midwinter. I watch the frozen world from my living-room window—resting my hands on the radiator to soak up some heat.

I miss Rose like mad. In the middle of the night, I get out of bed and lie down on the living-room couch, imagining her sleeping in her bed in her apartment, thirty blocks away. My living-room couch points north, straight at her, like the needle of a compass. I travel through walls, over the tops of buildings, gliding through the night air till I am lying next to her.

When I tell Brodsky how empty I feel and how much I wish I could be with my girlfriend again, he is completely unsympathetic. "Stop whining," he says. "Try growing up for a change." Brodsky's idea of "growing up" is to imitate him as much as possible. Work hard, stop complaining, be a man—like he was. He even tells me I should dress like him, get rid of my usual outfit of flannel shirt and jeans and get some good slacks and dress shirts, shave off my beard, cut my hair shorter.

This relentless tough-guy stance of his—he is like an iron fist in an iron glove—is really getting on my nerves. He is always interrupting me, making long-winded speeches, telling me the way things should be, just like my father used to do.

In the beginning of my treatment with Brodsky, when I was drowning, I needed his uncompromising strength to save me, but now that I was resuscitated somewhat, I kept looking for something different from him.

Maybe a little softness, a little quiet listening. But that, he said, was just more of my momma's-boy simpering. He told me that my problem was really very simple: I was completely self-centered, and the way to fix that was to just stop talking so much about myself.

Operating on this theory, Brodsky monopolizes every one of my therapy sessions—airing his pet peeves about sports, politics, finances, cars... anything he has heard on the radio or discovered in the *New York Times* that day. And if he isn't constantly taking up my session time talking about the Middle East or the latest football draft, he is talking about *his* personal life. I guess that is based on the same theory: anything *not* about me is therapeutic.

He tells me every little bit of gossip and personal history that pops into his mind. I hear, in great detail, about his trials and tribulations with his colleagues, the achievements of his children, both of whom, he says with a perverse smirk, hate his guts because he is, as he put it, "a terrible father." He even tells me that he was just thrown out of his weekly card game because he wins too much and his friends hate him for it.

I am sick of hearing about his life. "What the fuck do I care about your card games and all your problems? What about *my* life?" He smiles sarcastically: "Shit, Mr. Prince, it's your precious *life* that's suffocating you. If you paid more attention to other things and other people, you wouldn't be so fucked up!" Probably true, but maybe a few minutes here and there about me...would that be so bad? Forget it. No matter how much I complained, Brodsky's personal life was a permanent part of the treatment plan. Really, though, I shouldn't have been so surprised; it was that way from the beginning.

Just a couple of weeks after I start seeing him, I come into his office in my usual foul mood. I point out to him that he needs to empty the ashtray next to the client's chair. The sight of cigarette butts and ashes really irritates me; they remind me of my mother. "If you don't like ashes," he says, "empty the fucking thing yourself." I did—dumped them in the trash—along with the ashtray. "I don't know why you let people smoke in here," I tell him, "don't you know cigarette smoke can kill you?" To my amazement, his eyes fill with tears. I feel awful. What on earth did I say?

"What's wrong?" I ask.

"You reminded me of my wife," he says. "She died from lung cancer six months ago...." He grabs some tissues, wipes his eyes, and blows his nose. He looks at me, still teary. "Can you believe it. *I* was the one who smoked, for forty years. And she never touched a cigarette. A year after I quit, she gets lung cancer." He is filled with grief. I feel like I have to say something.

"I'm really sorry...what did your wife do?" "She was a nurse. Always doing something for somebody else. I'll tell you—she was a much better person than I am."

This constant revelation of his personal life never really stopped. Now, smack in the middle of my current downward slide, I am privy to all his little problems. The week before, I had arrived—as usual—early for my appointment. The door to his office was open, so I poked my head in. He was on the phone and motioned for me to wait outside. He was yelling, shouting at the top of his lungs into the phone. "Listen, you crazy bitch! I told you not to sell that thing. Why the hell don't you ever listen to me? OK, OK, I want you to just shut the hell up. You stupid jerk, if you don't do what I tell you, I'm not calling you anymore." He slammed the phone down and shouted out to me. "Come in!"

I walked into his office, stood in front of my chair. "Who was that on the phone?" I asked him.

"My mother."

"What!?"

"She's ninety years old but she's as dumb as she always was. I give her advice and she never listens to me."

"How can you talk to your mother like that? You're a shrink."

"Oh, do you think it would be healthy for me to suppress my feelings? You want me to wind up a neurotic wimp like you? My mother was always a stupid, thoughtless bitch and she still is." I shut my mouth and sat down.

Brodsky is a totally perverse bastard. He's angry all the time, and utterly isolated too, ostracized by everyone he knows. Obviously the only person in the world that had been able to put up with him was his wife, and she's dead. His only remaining companions, the only people who would listen to him at all, were his patients.

I told him I was having trouble getting to sleep. "OK," he says, "do what I do every night. I get in bed with a book—since there's nobody else to get in bed with—and just before I turn out the light, I drink one large glass of scotch."

If I was looking for sympathy, Brodsky was obviously not the one to supply it. When I told him how desperately I missed Rose and how much my home life was draining me dry, he told me that the problem (as usual) was very simple—all I had to do was make a choice. That's what grown people did, they made choices. He held up his left hand and grabbed the pinkie with his right forefinger and thumb: "One, you decide to stay home with your wife and kids and stop complaining...two," he drops his pinkie and grabs his left ring finger, "you move out and go with your girl-friend, but in that case, you accept the possibility that you might literally die of guilt."

The winter creeps on, day after empty day.

At the end of February, I have a message from Rose on my studio answering machine. The next day I call her at work. She tells me she has just gone to her grandmother's funeral; it had been an overwhelming experience for her and had set her thinking about what was really impor-tant in her life. "Mike," she says, in her sweet, earnest voice, "I really do want you to be in my life, but you have to tell me now...should I ever call you again? Should I stay away from you? I want to get on with my life." Whew! The cards thrown down, right there on the table. I told her I'd think about it and call her tommorow.

After she hangs up, I stand and stare at the phone. Stay in my house and live a life that was very much like a slow-motion nightmare every day, or leave my family and die of guilt. Simple choice. Not that Rose was ask-ing me to move in with her—though I'm sure she would have liked that. She just wanted to know if she was ever going to be part of my life again.

The next morning, I was out walking on Broadway, trying to decide what to do. East, north, west, south. Couldn't I just disappear into the city, find some crummy room on the Lower East Side and change my name? Drop them all—everybody who wanted a piece of me. Free. But my kids. But Rose...I look up and realize that I've walked a couple of miles. I am on Central Park South, and there, just coming out of a coffee shop, no more than ten feet away from me, is Rose.

I call her name, walk over to her, and we hug each other for what seems like an hour. I walk her over to Third Avenue and stand with her while she waits to get a bus back up to her office. I don't think we say more than five words to each other but clearly the choice has been made: just seeing her, just touching her, I know there is no way I could live without her. So now it is the same split, crazy situation as before. As long as I have her to run to, I know I can summon up the guts and energy to function in my family. Rose has me, I have her, and my double life is up and running again.

PART SEVEN
THE TALKING CURE

CHAPTER THIRTY-FIVE

S pring arrives. I take my kids out to the park on weekends and somehow live my life with Susan, going through the motions of conversation and occasional sex. I am seeing Rose whenever I can, at restaurants, in the park, at her apartment. I tell Brodsky I am seeing her again. He just shakes his head, tells me I am a hopeless jerk and reads me the latest baseball box scores from the *Times*.

A new magazine called *Wigwag*, started up by a bunch of disaffected *New York* magazine writers and editors, offers me a monthly column. They want me to write personal journalism, commentary on the various kinds of jobs people have—a thousand dollars a month for fifteen hundred words. With my handheld tape recorder, I interview nurses on AIDS wards, golf pros, funeral directors, then write the columns.

I do my radio show and live my fractured double life. Now, when I think back on that time, I see it as a kind of dream or a play I performed in, the reluctant main character, with a complicated life, complex lines to read, and absolutely no motivation whatsoever. A lost soul, just wandering in suspended animation, waiting, as I had always been waiting, for some supernatural figure, some heavenly beam, to shine on me and cure me of my ills.

At the end of June 1989, Susan tells me that "we" are letting the kids' full-time baby-sitter go. She says there just isn't enough money to pay the woman; Ben is entering an expensive preschool in the fall, and I certainly am not contributing much. I had long ago run out of paying creative projects, and what I get from *Wigwag* doesn't stretch too far with our current cost of living.

Since Susan is the main earner in the family, and I have no intention of going back to being a galley slave in an office, I don't really have any ammunition to fight the decision: from now on, I will be the kids' new nanny.

My first month is a real baptism of fire. After getting the kids up and feeding them, I take Sarah to her day camp on the East Side, then spend all day playing with Ben. He is four, sweet and cute, but to someone as self-involved as myself, the experience of concentrating on another human being so intensely for so long was an exhausting experience. Hours dragged by like days.

At three o'clock in the afternoon we go to pick up Sarah. More playing, then shopping for groceries, then cooking supper. By the time Susan comes home from her office at seven or eight, I am lying in a near-coma on the living-room rug, and I'm so furious at her for "putting" me in this position that I can't stand to look at her.

Naturally, I was over at Rose's more than ever. It was the only place I could go to recapture a little of myself. When the weekends came and Susan was around to take care of the kids, I ignored everybody in the house and disappeared into the television or out on the streets.

Now that I was nanny, the hour and a half I spent each Sunday morning in the radio studio was like a life preserver. It was a chance for me to get some privacy and solitude. I'm sure that sounds odd, privacy and solitude with twenty thousand people listening in, but that's the way it felt. I sat there, alone at the control board, talking fervently into the microphone, calling out to—I never knew who, but I knew I had to keep calling....

As the months wore on, summer into fall, fall into winter, the emotional drain was incredible—I began to feel like I was drowning. I remember sitting in the living room with the kids, watching for the ten millionth time their favorite Disney cartoon, *Robin Hood*. Robin Hood, Prince John, Maid Marian, foxes that sounded like Ronald Colman, tigers that had Peter Ustinov's voice, singing chickens...over and over again, till I felt like I was going to become a singing chicken myself.

In February, Susan and I had a big blow-up. A flaming explosion of an argument. She was sick and tired, she told me, of my passive aggression. I had better shape up or ship out. This sounded fine to me (shipping out), but just like before, I was afraid to take the step, scared to be on my own. And leaving the kids...

March. I was still trying to abide by the rules of family life, but it was becoming almost impossible to keep up the facade of normality. By April I was like a ghost wandering around the house. I didn't touch Susan, didn't speak to her unless she asked me a question, and then only a couple of words. To me she was virtually invisible. Once, enraged by my total disregard, she walked over to me as I was staring at the television screen. She looked at me, waiting for me to glance up at her, but I didn't. Then she burst out with, "I hate you! I want you to get out! I'm going to get a lawyer to make you get out!" I jumped up, a half inch from her face. "You fucking bitch, you ruined my life! Get away from me before I put you in the hospital!!" She backed away, walked into the bedroom, and closed the door. I sat down again and stared at the television.

The third week in April, I had two performances that David Rothenberg had set up for me at a nightclub on Seventy-second Street. There was a fairly good crowd because of an interview I had in the *Daily News* and listings in all the papers. I performed a new piece I'd come up with in the last two months—a kind of life story from age four, when my sister was born and my house came apart, right up to the present. My mother, shrinks, the radio, performing. I called it *The Talking Cure*.

Up on stage, I could see Rose's face very clearly in the audience, lit by the glow of one of the stronger houselights. I played to her. When I got off, she and I went to a bar only two blocks from my house. I felt like I was holding a lit stick of dynamite, looking for disaster.

When I finally got home, about three hours later, Susan didn't ask me where I had been. Business as usual. Impelled by two pints of alcohol in my blood and my taste for falling into the abyss, I broke my rule and had sex with Susan that night. It was exactly the way I figured it would be, or maybe the way I meant it to be—primitive and loveless. Around three in the morning, unable to sleep, I went into the living room, lay on the couch, and thought about Rose. Four A.M., I still couldn't sleep. I went over to the window. There was a bone-white moon hanging over the funeral parlor across the street. There was no traffic on Amsterdam Avenue. You could hear the switching mechanisms in the light poles as the traffic signals went from green to red.

By the time morning arrived, I had worked myself into a rage. About eight, Ben got up and wanted me to come into his room to play with him. I felt like I was going to explode—I was afraid of myself, of what I felt like doing to everyone in that house—I felt so oppressed and confined. I was afraid I was going to hit Susan, really hurt her. And she was as bad as me. In the past two weeks she had twice threatened to stab me, and once she even grabbed a block of wood and took a good, hard swing at my head. We were both on the verge of murder.

I played with Ben for about five minutes, then came into the living room. Susan looked at me with contempt. "That's it, that's all the time you have to play with your son?"

"OK," I yelled. "That is fucking *it*! I'm sick to death of you and your whole life! I'm leaving." I was out the door in two seconds. My time there was over. Whatever troubles would come, would come.

CHAPTER THIRTY-SIX

I lay awake, sweating, lying on my back on the single mattress on the floor of my room. It is near midnight and I can hear every little noise: the whoosh of car tires out on Riverside Drive, footsteps on the street, water rushing through the pipes in the wall, the skittering of the mouse that lives under my sink. Next to me, on a futon mattress pushed up against the wall, Ben is asleep. His regular soft breathing is the only sound that doesn't seem lonely or threatening.

It is late August, four months since I walked out, back in the Master Arts, this time in a different studio. My landlord-listener sold my old studio on the sixth floor and I had to move downstairs to the second floor. I can see a few trees in the park through the window, but not the river. The room is located over a pottery studio; lingering smells of baked clay, varnish, and alcohol waft upward through the floorboards, some of which are warped from water leaks. In one spot, near the sink, there is a six-inch patch missing entirely, and you can see the pipes and cables below. I tape a piece of cardboard over it. There are roaches and a couple of mice. I stuff up every hole I find with steel wool and leave a dozen roach traps in the closet and against the wall. Being so near the street, it is noisier, and I can smell the exhaust fumes from cars, but still it is freedom.

That summer, I continued watching the kids till Susan came home from work, playing with them, making supper—doing my job. It was wrenching to come and go from the house like that. Each day, when the kids asked me why I had to go away, I told them the closest thing I could to the truth: their mother and I were arguing too much. We didn't get along anymore. The kids wanted to know when—if—I was coming back. I said I wasn't sure but probably I wasn't going to come back.

Ben slept over on Friday nights and I played with him till Saturday afternoon. On Sunday afternoons, I picked up Sarah and we walked around the neighborhood or played pool in a family-type pool hall a few blocks away.

At first, right after I left, I had had that same relief, the same feeling of having escaped death, as the last time I had left. The days were warm and slow, the nights were quiet and comforting. Rose came by and slept over once in a while. I sat in my chair, looking out the window at the park while she lay on some cushions on the futon a few feet away. The studio would be dark, lit only by streetlight from the lamp on the corner and the apartments in the building across the street. We talked (I talked) for hours till Rose fell asleep. I kept staring out the window.

As the summer wore on, I felt increasingly confused and guilty over what I'd done. Every time I brought Ben to the studio to sleep over, I felt like crying. I wanted to be with my kids, but after a few hours with them I desperately needed to leave. I loved them, but it felt like they were killing me.

I had nightmares of big black dogs chasing me, biting me in the throat. On the street it seemed like everybody, especially policemen, were eyeing me suspiciously, as if they knew I was the worst sort of criminal. I kept looking at my door, expecting it to be knocked down by the cops, who would drag me away in chains to pay for my vile deeds.

I was in a perpetually confessional mode. In the middle of the day I'd wander into empty churches on the West Side and sit there, hoping somebody would come over and offer to help me, or at least listen to my tale of transgression and sin.

And the radio…since the day I had left my house in April, I felt like I was lying to my audience every time I got on the air. In September, right after Labor Day, I finally told my listeners that I had separated from my family.

I knew there were people who would hate me for what I was revealing. I had talked for ten years now about my wife, my marriage, and especially my kids—all my joys, my confusions, my triumphs over my twisted childhood. I'd been carrying the banner for thousands of people who were struggling just like me and now I had given up. I had betrayed them.

Over the next couple of weeks I got a lot of letters. Some people, to my profound relief, forgave me. They said they understood; they had the same awful problems themselves. Other people condemned me as a rank liar, a con man of the worst sort, thoughtless, heartless, deceiving. Mostly women. A few men. They were really hurt by what I had done. They couldn't listen to me anymore, they said. I could feel my whole audience drifting away from me, and as far as I was concerned, the punishment was no less than I deserved.

By the end of September I started to slip under the heavy weight of my remorse. The noises in my apartment seemed extremely dangerous. Though I had gotten rid of most of the roaches, sometimes I imagined I saw them crawling up the walls. The sink smelled funny; food was losing its taste and was becoming difficult to swallow. I worried all the time that something awful was going to happen to me or my kids, or Rose—horrible accidents and death seemed to lurk around every corner. I had trouble falling asleep, and when I did finally sleep, I awoke in the middle of the night, sweaty and cold.

Everything I had to do, no matter how small the task, seemed monumental to me. Being around the kids was becoming almost impossible. I finally told Susan she was going to have to find someone else to watch them. Going there every day, then leaving again a few hours later was too much to bear. It took her about two weeks to come up with someone. And that was it. I was on my own. My self-created exile was well on the way to completion.

I fixed on my shrink, Brodsky, as my last chance for maintaining my sanity. I counted the hours, then later the minutes before entering his office, where I could be safe from the demons that clutched and ground their teeth at me all day and night. I asked him to refer me to a psychiatrist to get some tranquilizers, maybe some antidepressants. He refused absolutely. "I don't see anybody who takes pills," he said. "If you want to take pills, then go talk to a psychiatrist. If you want to see me, then no pills."

"But I'm shaking myself to pieces." I told him.

"Good, shake yourself to pieces! When you're done we can put you back together and do it right this time."

I cried. I begged. No dice. No pills, no way to calm down. Work itself seemed like the only thing keeping me sane. I still had my column in *Wigwag*. Every month I had my deadline to meet, editors to whom I was responsible, money I had to earn.

I talked to Rose on the phone for hours; sometimes I slept over, but I felt guilty sleeping overnight in her bed. It just didn't seem right. *She* wasn't my wife. *This* wasn't my house. In the dark hours of the morning I jumped up and ran.

Sarah was angry at me—she had no sympathy for my disappearance. Why should she? We spent shorter and shorter amounts of time together on Sunday afternoons. Sometimes after less than an hour together she told me to take her back home.

At least Ben wasn't judging me, not yet anyway. On Friday nights, I ordered in supper for us, then we played on the floor. After, he brushed his teeth and changed into his pajamas, and we lay next to each other on the futon while I read to him. Around eight-thirty, he got sleepy. I put a tape on the stereo set—*Children's Lullabies from Many Lands*—that I had recorded off one of his favorite records at home. He loved that tape, and so did I. I got him under the covers, kissed him, smoothed his forehead. He lay with his head up against my hip as I sat on the mattress next to him. And the lullabies came softly out of the speakers. English, American, French, African. I didn't understand some of them, but they were all wonderful. The one I liked best—I don't remember the title—was translated from Yiddish. It was sung, in the usual minor key, by a woman with an achingly tender alto voice. It was so comforting, so beautiful, it was as if all the mothers that had ever lived were singing that song in my room.

November. I slipped further. I was losing weight so fast, I had to make new holes in my belt so that it would hold up my pants. I was cold all the time and slept in jeans and a flannel shirt. I was afraid to get in the bathtub; being naked and in water seemed especially dangerous.

Thanksgiving morning, I was by myself. I couldn't be with my kids, and I didn't want to accept Rose's invitation to come out to Jersey to be with her and her family. Then I went over to Steve Post's house to speak with Steve and his wife, Laura. I poured out my troubles and was able to be a little more relaxed than usual after they graciously bestowed one of their Valiums on me. Around noon, they left for a Thanksgiving family dinner.

I walked slowly up Broadway to my studio. The sun was trying to break through a slightly polluted haze. The stores were closed, the streets, for Manhattan, were virtually empty. Everybody had flown off to Iowa, or Connecticut, or back out to Queens or Brooklyn for the family dinner. I, alone, like the survivor of a nuclear attack, patrolled the ravaged wasteland. But wait! I wasn't alone. There were other survivors drifting past. Who were these people? Women, overweight, their dresses hanging not quite right, their shoes squashed and a little tilted, walked arm in arm with pressed-jean, pastel-sweatered men, wrapped in an invisible cocoon of false cheer and melancholy affection. A solitary man in his fifties, well dressed in tweeds and shined shoes, his beard neatly trimmed, walked along thoughtfully behind a half-crippled, gray-muzzled dog. Old people balanced painfully on their canes, their clothes threadbare, their skin blotchy and unhealthy, lined and careworn. A wild-eyed man in his twenties, holes in his pants, a rope for a belt, his hair all matted and filthy, walked rapidly muttering curses. And against the steel-gated store entrances, lying with legs extended were the wrecks of human beings, shapes of people, once men and women but now reduced to rag-wrapped, shapeless forms, fluids running out from under their layers of coats and blankets, their red and dirt-seamed hands clutching the necks of dark green bottles. I was in a shadow world, a parallel universe, a parade of sad and deliberate ghosts, drifting up the empty sidewalks of Broadway.

Chapter Thirty-seven

D ecember. My confusion, my guilt, and my sense of panic are increasing. As I wait, pacing in anxiety, outside the radio studio one Sunday morning, I have an image of a dagger, stuck straight down into my brain from the top of my skull. I try to pull it out by sheer willpower, but it is stuck there, like the mythical sword in the stone, and I don't have the special power to extract it.

It has become impossible for me to keep my increasing loss of rationality and my ingrown, morbid fantasies about madness and death out of my on-the-air monologues. I wonder if anybody is listening to me anymore or if I am just talking into a great, dead vacuum.

Inevitably, my mother reappears in my life—a huge, hovering, black presence. It is toward her and my other judgers and accusers (my wife, my shrink)—and away from my friends, my children, and Rose—that I turn to preserve my sense of self, to maintain my familiar identity. Failure, fool, disturber of the peace, betrayer of sacred trusts. Murderer.

One afternoon, pacing around my apartment, seeing roaches on the walls, gray shadows running along the moldings, I am stopped dead by a tremendous pain in my side. It is an astounding, stabbing, wire-hot pain that literally brings me to my knees. Oh, Christ, I think, what am I doing to myself now. I take two tranquilizers. The pain doesn't go away; instead it only increases. I break out in a sweat over my entire body. I feel like I am going to faint. I crawl across the floor, reach for the phone, and dial up my doctor. No use, it's Saturday. I try to calm down; the pain gets worse. I call Brodsky but, of course, only get his machine. I call Rose, no answer. The pain spreads to my groin, down to my penis, up to my chest. I get up, stumble out of the apartment, and take a cab to the emergency room of New York Hospital.

I sit in the crowded emergency room, practically passing out from the pain. Finally I am on a gurney, rolling into another room. X rays, prodding, poking. I am living in the pain now, as if it is a house I inhabit. They take a urine sample, roll me back out into the hallway, and park me there till they can get the X rays and tests back from their lab.

I have a kidney stone. They give me an injection of Demerol, and in a few minutes I drift off into never-never land. A little while later, they get me up, issue me a vial of Percodans, and tell me to go home and drink a lot of water till the stone passes. They ask if I have anybody to see me back home. The first person I think of is Susan—how could she refuse to help me at such a time? I call the house. Sarah picks up. "It's Dad, can you put Mommy on?" Susan's voice on the line. "Yes?"

"It's me. I'm here in the emergency room at New York Hospital."

"Hmn-hmn."

"Can you pick me up? I'm really woozy from pain and the pills they gave me."

"Mike, I'm not responsible for you anymore. You have a girlfriend now, why don't you call her?" She hung up. Of course she's right. I have no business asking her for anything.

Approaching Christmastime. I've lost nearly twenty pounds. I hardly eat. I sleep maybe two hours a night and have violent nightmares. I think constantly of killing myself.

I conceive a picture of my mother as a gigantic black and red bug, about the size and shape of a snapping turtle. Sometimes, when I'm out walking on Broadway or taking the train down to do my show, I feel her high up on my back, teeth digging into my spine right below the base of my brain, legs hooked onto my back. It seems so real, I almost want to reach behind me and brush her off, or smash her hard and crack her into bloody oozing pieces. If I manage to calm myself, the bug-mother slips down my back and eventually drops to the pavement, and I am able to walk away.

I think of my mother all the time. I am filled with a blinding hatred and an abject terror of her. I want her to go away and leave me alone. I want her to come back from the dead so I can kill her again for all the awful things she has done to me.

I am appalled by my insane, brutal daydreams. My mother is dead; she left me a long time ago, so why can't I leave her?

One afternoon I walk into the orthodox synagogue across the street from the Master Arts. I ask to see the rabbi. I haven't been in a synagogue for decades—I am filled with childhood memories. My grandparents, my aunts and uncles. Old, musty men, chanting sad prayers, singing and dancing, weeping, laughing. Wine and food...funerals, weddings, bar mitzvahs. I fish a yarmulke out of a wooden box, put it on my head, and sit on a folding chair in front of the ark.

The rabbi, a big, round, solid man in his late thirties, comes over and sits down next to me. He has a full black beard, long, wispy sideburns, a buttoned-up white shirt, and black, shiny suit and shoes. As orthodox as they come, a missionary, a Lubavitcher Hassid from Brooklyn sent out to minister to the heathen Jews of the Upper West Side.

He radiates compassion. I immediately begin to cry in a silent, sustained way, the tears falling down my cheeks and dropping onto my coat. "How can I help you," he asks.

"It's my mother," I say. "I want to do something for my mother. She's dead."

He puts his hand on my shoulder. "I'm sorry," he says, "when did she—"

"Fourteen years ago—she killed herself." I can tell he is surprised. He probably assumed, from the way I am carrying on, that she had died just recently. He nods, passes his hand slowly over his head, and strokes his beard. "We can say a prayer. What is her Hebrew name?"

"Ruth. Ruchel."

"Ruchel." He takes a notebook out of his pocket. "What is her date of birth and the date of her passing?" He writes the details down. "I'll have to check these dates with the Hebrew calendar, then we can say a prayer at the appropriate time...."

"Thank you."

We sit there for a while. Then a little girl calls out from the back of the room. "Abba, Ema says it's time to eat." He gets up, touches my shoulder again. "I have to go now. We have to lock the place up." I get up and follow him to the glass doors. "Come tomorrow. You'll come tomorrow?"

"I don't know," I say and walk out. The sun is setting, long shadows spread down the street.

I get a call from David Rothenberg. One of his clients, the Cafe Ariel Theater on Forty-second Street, is looking for shows. They have one week available—four shows, the first week in January. Am I interested? I tell him I am. I need the money, whatever I might wind up making, because I have just found out the week before that *Wigwag* is folding, after a year and a half. No more thousand dollars a month. No more money from anyplace. I can't pay any bills. Envelopes with red warning signals—from Bell Telephone and Con Edison—are piled up, unopened, on the shelf beneath my window. The last bill I paid was my quarterly life-insurance premium.

I've already made up my mind that if I want to stay alive, I'm going to have to go into a hospital.

I struggle with Brodsky, a last desperate, bloody war, week after week. I call him every day and threaten suicide, and blame him for what I am about to do. He tells me not to threaten him—he doesn't need my shit. He also tells me that if I leave him and go to the hospital, not to expect to see him when I get out.

Ben sleeps over one more time near Christmas. That night, before I put him to bed, I tell him I am going to have to "take a break"—just a little kind of vacation.

"Where are you going?"

"No place special, maybe someplace near here, but I won't be gone long."

"Can I come with you?"

"No, you can't. But don't worry, I'll call you if I go away." I tell Sarah I'm not going to see her for a while. She is silent, staring at me from the doorway of the apartment, then she shuts the door on me.

CHAPTER THIRTY-EIGHT

The last week of December. I rehearse my show *The Talking Cure.*

I am behind the curtain upstairs at the Cafe Ariel Theater, right across the street from the West Bank Downstairs Theater Bar, where I began my ascent to "stardom" four years ago.

I peek around the curtain. There are about twenty people out in the audience—not even half-filling the small house. Rose is sitting in the last row with David Rothenberg.

As I pace, I forget the show and concentrate on the next couple of weeks of my life. I have no medical insurance and practically no money left. I found out that since I have no cash and no assests, I am eligible for emergency Medicaid—to pay for the hospital.

I call Susan and ask her if she will help me get into Columbia Presbyterian in Upper Manhattan, reputed to be a decent place. She refers me to a woman, a psychologist she knows who works there. I make at least a dozen calls, urgent appeals, wading through a swamp of bureaucracy. Finally, the day before Christmas, they tell me I am cleared. I can commit myself whenever I want.

I hand my radio show over to Lynn Samuels, who already has a regular show on WBAI. I tell her to tell my listeners I'm working on a journalistic assignment—I have a deadline to meet and can't be on the air for a while.

When I see the lights go down in the house, I walk onstage and sit on my stool.

To my amazement, I do a good show. I remember every bit of the story as it unfolds, the sequences, the transitions, bits of dialogue, portraits of characters—the whole thing goes off almost perfectly.

Afterward, backstage, I sit on a folding chair, staring at some costumes from another show hanging on a rack. Rose stands over me, hands me a glass of water, and congratulates me on the show. I'm wondering how I was able to remember an hour and fifteen minutes of the most complicated story, getting all the dates and the pacing and particular lines just right, down to the last little pause and nuance—even manage to be funny and make people laugh. How is that possible when I can hardly walk the streets, ride the trains, eat, or sleep without shaking in terror?

The next morning, Rose and I take the subway uptown to the hospital at 225th Street. There is a newsstand right next to the subway exit. Screaming headlines, two inches high. "Troops Poised To Attack!" "President Bush Draws Line in the Sand!!" "Saddam Threatens Israel with Biological Warfare!" I stand there holding my suitcase, looking at the papers, shivering in the cold. *That's right,* I think, *pick on the Jews. Well, here's one Jew that's headed for the bunker right now. You all go playing in the sand; I'm out of here.* I feel sorry for my kids, leaving them to this crazy world.

I help Rose negotiate her way across an icy footbridge on Broadway over the Harlem River to the driveway that leads to the entrance to the hospital. In admissions, with Rose standing there watching, they take my suitcase and put me in a wheelchair for the trip up to the ward. I find that irritating. "I don't need a wheelchair," I tell the attendant. "Hospital policy," he says as he straps me in like a baby in a stroller. I look over my shoulder at Rose as they wheel me into the elevator.

CHAPTER THIRTY-NINE

From the minute they brought me into the ward and installed me in a small, clean private room, I felt as if I'd been rescued from drowning—that half my troubles had immediately dissolved. I was sitting in a comfortable chair, overlooking the driveway of the hospital, my suitcase lying nearby on the small bed. What seemed like a whole team of attendants and nurses surrounded me.

I had my blood pressure and temperature taken. I answered a lot of questions about how I felt. All these nurses and attendants, concerned about *me*. I took a few deep breaths, letting a couple of months of tension flow out of me.

The more questions the nurse asked me about why I had come there—what my problems were—the more I realized that save for my shrink and my wife, my troubles were mostly in my own head, all starting with my mother. I had no real enemies. What *were* my problems, anyway? It was hard to come up with enough of them to fill out the nurse's form. I had two kids who loved me, friends who tried their best to help me, thousands of listeners who tuned in to hear me talk each week, and a woman who was so devoted to me that my worst craziness didn't faze her. No more than twenty minutes in the hospital—I was able to see my willfulness and selfishness for exactly what it was. I shook my head and smiled ruefully.

"What's funny?" asked the nurse.

"Nothing," I said.

The nurse sat there, waiting, her pen touching the form on her clipboard. I pulled myself together—I had to tell the woman something. I didn't want them to think I wasn't sick, that I could, God forbid, take care of myself.

I told her that I felt guilty. That I hated myself for abandoning my kids, just as I had been abandoned. That there was a woman who loved me, but I didn't deserve her love. That I wished I could just hide from them all—at least for a while, till I could figure out what to do.

The nurse made some notes and told me that a psychiatrist would be in to see me in a couple of minutes. Outside my window, which, now I could see, overlooked the emergency entrance to the hospital, ambulances were pulling in and out, their red lights flashing in the spreading afternoon shadows.

The first couple of days in the hospital were like a vacation. I gained back five pounds in three days. I slept soundly, no waking up in the middle of the night, no shaking from nightmares, bathed in sweat. In the rec room I was the ping-pong champ of the ward. Forty-five years old and still had the old reflexes. Not bad.

I was doing pretty well till the drugs kicked in and I entered the World of Pills. In the two decades since my last appearance in the bin, the medical model for treating mental illness had gained total ascendancy. The standard treatment for all mental patients was three to four weeks of hospitalization. Find the right medication, then boom—shoot them back out into the world, where with proper medical maintenance they would do just fine, or at least they wouldn't be bothering the doctors with their silly and irritating personal problems.

The doctors came up with a diagnosis for me: manic-depressive—bipolar 2 (I was only in the minor leagues of bipolarity...to earn a coveted "1" required wider swings than I could manufacture). Bipolar sounded very scary to me. I kept thinking about bouncing back and forth, not between up and down, hot and cold, but between the Arctic and the Antarctic. Wolves, glaciers, howling winds, and thousands of square miles of frozen white nothingness. I saw myself sailing high over the temperate zones, past the equator, faster than a speeding mood swing—right into the dripping jaws of a waiting polar bear.

I was given a small dose of some powerful antidepressant called Imipramine. The medicine had two bad side effects—it lowered my blood pressure and blurred my vision. No more ping-pong for me. After a week on this stuff my blood pressure was so low that I shuffled when I walked, and I was cold all the time. I was often on the verge of fainting. The condition stabilized somewhat after a while, and I got some energy back, but I lived in a permanent fog. It was a struggle to stay awake and aware. My brain was stuffed with a kind of white anesthetic gauze—beneath which I could still sense the circling sharks of guilt and doubt. In the afternoon, I skipped group therapy and crafts. In my room, I slipped into a dazed trance, my head resting on my arm, soaking up the warmth from the radiator beneath the window and vaguely dreaming. I complained to the psychiatrist whenever I could catch a glimpse of her about the side effects of the antidepressant, but she had no time to waste on my problems. It was truly a new world, everything was pills. The concept of talk therapy, Freud's "talking cure," had gone the way of the great auk and the dodo. Neurons, synapses, serotonin. Prozac and its brothers and sisters had arrived. "Happy days are here again!"

As I remembered from Downstate, patients who bothered psychiatrists with their problems were considered annoying. Now, twenty years later, I could see that talking about your problems was not only irritating, it was a symptom in itself! If the pills were working correctly, you would be better and have no problems you would need to talk about.

When I finally insisted on seeing my psychiatrist, a cold, slightly corpulent young woman in her early thirties, she snapped at me: "Alright, five minutes—where's your room?" She sat opposite me, stone-faced and glancing pointedly at her watch every minute. "What's the problem, Mr. Feder?" I could tell I was on a timer. I scrambled to put my troubles into clear, short words. "This medicine is making me feel worse—I feel faint, tired, I actually think the pill itself is depressing me."

"Mmn-hmn."

"I want to reduce the dose."

"We've been over this before: you just need to get used to it."

"Look, I'm not a child, I'm not an idiot…I know when something is making me sick."

"Mr. Feder, I don't really think you are in a position to know how you are really feeling at this point." She got up to leave.

"Wait!"

"What is it?"

"I have some things bothering me."

She frowned, looked at her watch, sat down, and stared at me. "Yes?"

"What really bothers me is, I don't know what to do when I get back in the world. I don't know how to handle my kids and I can't figure out what to do about…Well, there are two women, my wife and girlfriend, and I'm still very confused about my mother and—" This was too much for her. She stood up again and walked to the door.

"Mr. Feder, these are problems that you will have to resolve for yourself when you are discharged. Perhaps," she said with complete disgust, "you can get *psychotherapy.*"

There was a general pull, kind of like a tug-of-war going on in that hospital. It was an invisible battle being waged between the patients, who had a burning desire to talk to someone, and the doctors and most of the nurses, who kept beating them back with pills. It was so sad to see this. All the patients wanted to sit in a room and tell their troubles to a kind and patient listener. The staff wanted the patients to shut up and take their pills—"stabilize" and get the hell out. Part of the problem, of course, was the health insurance companies. They would pay for no more than a month in the hospital and preferred two to three weeks when they could get it.

Late in the evenings, after sucking down my boiled chicken and vanilla pudding—when the afternoon dose of my antidepressant had worn off and before I got my bedtime dose—I was able to feel and think more clearly. Then all my real-world problems came flooding back. Guilt reared up in me like a thing with teeth.

Pills didn't seem quite as bad to me at moments like that. I just didn't like the feeling of not being able to think and feel and speak correctly—it was like being wrapped in invisible chains. It was easy for me to denounce the medical model; I really didn't need it that much. For some people, there was no contest; numbness was absolutely preferable to hell on earth.

There were, just like the last time I was in the bin, many people who were much, much worse off than I was. Poor, driven wretches who howled and cowered from frightening visions, who muttered confessions and curses to invisible entities that followed them wherever they went. People who ran through the halls, laughing and crying, or made sudden frightening lunges at other patients and had to be tied down to their beds. Others who stared for hours, wordless, motionless, out the window or at a spot on the dining-room wall.

The most violent person on the ward was an orthodox Jewish girl, Hannah. She was a looming, menacing presence, maybe six feet tall, two hundred pounds, built square like a football player, with a round, fleshy face, dyed-blond hair, and tiny mad black eyes. She never relaxed, always talking, pacing, laughing, getting in people's faces, stalking the attendants and the nurses. Every other day she'd wind up in a fight with another patient, sometimes gouging and punching till the attendants came and pulled her off. They'd drag her to her room, slap the leather restraints on her, and shoot two quarts of elephant tranquilizer into her. Even then, it took her close to twenty minutes, howling and cursing in English, Hebrew, and Yiddish before she blanked out: "Fuck you, you anti-Semites! God sees what you are doing! Baruch atah Adonai...fuck you! Killers! Meshuges! My rabbi fucks you in the ass!! God help me, help me!" Sometimes, why I don't know, they didn't tranquilize her. She would yell for hours, driving everybody on the ward crazier than they were already.

In her relatively sane moments, Hannah put herself in charge of the TV in the patients' lounge. Whatever somebody was watching had to be approved by her. If she didn't like a show, she just switched it.

Bolted in ten feet high on the wall in the lounge, presiding over a room full of shaking, pacing, fidgeting patients, the TV was playing the Gulf War show, courtesy of CNN. There were enough patients in the ward, even me when I wasn't too self-involved or bored, who wanted to watch how the world was eating itself alive. Every day General Schwarzkopf threw his pail of fish at the newspaper seals, and after they gulped it down and flapped their flippers in approval, the picture would switch to

Bernard Shaw on the roof of some luxury hotel in downtown Baghdad, his silly face floating on top of his foreign correspondent's overcoat. Same old pompous rhetoric and clichés. The only thing that was interesting to most of the patients was the bombs, or "fireworks," as most people on the ward called them. The display was great, but how many fireworks can you watch before you get bored?

Besides Hannah, the other really extreme case on the ward was Jimmy, a stocky, pockmarked Irish kid about seventeen years old, who paced the hallways denouncing Jews at the top of his lungs."Fucking Jews are the devil. Ha-ha! The devil is Jewish. Fuck the Jews...the devil has a circumcised dick! They killed Christ! Shoot 'em all!"

Of course, this not being the "real" world, Hannah and Jimmy got along just fine. He screamed about the filthy Jews, she cursed the filthy Christians. They passed each other in the hall, ranting and raving, stopped for a second, smiled at each other, and moved on, taking up their raging and cursing exactly where they had left off.

CHAPTER FORTY

A t about nine o'clock each night, I made my calls from one of the pay phones on the ward. Except for the first night in the hospital, I had been calling my kids every night. I wanted them to know I was still alive and thinking of them. Sometimes I called my friend Ralph in Park Slope. He was one of the few people in my life besides Rose who didn't think I was a hopeless lunatic.

I didn't call Rose and dreaded when she called me. She'd visited me twice the first week, but after that I tried to avoid her. It embarrassed me for her to see me this way. I also had another, important reason for keeping her away....

After the first week in the hospital, and as I continued to call to say good night to the kids, I'd get Susan on the phone first. In the beginning, she was cold and formal—handing the phone to Sarah, then Ben. After a while, though, Susan asked me how it was going in the hospital. What pills they were giving me, how I was doing. I was so steeped in guilt that her simple expressions of interest in my condition were like blessings to me. When she started being even a touch personal, I told her how sorry I was to have done the thoughtless things I had done to her. Not just over the past six months, leaving her alone with the kids, but all the way back to my despicable behavior about Ben, her pregnancy. Every crime I'd ever committed came tumbling out of my mouth.

357

Several days into my marathon confession, Susan's tone seemed to change. She seemed almost, for her, tender, and even the slightest bit forgiving. I sensed, I suppose partially because I wanted to and partially from her tone, that there was a chance, a dim yet perceptible possibility that I might be able to return to the family.

I tried to forget about Rose. Easier said than done. She called all the time—anxious to see how I was doing, and then even more anxious when she didn't hear from me. She could tell that something was going on, and I'm sure she knew what it was. After all, I'd made such U-turns before, and she had an unerring instinct for my moods. She became more upset as the days went on. Near the end of my third week in the hospital, after I had ignored her for three days, she got me on the phone. She was practically hysterical. I didn't want to tell her that I was hoping to return to my family, that she was headed for the trash bin again. I didn't want to hurt her, and I suppose, God forgive me, I thought of her as insurance, just in case things didn't work out with Susan.

Rose wanted to know why I was avoiding her. I said I wasn't—it was just that I was having a bad time. She didn't believe me. Finally, she broke down entirely: "I should be in the hospital instead of you!" she cried. I got off the phone, shuffled down the hall, and lay down on the bed in my room.

After the first week they had moved me into a three-bed room. One of my roommates was a teenage kid who was suicidal. The other was a gray, depressed Jewish man from the Upper West Side, about fifteen years older than me. He'd been on the ward, he said, for almost five months. I was surprised to hear this. He didn't really seem that sick to me. He read the *Times*, did the crossword puzzle, read books, and appeared to be fairly sane and reasonable. I couldn't understand why he'd been there for so long.

One afternoon, he wasn't around for lunch. When I saw him at dinner, I asked him where he'd been. "Oh, I went down to my apartment on a day pass."

"Yeah, what happened?"

He shook his head. "It's still too depressing for me there. I just get lonely and I have to come back." So, *that* was his story. He stayed in this place because he lived alone. He had no family and no friends. He was in a mental hospital because he was lonely!

Jack, his name was, was lying in his bed when I came back to the room, feeling like a piece of shit after my phone call with Rose. I lay down on the bed. "Bad phone call?" he asked.

"Yeah, my girlfriend."

"You're married," he said, "and you have kids—I never heard about the girlfriend." He sounded jealous and started to preach about how ungrateful I was for not appreciating all the things I had, all the people in my life. "For God's sake," he said, "you even have a radio show, thousands of people listen to you."

I shook my head. "Yeah, but—" Then I stopped. I'd never told a soul in this place that I was on the radio. "What do you mean, radio show?" He sighed his deep, self-pitying sigh, "I'm a WBAI subscriber."

"Oh," I said nonchalantly, "you were a listener?" He turned over to face the wall. "Yeah, but I never liked your show—you talk too much." Two minutes later, he was snoring.

I couldn't sleep, not even with a double dose of my antianxiety pills. I got up about midnight, wrapped in a fury of guilt and ambivalence. Here was Rose, beautiful, loving Rose, who wanted nothing more than to be with me—just purely and simply be with me. A decent, sympathetic, tender woman. And here was Susan, the woman I had pledged to love, honor, and obey till death do us part—the woman who had had my children. I felt both their presences, out there, beyond the protective walls of the hospital, waiting for me, ready to ambush me with love or responsibility the minute I set foot outside the grounds. I had to talk to somebody about this or blow up! I banged on the thick Lucite of the nurses' station, waited there with my nose pressed up against it till the head night nurse came out. She took me into an empty room. "What's wrong, Mr. Feder?"

"I don't know what to do. My wife may be ready to take me back into the family—my kids. My girlfriend loves me so much, and I feel happy when I'm with her. If I say yes to one, then—" She held up her hand to interrupt me, all business.

"Let me ask you a question," she said, "and I want you to answer me without hesitation. OK?"

"Yeah..."

"If you could choose one of these women, your wife or girlfriend, to get hit by a bus, right this second, who would it be?" I hesitated.

"I don't—"

"What's your answer?"

"My girlfriend," I said, without another moment's thought.

"That's it," she said. "Now just proceed accordingly." She got up to go. I followed her to the door. "But—"

"You made your choice, now follow it."

I felt like the worst piece of shit in the world, a murderer, but at the same time I was immensely relieved. Now the decks were cleared for me to get back to my family.

During the third weekend of my stay, they approved me for my first overnight pass. I called my friend Ralph and he agreed to pick me up and let me stay at his apartment in Brooklyn. I called Lynn Samuels and told her I would be taking my show back, at least for the coming Sunday morning, maybe permanently. I had already been going out on three-hour local passes, just to walk around the neighborhood—get used to the outside world.

I'm waiting at the door of the ward, excited and anxious as a child waiting to go on his first camping trip with the grown-ups. It's the night of my big sleep-over at Ralph's. I have my clothes packed, my toothbrush and my soap, in its little plastic carrying dish, ready. Ralph arrives, signs me out, and we're driving to Brooklyn. I haven't been in a car in months. Everything is going by so fast; the lights are so bright. I concentrate on talking to Ralph, concentrate even more on listening, something I'd given up doing for the last couple of months.

We arrive, back in Park Slope, my old neighborhood. Up the four flights of stairs to his apartment and...the entire place is a disaster area—strips of wallpaper hanging down, paint cans lying around, holes in the wall, insulation and wires hanging down from the ceiling. Ralph walks me into the spare room. "OK, here's your bed." I'm horrified. There is no way I am going to sleep here—rats and bugs could crawl through the holes in the wall, the hanging wires look like snakes—there is junk piled everywhere, books in stacks on the floor, records, tools, paintbrushes, easels, canvases; Ralph's dog runs in and jumps on me, barking. I yearn for my clean, warm, sterile little hospital room.

"What happened in here?!" I ask him.

"Oh, just renovating."

"I can't sleep here, man." He looks around. "I guess I didn't think about that much." So, what to do now. I'm out here in the big scary world, I can't sleep here, and it's already nine-thirty—not enough time to get back to the hospital by ten, which, for some reason I don't understand, is the cut-off point for patients to reenter the ward. What am I going to do?! Ralph suggests I call Rose—she'll take me in. No. I can't. I have been avoiding her, keeping phone conversations as brief as possible. I can't see her—that's over. I can't go to my studio. The place scares me. There is only one place I can think of to go. I pick up the phone and call Susan. "Look, I know this is weird, and I really apologize, but I was supposed to sleep at Ralph's tonight, an overnight pass, but I can't sleep here, the place is a mess."

"Hmn-hmn."

"Well, I know I don't deserve any favors from you after the way I've been, but could you just let me sleep the night there? I'll be gone in the morning to do my show."

There is a long silence. I'm getting more panicky all the time. Finally, "OK, if you have to."

We drive back across the Brooklyn Bridge to the Upper West Side. Ralph rides up with me in the elevator and leaves me at the door to the apartment. "Pick you up for the show tomorrow morning."

"Yeah, OK."

Susan opens the door, a wry smile on her face. I walk in and set my suitcase and my little plastic toiletries bag on the floor. It is so strange standing in this apartment, as if I've entered a dream of a previous life, one that I'd lived centuries ago.

The kids are asleep. Susan and I sit, me on the couch, she on a chair far across the living room, looking at each other. She is smiling a little, eying me carefully. "How're you doing?"

"OK, considering…how are the kids?"

It is awkward and familiar all at once.

This is my wife, whom I have known for more than fifteen years. We have slept together in the same bed for years, had sex hundreds of times, exchanged marriage vows, furnished apartments, made plans for our lives, created and taken care of children together. But I am also just a visitor, an unexpected, disturbing overnight guest who will be gone in less than ten hours.

Close to eleven, past time for my pill. I hate taking it. As soon as I do, I lose whatever clarity I have, my body tingles with chills, I feel weak and numb.

"Can I get a glass of water?" I ask her.

Susan shakes her head, that pained, pitying smile never once leaving her face, "Yes, you can have a glass of water."

I swallow the pill.

"Mike," she said, "you don't need those pills."

"You're right, but…"

"You just need to find a decent therapist."

I feel the pill taking effect almost instantly; soon I'll be too tired to talk. I lean forward on the couch. "Look, you know how we were talking when I called from the hospital." She nods.

"Well," I continue, "do you think there's a chance—that there might be a possibility of me coming back here?"

"I don't know. Maybe, it would be a while…you know, I'd have to make sure you were stable, that you had a job, that you weren't going to start acting the same old way again."

"Oh, I wouldn't. I've seen some things about myself. I know I could—"

"And, you know—that woman would have to go. You'd have to promise me and mean it."

"Oh, don't worry about that, I stopped having anything to do with her."

Susan looked at me skeptically. "No," I said, "I'm really serious, she's out."

"Well, we'll see—the kids really miss you." I'm filled with joy to hear even that qualified response. Oh, I'll be good if she lets me back home. I'll do anything she asks, do the chores, watch the kids, get any kind of job, whatever she wants. I thought I detected a hint of affection in Susan's smile, of nostalgia for the old days.

It's almost midnight.... The pill is really working in me now, I'm extremely sleepy. "Well," I say, "I guess I'd better go to bed." There is a long, expectant pause—a sharp, clear moment. We look at each other. I'd do it if she would. I want to sleep with her—it would be proof that I'm still the man I once was, not an irresponsible child, a useless, disturbed vagrant. I'm waiting for her to say it. Then the moment passes. She gets up. "You can use the extra bed in Ben's room."

I get my suitcase and my toiletries bag, brush my teeth.

I poke my head into Sarah's room. It's like a sharp pain, seeing her there, all twisted up and flying around in her sleep, the way she always does, her dark blond hair all over her face and the pillow. How many thousands of nights have I seen her sleeping, covered her up, smoothed her hair?

In Ben's room, the same stabbing ache. He's sleeping, as always, on his side, composed and perfectly calm. I sigh. Susan's put a quilt on the single guest bed in the corner. She goes out for a minute. I take off my pants and get under the covers. The bed has a futon mattress; it is much softer than the hard, plastic-covered mattresses at the hospital. I sink into it, tranquilized from the pill, so happy to be in the bosom of my family again, watched over, protected, in a fuzzy, childlike dream of serenity. I look across the room at Ben. His bed is surrounded by stuffed animals: bears, seals, dogs, lions. Susan comes back in, walks over, and stands looking down at me, all comfy and safe in my little bed. She shakes her head, laughs a little. "You sure you don't want a stuffed animal, maybe one of Ben's bears." I tell you, it sounds good to me; but for that rueful look on her face, I might have taken her up on it. I shake my head, smile. "No, thanks." She goes out...and I sink into a deep and happy sleep.

Next morning. The minute I open my eyes and realize where I am, I'm in a panic. I get dressed and sit in the living room, holding onto a cup of coffee with shaking hands. The kids are up. "Daddy!!" It's like Christmas for them. They throw themselves at me like huge beanbags, gripping, kissing.

Ah, if only I could grasp this happiness. I stretch my will till I feel like I'm going to snap. *Give me this one thing, please.* No hope—I can't do it; something has twisted back in the night. Almost immediately, I'm shaking again—I want more than anything in the world to be out of there. I look at Susan sitting in the rocking chair across from me. Those X ray eyes, that tight condemning mouth. Horrible! I'm counting the minutes till Ralph comes to get me.

With Ralph's help, I manage to get through my radio show. We talk about the Gulf War, we play a few records, take a couple of calls. Half the time I want to jump up and run from the studio, but I'm able to keep it up for an hour. At the end, I sign off and tell the audience I'll be back next week—as usual. Wherever I am, hospital or halfway house, I know I have to keep doing that show.

CHAPTER FORTY-ONE

At the end of four weeks in the hospital, I'm pronounced officially cured. Steve Post and his wife, Laura, have offered
to take me in. Of course, just temporarily, only a short stay. During my last
week in the hospital, I'm on the phone constantly to Susan, trying to get
some firm answer about my future. Is she going to let me back? She never
says, "Yes, hurry on back," but it appears to be merely a matter of fulfilling
certain probationary rules for me to be reinstated. Mostly it is based on the
kids—they need a father.

Susan says I have to find a job, bring in some money, and *no more girlfriend*. All this sounds OK to me. I haven't spoken to Rose in ten days—
not since the night I shoved her in front of a metaphorical bus.

As far as a job—my old lawyer Jake says he'll give me part-time work
as a file clerk. I know he doesn't really need anybody—he already has a
secretary who does the filing—so it was pure charity on his part. It is a little humiliating, considering our original relationship—lawyer and star—
but I'm grateful to him for the handout.

I'm camping out in the Posts' apartment on Eighty-seventh Street, just
eight blocks from Susan and the kids, sleeping on a big comfortable couch
in the living room. Steve and Laura are home most of the time, so I always
have company when I am feeling panicky, which is often. Laura is a great
audience—she has lots of practice, living with Steve for twenty years.

365

I still feel scared being out on the street, the crowds overwhelm me, the noise, all the lights and cars. It is an adventure merely going around the corner to buy a sandwich and soda. I'm going to an outpatient program at St. Luke's Hospital twice a week, seeing a psychiatrist—a fierce individual with a big black mustache, named Dr. House. He checks my blood pressure and regulates my medicine. I tell him the antidepressant is driving me nuts, that I practically fall over onto the subway tracks on the way uptown to see him. He tells me I have to keep taking the medicine or get back into the hospital. "But don't you hear what I'm saying? It makes me dizzy and faint, I can't see anything clearly, like I'm looking through the bottoms of Coke bottles!" He narrows his eyes at me, bristles his mustache, and raises his finger in the air. "Don't question the medication, Mr. Feder."

"Well, I *am* questioning the medication—I'm telling you it makes me sick, it's even making me fucking depressed! What am I supposed to do?"

"I'll tell what we do!" his eyes blazed and he thumped his fist on the desk like a combat general. "We *attack* the depression! We aggressively up the dose!"

"But—"

"Do you want to be back in the hospital, Mr. Feder—do you want to risk suicide?"

"No."

"Then take your medicine."

I start working in the law office the week after I get out. I file forms for three hours, then, in the mid-afternoon, take the train, always careful to stand with my back against the wall so that the track is as far away as possible—back up to the West Side to Post's place, just in time to sit in the south-facing window and catch fifteen minutes of sun squeezing between the buildings opposite. Directly across the street is a big Catholic church. During the day and in the early evenings, I can see the altar, the hanging lights and colored candles. I watch people hurrying up the steps and coming out a little while later, calm and serene looking.

I'm so comfortable in Steve Post's living room, I consider taking out a six-month lease. Late at night I lay on their couch, wrapped in a big quilt, all warm and cozy, and imagine I've been adopted by kindly parents.

Near the end of my second week out of the hospital, on Valentine's Day, I finally go over to see the kids. I stop in at the Party Store two blocks from the house to buy them some heart-shaped chocolate lollipops. People are streaming in and out of the place, breathless, on last-minute impulse-buying sprees, candy, cards, costumes, hearts of every size.

I think of Rose—Valentine's Day was her holiday. The box she sent to the radio station on my birthday almost six years ago held a heart-shaped red paper clip holding together the two sheets of her letter to me. Hearts, of course. Rose was entirely a beating heart. *But enough of this mushy nostalgia, I have something to do!*

I walk over to the apartment and go up to see the kids. I give them the lollipops; they give me, with great ceremony, a huge heart-shaped red paper Valentine that they have made themselves. Really it's from Sarah, the artist. The heart is covered with words, collage fashion, that she has cut out of magazines and newspapers. *Terrific. Great. Lovable. Smart. Dad.* Ben has contributed by drawing a couple of wobbly yellow hearts on it in crayon. We talk for a while, then Susan says it's time for them to go to bed.

At the door I hug the kids, then Susan walks forward and, leaning over both of them, gives me a hug; tentative, a little awkward, the first time we'd really touched in almost a year. I could have wept in gratitude.

I see the kids every couple of nights for a visit, a little longer each time, and speak to them each night on the phone. After they get off, I report my life's progress to Susan, how I had gone on a paralegal job interview that day, how the medication is keeping me stable. Not exactly true, but I want to sound perfect.

Still I'm not hearing what I want to hear from her, a definite date. The Posts, genial hosts that they are, have already made a couple of polite inquiries about the length of my stay.

I finally get up the nerve to tell Susan that I wish to know what is happening, when I might actually be coming back. I had all my hopes pinned on it. She tells me she'll think about it and for me to call her the next evening, about eight, when she gets home from her office—she'll let me know then.

All day I pace around, hardly able to think, waiting to call her. By eight o'clock, I've been hovering around the phone for half an hour, looking at my watch every half minute, waiting to dial. "Hi."

"Hello."

"So, what—when do you think?"

There was just a slight pause, then a sudden change in the temperature comes through the phone, a sense of formality.

"I have been thinking very carefully about this," Susan says, "and I've talked to many of my friends and colleagues. They have convinced me that it would not be in my interest to have you come back to live here." I am floored, almost literally. I reach out to hold onto the wall, slip down onto a hassock next to the couch. "What are you saying, you're not letting me back—ever?"

"I have the children's interests and mine to think of."

"But I thought you said that the kids needed me—and that if I never saw my girlfriend again and got a job that—"

"I'm sorry, but that's my final decision." The phone receiver was slippery in my hand. I can hardly speak—a black hole seems to open up in the air right in front of my eyes. Where will I go now; what is going to happen to me? Susan's voice comes over the phone again. "I want to say one more thing. Remember, if you kill yourself, it's not my fault."

I hang up, poleaxed, and fall back onto the couch for a few seconds, suspended in space. Then I jump up and run into the bedroom, shaking, to tell Laura and Steve what has happened. They don't seem very surprised. I'm practically babbling, getting more agitated by the second, like a jet engine revving up for takeoff. "She promised I could come back! If— why would she say that to me about killing myself?—does she *want* me to kill myself?"

I run out of the room, grab the phone, dial up my psychiatrist, and only get his answering service. "Is this an emergency, sir?"

"Yes, it's a fucking emergency!"

"We'll page him for you, sir." Pacing, pacing, in and out of Steve and Laura's bedroom...frantic.

Half an hour goes by, the doctor doesn't call back. Motherfucker obviously doesn't care if I live or die. Up *his* dose! I pace and pace, pick at my fingers until they bleed, twist my hair into knots, and get some Valium from

Laura, but no matter how much I take, no matter how many miles I walk around that living room, I can't calm down. I look over at the bookshelf where I had propped up the kids' Valentine's Day card. I'm never going back, never going to live with my family again. I feel like my life is over.

Going on 11:00 P.M. Now I call the hospital and speak to the nurse about coming back. Maybe I can take a cab. She says there are no beds, and anyway it would take days to reinstate my emergency Medicaid. They advise me to go immediately to the emergency room of a city hospital if I think I'm going to hurt myself. Hurt myself? What a stupid euphemism. There's my gravestone. *Mike Feder. Beloved Husband and Father. He Hurt Himself.*

I'm not going to any city hospital. I'd rather be dead than to be in one of those places again. I throw on my coat and race out of the apartment, down the stairs, and out into the freezing night. I look both ways.... What to do? Where to go?

I notice the church across the street and walk toward it, right in front of a car—screeching brakes, cursing. *Who cares*? Up the steps, into the church. People at the front kneeling, priest, robes, I can't sit down, have to move, up the side aisle—there's a giant crucified Christ, his horrible sad eyes, thorns in his head. Man, you're not the only one—can't stop moving—everybody looking over at me. A man walking toward me...red uniform. Usher? Cop? Cops are all Catholic. Maybe a Roman. Where's your spear, officer? Jew. I don't belong in here. But I didn't kill him! Anyway, *he* was a Jew, him and his mom and his dad...all. If I pray? Blood of Christ, drip on me now—like Ben Hur—it healed the lepers. Usher's hand on my arm, "Can I help you, sir." "You can get the fuck out of my way." Careful, careful...turn the other cheek.

Out of the church, down the steps, almost tripping over a bum, rolled up in filthy blankets...in my way, in my way—what does he want? Help. Everybody wants help, fucking smelly piece-of-shit bum. I should kick him in the head. But I'm a bum, I live off other people, I beg...

Walking, walking, over to Broadway. Blast of car horns, brakes... radios thumping...Tower of fucking Babel. Machines. The ghost in the machine. Hamlet's ghost. Bus—full of foolish faces following me. I'm not the problem, assholes. Walking, walking, up Broadway. Hot-dog stand.

Disgusting smell, I could retch…red beef, mustard, dead cows, blood of the cow, body of the cow, washed in the blood of the cow. How could she say kill yourself—insurance—better dead than alive, better red then dead. Red light, green light—which one is stop and go—like a mad river, steel lights, bumper-shine.

They'll kill you—step off—curb like a cliff hurtled to his death. Did he jump or was he pushed? No clues, inspector. Details. Details. The man's life. Ask his radio audience—they know—radio… what? What kind of job is that? Talking. He talks, officer, he tells stories. From that you'll make a living? Be a professional. Be a clown—all the world loves a fucking clown. Walk, walk. Block, block ends, lights, cars…. keep going, they have to stop, it's a law, no, in Los Angeles they stop—OK, not here, it's only a quick bump, then you get up. I saw it in hygiene class in high school—or was that driver's ed—watch out for pedestrians…children killed every day, hit and run, ball between the wheels, I couldn't stop on time. Bullshit!! Murderer! Murderers of children, ninth circle of hell. Didn't leave a note—but she did! Block letters, I CAN NO LONGER LIVE WITHOUT THE RESPECT OF MY CHILDREN. Live and be well—you should. I can no longer live without. Children…my children. I couldn't have children. Dad. Not me, Dad. I never called *him* that. OK, that's the way it goes, those are the cards you were dealt…walk, walk…over to the river…the park, twisty tree branches, reaching, I'll get you my pretty one! Dark park…they say it's full of maniacs—well, make room for Daddy, boys. Into the trees, down to the river, cold as hell—cold dark quiet peaceful river…under the bridge, dark shapes, scurry little rats, get the fuck out of my way, a man in the bushes, "Hey, buddy." "Fuck you!! Back away, no more, man"—they kill people down there—*I* kill people. I killed her, here's my credentials, an autographed note…broke her heart, she told me. Shit, babe! Nobody dies of a broken heart. I did—I died of one. Stop, here. The river…slow and cold. I can stop. Stop. Here. This rail…stop.

The lights on the other shore, a mile away—all twinkly and bright in the black, sharp air. One boat, a tug, whooshing its way down to the ocean. Bushes, trees, whispering in the wind. Still night. Holy night. There is something holy about the night. There is something holy in a heart, even a broken one, still beating.…

I take a deep breath of knife-cold air and slowly return to myself. Everything comes back into focus, and then *more* than everything—inside and out—suddenly seems perfect: crystal clear.

I walk back up the slippery slick grass hill, out of the park and back onto Broadway, back to Steve and Laura's apartment. Upstairs, one in the morning. One red light glowing in the dark church. Everything quiet. I open my bottle of antidepressants and dump them in the trash, lay on the couch, composed, relaxed.... but awake, it seems to me—for the first time in years.

Two days later, I'm walking out of the subway, returning from my filing job.... holding onto the guardrail of the steps. My balance and vision are better since I dumped the pills, but I'm still a little wobbly. I blink in the bright sunshine.

Since I went off the deep end and returned the other night, since I stopped taking the medication, the whole world looks different to me, as if someone had peeled away a huge opaque plastic covering. Every object— trees, street signs, magazines, fruit in the deli—glitters in a kind of quiet perfection. Every person, not just the young and the beautiful (and the West Side is full of them), but the old, the angry, the twisted and depressed—all seem *right* to me—appearing just exactly as they are meant to. And this is an experience of the world I can distinguish from those temporary highs, the periods of manic pseudo-clarity I'd had before. This is a simple, stark reality. No racing pulse or soaring thoughts are required to lift everything above itself. Things seem just as they should be, funny, sad, ugly, beautiful. But I know this vision won't last. Life, no matter how desperately I try to make it one, isn't a fairy tale. It changes in tiny stages, I'm beginning to see. But still, as I stand on the street corner, listing a little in the breeze, I feel I have crossed some small bridge, heading toward a better destination.

I cross the street, shading my eyes against the sun. As I step onto the opposite sidewalk I see Rose walking right toward me. I step back, almost over the curb, back into the street. She reaches out her hand to steady me. "Mike, are you alright?" I haven't seen her or talked to her in almost a month. It is almost like seeing an apparition. "Yeah, just a little wobbly— no big deal."

She looks absolutely beautiful, standing there in the bright sunlight, her hair shining, her beautiful eyes, her rosy-flushed face. I have no idea what to say to her and just wait for her to talk to me. I think she might— she has every right to—turn around and leave me standing there. Not Rose—she isn't the type who walks away.

Two, three, four blocks, we walk next to each other in silence, till we are in front of a coffee shop. We go in, take off our coats, sit, look at each other awkwardly for a minute. I take a deep breath."You have to hate me for the way I acted toward you." She sighs. "Oh, Mike, don't you understand yet. I don't hate you. I love you."

"If you treated me the way I treated you, I wouldn't be sitting here, holding *your* hand."

She smiles. "Well, I guess we're lucky I'm not you."

I fill her in on the last few weeks. It's no surprise to her that I ditched her one last time to get back with my family. In fact, nothing I did seems to be much of a surprise to her, except my constant inability to understand how much she cares for me.

We get up finally and go outside. I walk Rose over to the subway. She has her arm through mine. "So," she asks, "when will I see you again?"

"What about tomorrow," I say, "is tomorrow good?"

"Well, let's see," she says, frowning, "I'm *very* busy, so—" I must look stricken because she laughs and says, "Tomorrow is good and probably the day after tomorrow is good, and I'm sure the day after that is good too—" I hold up my hands: "Alright, alright, I get it."

She looks at me and sighs. "I really hope you do."

A few days later, with Rose along as bodyguard to protect me from scary monsters, I go back to my studio for the first time since I retreated into the mental hospital. Everything about the place—the holes in the floor, the musty smell, the mattresses covered with dust, the very walls—fills me with sadness and disgust. I can recall only brief moments of contentment and peace in ten dark months of anxiety and decline…. Ben, tucked in, drifting off to sleep while lullabies play on the stereo.

I pick up some papers, records, a few books, some clothes, stuff them into a big laundry bag I have brought with me. I leave the rest of my stuff, the dishes and silverware, my old broken-down stereo, the mattresses, the chair—leave them and walk out, the door unlocked behind me.

Rose and I walk back up Riverside Drive to her apartment. The March air is cold, and colder still is the wind coming in off the Hudson, which you can see through the bare trees, glistening in the warm sun.

HERE AND NOW

When I swim up from sleep in the morning, usually around six-thirty or seven, Rose is already up. She stretches, gets out of bed, goes through the living room, opens the front door, gets the paper—then a glass of orange juice—makes her sandwich for lunch; showers, dresses, has her cereal and vitamins; brushes her teeth, a few last touch-ups to her hair and clothes, a pause…a kiss good-bye; then out the door and off to work at the hospital.

I hate to see the door close behind her. I'm alone again, and I don't really believe she will return. The apartment is as silent as a funeral parlor for the first few minutes—I am faced with myself, and I need some rituals of my own to sustain me. Eventually, I develop a few.

I make myself a cup of instant coffee, drip in some maple syrup, add a little milk, stir it, put the spoon in the sink. I take the cup and a box of matches and walk into the living room. I set the cup down on a cork coaster on top of the radiator cover near the living-room window, and walk over to the small wooden table against the opposite wall where I've set up a little altar. A white candle in a brass candlestick holder, just behind a small, tarnished bronze statue of an old Buddhist priest on a horse. He's riding side saddle, looking at the scenery as he passes slowly by. I pinch off most of the carbonized part of the wick, then light it, shake out the match, bring the box of matches back into the kitchen, throw out the match. Back into the living room. If it's fall or winter, I turn on a couple of lamps to chase away the gloom. Then I sit back in the reclining chair, gaze out the window at the small patch of sky above the surrounding buildings. I watch the candle flame and meditate—first on the people who have gone...

I think of my mother and father—poor, tortured souls that they were. At first, when I began this morning practice, I felt they were close to me, almost too close. I have spent years trying to forgive my parents, and I wonder if the job will ever be quite finished. When I stumble, whenever I'm brought up short by some fault—a spasm of stinginess, a burst of irrational fear or violent anger, or worse, a coldness over my heart that separates me from Rose or my children—I think of my parents: "If only you hadn't been so crazy and mean..." "If only you hadn't gone so far away..."

But lately, I have a sense that they have drifted far, far away—an immense distance, to another plane where human misery is not even a memory. Have they become so remote in the natural course of things, or have I let them go?

When I was four months out of the hospital, just after I moved in with Rose, Vicky called me. I hadn't seen her for almost a year, since I moved out of my house. She came up to the West Side and we went out for coffee. She'd quit her job at the theater and was doing freelance play editing and reviews. Vicky, awkward and basically shy as she was, never had any close friends. Like a lot of theater people, she had a million acquaintances, people to have lunch with, to go to plays with, but no one to sit with for hours and trade secrets. She lived in a tiny basement studio in Brooklyn Heights, spending too much of her time alone, reading and writing, drinking pots of black coffee way into the night.

When she came up to visit me that day, it was dificult for both of us. Vicky never had much patience for my run-on psychoanalytic monologues, unless I was performing them onstage. So I didn't bore her with my various woes. And she hardly was the one to talk about herself. So we walked down near the river, talking about art and theater, about storytelling. She wanted me to brush up my *Talking Cure* story and perform it in a college or a theater.

I told her I was done with that. I was keeping a low profile from now on. I was working on my relationships with Rose and my kids. My sole artistic endeavor was my regular radio show, and that was only possible because I could sit alone in the studio while I talked.

Vicky wanted me to go the theater with her, but I told her I couldn't. All I did was go to work in the morning and then go home. Maybe, I said, when I was feeling a little better, when I developed slightly more energy than the average snail, we could get together again.

I didn't hear from her for more than six months. Then, in the depths of the winter, I got a long reflective and emotional letter from her, recalling all the good times we had had together, how much working with me had meant to her. She promised not to bug me about performing. She just wanted us to be friends again, go to the plays, have dinner, and talk. There was a deep undertone of loneliness and desperation to her letter—that was odd for Vicky, since she was usually so reserved and proud.

It took me a couple of weeks to write back to her, not knowing exactly how to tell her that I didn't want to see her again. I didn't want to shoulder her loneliness and pain. There were already too many claims from Rose and my kids on my limited fund of affection and responsibility. All I could see when I read Vicky's letter was another sad, disappointed woman who wanted me to cheer her up—but I had done that enough for several lifetimes already.

I wrote her back, saying I, too, missed all our times at the theater together, working with her, talking for hours over coffee, about performing, creating. That was true enough, I did miss all that. I especially remembered, I told her, a performance of La Bohème that we'd gone to. It was done at the Met, directed by Franco Zeffirelli (Vicky had gone for the directing as much as the opera). The voices were a little lacking, but visually it was the most beautiful thing I'd ever seen on a stage. Sets that took you far from the boring, disappointing present, crowds of gorgeously costumed people...snow falling on the cobbled streets...a suspension of life—like a magic spell. I turned to look at Vicky. She inclined her head a little and smiled at me. We were in church, the Theater.

I told Vicky she had made a valiant effort with me over the years—attempting to make a silk purse out of my native pig leather—and I appreciated it. I told her I was sure I would never forget all the things we had done and gone through together, but I couldn't see her. It was all I could do to get along each day—be with Rose, see my kids. Maybe one day…I hoped she could forgive me for being so selfish. I sent the letter off.

I never heard a word from her, not that I would have expected to, considering what I had written. Then, early that fall, I got a formal black-bordered card in the mail: my presence was requested at a memorial service at the Public Theater for Vicky Elliot, celebrating her life and mourning her death in August from cancer.

The announcement was from Vicky's older sister. I was afraid to go, ashamed to show my face. I had abandoned Vicky, rejected her when she needed me to be her friend. She probably knew she was sick when she wrote me that letter. Rose persuaded me to go, pointing out that I wouldn't have been invited in the first place if I was a known criminal.

In the lobby of the Public Theater, certainly Vicky's favorite place in New York, an easel was set up with a blown-up photograph of Vicky as a little girl, all dolled up in a go-to-school dress, with long curly hair and a big, happy grin on her face. The place was crowded with all her friends from the theater, a lot of whom I'd met over the years. We stood around the lobby, trading stories about her.

A woman, about sixty years old, walked over to me. She introduced herself as Vicky's sister. I cringed, expecting the worst. I dreaded hearing about that last letter I wrote to Vicky, but she didn't say anything about it, just said she'd heard a lot about me from Vicky and thanked me for coming.

She filled me in on the details. Vicky had discovered last winter that she had ovarian cancer. She left New York in March to go down to stay with her sister and get treatment. Despite the chemotherapy and radiation the cancer spread. She knew by the summer that she was dying.

"Vicky wasn't a complainer, you know," her sister said.

"I know."

"Even at the very end, she never said a word about the pain." We stood there a moment in silence. Then I couldn't bear the guilt anymore. "She wrote me a letter," I said, "last winter—she wanted to see me, but I was—" I couldn't say, "too wrapped up" in my own life. Vicky's sister put her hand on my arm. "Vicky told me about that letter and the one you wrote her back, Mike. You shouldn't feel bad for a second. Vicky never talked about you except to smile and say what a good time you used to have together."

Everybody was called into the theater for the readings and a service, but I couldn't bear it. I walked out of the place and went home. I heard what her sister said but it didn't really penetrate. All I could remember— I could see those letters again—was Vicky, reaching out to me from her heart and me rejecting it.

Carlos died—he couldn't have been more than forty-five or forty-six—in the summer of 1996.

In the early 1990s, right around the time I was recuperating from my second breakdown, his hard drinking had caught up with him—with a vengeance. He had had a couple of serious operations, had been on the verge of death. When I saw him again after I got out of the hospital, he had lost a tremendous amount of weight. I have a black-and-white picture I took of him then—he's sitting across the chessboard, with the sun coming in the window behind him. His hair is thin and graying, his face is pale and lined. He looks like a ghost.

His old, loud raucous laugh was gone, replaced by a kind of melancholy wistfulness. His irony was intact but definitely muted by his brush with death.

I saw him two or three times over the next couple of years. He called me once in a while, wanting me to visit him or drop in on some galleries. To laugh a little, talk about the world, about art, about life. And all I could see was another pull on my life. All the man wanted was to be with a friend. In Carlos, as in Vicky, I felt that old, twisting force, another person living through me, draining me. I avoided him, put him off. He was disappointed in me, but he was too nice—too much of gentleman—to say anything.

The last time I saw him was in the early spring of 1996. We visited some galleries in Soho together. He still looked pale and wasted to me, but he said he was doing better, taking long walks around the city. He was hopeful, as always. Optimistic about getting together a show of his paintings.

We took the train back uptown. Carlos stayed on when I got off at 110th Street. As the the train pulled away, I waved at him. He smiled and waved frantically—a joke—like I was his long-lost brother who he had just seen after ten years.

He called me three months later—in June, I think it was. He was depressed, just out of the hospital after more major surgery. He wanted me to come visit him at home. I could hear his mother's drunk, hysterical voice in the background. I told him I would as soon as I got a chance. As if I were so busy, as if I had to fit him in between board meetings. The truth was, I didn't want to see him. I didn't want to go up to the Bronx and sit for hours in that cramped, sad, crazy apartment with his crazy mother. And seeing Carlos reminded me of my humiliating flop years ago, when my grandiosity had practically destroyed everything. I wanted the ghosts of my past life to stay dead and buried. To me, Carlos was one of them. So, despite my promise, I didn't go to see him.

Two weeks later, near July, his mother called me. She told me Carlos was feeling really bad—sick and depressed—it would mean the world to him if I could come and visit. I told her I'd try, but I never did.

In August, a mutual friend called and told me Carlos had died of a heart attack a couple of weeks earlier.

Another memorial party—in a loft in Chelsea. People reminiscing, me sitting there, waiting for someone to unmask me. But there was no denunciation, just quiet, sad conversation. Somebody had picked up a couple dozen of Carlos's paintings from his house and we each chose one to take home with us.

In my mind, Vicky and Carlos appear together, like twins. I don't think a day has gone by that I haven't asked for their forgiveness or, failing that, sent them a gift—some silent observation or twisty little joke for them to appreciate.

The first year of our life together, Rose was more a visiting nurse than a mate or a partner. She saw me through the aftershocks of my breakdown, my near-suicidal guilt about my children—every panicky moment when I couldn't breathe or woke sweating and shaking from a nightmare.

During the first few years I was with Rose, I could never refrain from battling with Susan—divorce contract, custody, money. Rose still felt she was "the other woman." And, in a way, she was right. Waking and sleeping, my heart and my mind were pulled in the direction of my kids and the old, awful battleground of my marriage. In fact, I really wasn't living with Rose so much as I was living in midair someplace, hovering equidistant between my old apartment and my new home. It wasn't until Rose and I actually got married, in the summer of 1995, that she finally felt secure. As for me, it's only in the last couple of years that I feel like I actually have a new, safe home.

In the last ten years I've watched my kids grow up—I was going to say without me, but that's not true. They slept over every week (Ben still does, but Sarah is off to college). On weekends we walk around the city, go to movies, watch videos.... And of course, we talk. I tell them about books, about nature, language, religion, about the things I've done, the adventures I've had. I tell them stories. The only thing I have to remember is to shut up once in a while and give them a chance to talk.

Being a father to my kids, being Rose's husband—these are strange, difficult parts to play, parts I sometimes have to make up as I go along. But I seem to be getting the hang of it. Now, in my old age, I'm discovering the rudiments of love, or more particularly, I'm rediscovering something that was buried fifty years ago and is poking its way back to the surface again.

This past Sunday, three days after the anniversary of my mother's death, I got on the train and went out to Long Island to visit her grave—something I hadn't done since the day she was buried, twenty-four years ago.

It was a warm day and a long walk—past thousands of tombstones—to get to her grave. A great city of the dead. I suppose the average person would be nervous, running the gauntlet of so many ghosts. But of course, I immediately felt right at home. The dead and I were old friends.

I got to the location (marked out on a map they gave me at the office), searched around for a couple of minutes and suddenly there I was, standing right in front of it—of her. RUTH FEDER, BELOVED MOTHER, JUNE 5, 1921–SEPTEMBER 27, 1976. Beloved Mother. My sister had picked out the stone, told them what to write on it, and commissioned a single rose to be carved at the top.

I kneeled down in the dirt and stared at the stone. I suppose I knew enough not to expect a Hollywood crescendo, a sudden transformation.

So many feelings, so many thoughts and memories swirling around in me. I felt myself, as I had so often in my life, freezing, turning to stone in the presence of my mother. But this rigidity only lasted for a moment, then I was just still. Not a sound in my mind or my heart, not a ripple.

And out of that stillness came a feeling—more a knowledge—that was in fact new to me. I was kneeling at the grave of a *child*. Not a grown woman—a child. A sad, angry, helpless child. My mother's purpose in life was to be taken care of—to have her fears soothed, her wild imagination calmed. And our job, all her family, whether parent or sister, husband or child, was to do that soothing—to take care of her. What terrible folly it was for me to ever have expected her to take care of me. What years, what a life I had wasted hating her for something she could never do. And (Hollywood climaxes aside) I discovered something else new to me: a total absence of bitterness; my lifelong anger toward her had disappeared.

It's been a week since I went to see her and the feelings I had standing in front of her grave have remained. I'm superstitious about saying such things out loud, but I don't believe that anger and bitterness will ever return. What has replaced it is sadness. A deep, abiding grief that seems to stretch all the way back to my childhood days with her. That is what I will feel now—for how long I don't know. For as long as it takes.

Before I left the grave, I took a photograph out of my pocket and placed it on her tombstone. It was taken when I was twelve years old. My mother was sitting on a big, stuffed chair, her face distorted by anxiety, doubt, sadness; her mouth parted in an attempt to smile. Her hair was gray but somebody had gone to the trouble of brushing it. And right next to her am I, half standing, half perched on one arm of the chair, with my arm around the back of her neck, my hand cradling her left shoulder. I'm smiling a big, cheerful smile—as if to say: don't worry, Mom, *I'll* take care of you.

Beloved Mother.

Of course.

November 2000